T0287397

THE NAZIS
THE HIDDEN HISTORY

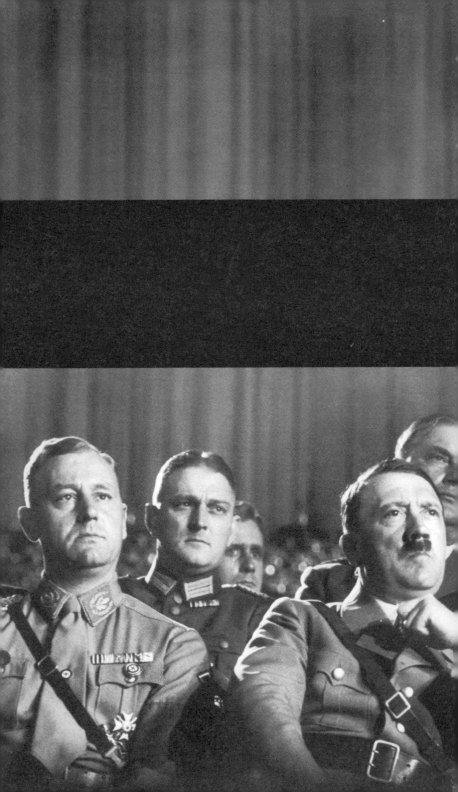

THE NAZIS
THE HIDDEN HISTORY

The catastrophic impact of the Third Reich

Jonathan J. Moore

NEW HOLLAND

Thanks to my mum and dad who have always
had walls of books to read and inspire.

First published in 2017 by New Holland Publishers
London • Sydney • Auckland

The Chandlery 50 Westminster Bridge Road, London SE1 7QY, United Kingdom
1/66 Gibbes Street, Chatswood NSW 2067 Australia
5/39 Woodside Ave Northcote, Auckland 0627 New Zealand

www.newhollandpublishers.com

A record of this book is held at the British Library and the National Library
of Australia.

ISBN 9781742579733

Group Managing Director: Fiona Schultz
Publisher: Alan Whiticker
Project Editor: Bill Twyman
Designer: Andrew Davies
Production Director: James Mills-Hicks
Printer: Hang Tai Printing Company Limited

10 9 8 7 6 5 4 3 2 1

Keep up with New Holland Publishers on Facebook
www.facebook.com/NewHollandPublishers

Contents

INTRODUCTION

Adolf Hitler was a simple man with simple aims.
He wanted to impose the world view that was inside his head onto the rest of Western and Eastern Europe. He sought to make millions of people and entire nations fit into his rich internal fantasy life.

That this might involve the death of 150 million individuals and the extermination of several races wasn't such a problem – it was all for the greater good according to the 'Austrian corporal'. With the aid of thousands of years of anti-Semitism and 400 years of Prussian military experience Hitler almost achieved his goals.

The *Neuordnung* (New Order) envisaged by Hitler involved the creation of an empire stretching from Britain, across Europe and on to the Ural Mountains that divided the West from Asia. At the heart of this *Grossdeutsches Reich* (Greater German Empire) would be the ancestral lands of Germany – a generous rewriting of Imperial History would lead to all of the Czech Republic being considered part of the Germanic heartlands, as well as Alsace-Lorraine, Austria, Slovenia and the provinces taken from Germany in the Versailles treaty.

Western and Southern European states would have varying degrees of autonomy although their foreign and defence policies would, of course, be guided by the 'wise and benign' Nazi leadership. As long as communists, Jews, homosexuals, gypsies and the mentally or physically retarded were eliminated from their territories, these client states would be permitted to run their own domestic agenda with little interference from the Reich.

The possession of the vast lands to the East was the key to Hitler's dream.

It was here that the warped strands of his delusional imaginings combined to create the bedrock of his ambitions. All other goals were subordinate to his plans for the east. The hated Jewish Bolsheviks were to be destroyed in a war of annihilation. The *Untermensch* (subhuman) Slavs who served their evil masters were to become subjects of the new Aryan conquerors and serve on the plantations and estates of the Germanic colonisers. Once the new *Lebensraum* (living space) was secure and resources from the eastern provinces were pouring into the Reich, massed sterilisation, deportation and destruction of the *Untermensch* Russians and Poles would allow the new lands to be truly Aryanised.

While inferior races were allowed to wither on the vine, Nazi breeding policies would ensure that the German population grew sufficiently to settle the new territories. Married German women were not allowed to work but would instead vie with their friends for the Gold Mother's Cross, awarded to those giving birth to eight or more children. Hitler's racial theories allowed children, even from Slavic families, to be adopted into the German community if they were blonde and blue eyed. The German race would have guaranteed its existence.

The Eastern border of the new empire was to be called the A–A line – the proposed line ran from Archangel in the north to Astrakhan on the Black Sea in the south. Any remnant Soviet or Slav power east of this line was unimportant. They would be denied transport infrastructure and access to the industrial and agricultural heartland of European Russia. Continued military activity along the border would ensure surviving Russians lived in medieval squalor. As the German population of the newly captured territories grew they would be able to handle their own defense needs allowing the triumphant Wehrmacht to downsize to a peacetime establishment.

The empire was to be ruled from the new capital Germania. Berlin was to be entirely remodeled with old decrepit apartments being replaced by modern accommodation. The *Sportsplatz*, which had been built for the 1936 Olympic Games, was to be superseded by a new stadium capable of holding 400,000 people. At the centre of the new Berlin was to be the vast Grand Hall, which would have been the largest enclosed space in the world. Its dome would have been 16 times larger than that of St Peter's in Rome. The structure would accommodate 180,000 individuals at Party rallies and such was its scale that the exhalations from the adoring crowds would have formed clouds within the mighty cupola. Determined to outdo the French, Hitler envisaged a 117 metre tall Arch of Triumph. This was planned to dwarf the Arc de Triomphe of Paris and its dimensions were carefully calculated to allow the name of every German soldier who was killed in WWI to be engraved upon it.

Germania would be at the heart of a superlatively modern transport infrastructure. Autobahns would crisscross the empire and German standard gauge railways were intended to replace existing lines. The Greater European Rail Network would link Kazan, Stalingrad, Leningrad, and Odessa within the conquered territories. No doubt Stalingrad and Leningrad would have been renamed to more appropriate German forms. Maybe Blücherburg or Clauzwitzhof.

Within the Greater German Empire different nations would meet different fates depending upon Hitler's biases and prejudices. England was to be largely left alone. Hitler was something of an Anglophile and admired the British although he acknowledged them as a threat. France would lose Alsace-Lorraine and some Alpine provinces but a right-wing puppet government would ensure that the French police were doing the Nazi's bidding. Swiss neutrality was acknowledged, they were of good German stock so would be allowed to manage their own affairs. Hitler's industrial backers made sure of that.

For the peoples of the East, things weren't quite so rosy. Drawn up in 1939–1940 was the *Generalplan Ost*. This was subdivided into two phases, the 'Little plan' and the 'Great Plan'. The first was largely restricted to exploiting the resources of Poland while the latter outlined the future of all of the occupied territories that were in the sights of the Nazi operational planners.

The initial step was to identify peoples who would be suitable for Germanisation. The Baltic States were considered to be particularly fruitful grounds for developing the German way of life. Their proximity to the Aryan heartlands of Scandinavia and the fact that there had not been too much interbreeding with their Slavic neighbors meant that they were an 'uncontaminated' population. When the Reich Main Security Office drew up the plan they also estimated that approximately 35 per cent of Ukrainians and 25 per cent of Byelorussians were also racially acceptable.

For most of the other inhabitants of the East, the broad-featured Slavic populations of Poles and Russians, the future was bleak. Some trusties might be able to stay on and help with the German colonisation but the majority would be deported. Plans were drawn up to clear the *Ost-Reich* of 20 million Poles by shipping them to western Siberia where they would be dispersed among the indigenous population to ensure that no new Polish nation would emerge. The Tartars of the Crimea were seen as occupying the ancient Gothic heartland and Hitler was particularly keen on clearing out the entire peninsula and settling it with a new, pure, population of Germans so that they could live in the racially ideal *Gotenland*, The Land of the Goths.

Just as Eastern territories would be cleared, within the Germanic part of the empire, society would be cleansed 'for 600 years'. Those suffering from genetic disorders, birth defects or chronic mental disabilities were to be eliminated and a death certificate citing 'complications from pneumonia' would be forwarded to loved ones. Alternatively the less radical option of forced sterilisation could ensure that the causative genes for alcoholism or melancholia would not be passed to future generations. Hitler's ideas on racial purity did not emerge in a vacuum. Throughout Germany, and particularly in the Nazi heartland of Bavaria, scholars had promoted ideas of racial purity for centuries. This combined with hundreds of years of anti-Semitism produced masses of 'scientific' literature giving an ideological and scientific basis for the extermination of entire races of humanity. The atrocities committed by the likes of Joseph Mengele did not emerge due to one man's sadistic nature.

But just as pseudo-scientific theories gave a moral justification for mass murder and almost unprecedented human rights abuses, concrete military theories allowed these deadly ideas to spread throughout Europe. Hitler was handed a weapon that brought the independent states of Europe to their knees. Rather than vague formulations based on dubious racial histories, *Blitzkrieg* (lightning war) was a well thought out development of Prussian tradition and military innovations which for a period of time made the German Wehrmacht (army) invincible. Hitler's warped perceptions became a reality for millions of conquered people as the military crushed any opposition in lightning swift campaigns that reduced once mighty foes to a laughing stock.

Seeking to break the deadlock on the Western Front in WWI the German High command had developed a new type of warfare. At the heart of this warfare were the *Sturmtruppen* (Storm Troopers). Selected men were organised into *Sturmabteilung* (Storm Detachments) and given the task of breaking through the opposing trench lines. Preceded by a short sharp barrage they would attack the enemy strongpoints. Rather than hitting them head on, the *Sturmtruppen* were trained to bypass resistance and head into the opposition rear areas where they sowed confusion and death. Should unexpected resistance appear the elite soldiers would use mobile artillery assets, submachine guns and showers of grenades to wipe out their opponents. Once in the rear of the enemy trenches they would roll them up from the flank.

Some spectacular successes were achieved with this new style of warfare but it was introduced too late in the WWI to prevent the balance of resources tipping in favour of the *Entente* forces.

Between the wars military theorists such as Basil Liddell Hart adopted these new techniques to a modern battlefield. But it was the German General Heinz Guderian who welded disparate theories into a combined style of war that was embraced by the military. Tanks supported by flying artillery in the form of the new Luftwaffe (air force) would break through enemy lines. Supported by motorised infantry, artillery, anti-tank guns, flak (anti-aircraft guns) and sophisticated radio communications networks they would drive for the distant rear of enemy formations. Two new weapons of war were introduced which revolutionised combat – the internal combustion engine and the radio. Ponderous armies trained in linear warfare had no hope against this coordinated, mechanised onslaught.

As in some fevered Wagnerian opus the armed forces of Nazi Germany strode across the European landscape. Destroying their ungodly foes with massive armoured thunderbolts. Unstoppable and powerful the triumphant German soldiers smashed the mere mortals of smaller nations. German weapon systems even penetrated the stratosphere, seemingly about to lift man from beyond the constraints of the globe.

Following behind the armed forces were the ideological enforcers of Nazi state – the black-clad SS (*Schutzstaffel*, literally the Protection Squadron). They herded millions of 'undesirables' into pits where they were 'cleansed' from the earth with a bullet in the head. Others were beaten to death in a dank basement in one of the myriad Gestapo headquarters that appeared throughout the newly-conquered territories.

In September 1941 there was nothing to stop the armored fist made, up of the German Panzers, as they stormed towards Moscow. France had fallen, the British military was a shadow of its former self. Poland was wiped off the map and most of the minor European states were allied with or conquered by the Third Reich. It seemed nothing could stop Hitler's crazy dreams becoming reality. Once Moscow fell, the loss of transport infrastructure, industry and population centres would mean any further Russian resistance would be token only. Earlier encirclement battles had led to the Soviet Western field armies of three million men being captured along with their equipment and supplies.

There was nothing to stop Hitler's dreams of *Lebensraum* and racial purity becoming reality. But the Panzers were stopped – not by mud or snow, not by the Russians, not by the German High Command. They were stopped by Hitler. A six-week window to conquer the world passed.

The German high command and the top Nazis were not surprised. In previous crises dating back to the Beer Hall Putsch in 1923 Hitler had shown a propensity to panic. The brilliant political operator had one fatal flaw as a military commander – an unwillingness to finish off a beaten foe. There was one factor which stopped the Germans winning the war – Adolf Hitler.

However, for 12 years Hitler was able to fulfil his demonic vision. In that time countless millions experienced appalling deaths and privations. Had he established his empire it would have been a catastrophic end to hundreds of millions of lives.

1

DICTATORSHIP

The *Fallbeil* – drop axe

The Nazi regime used many methods to get rid of recalcitrant citizens. Some would disappear in the dead of night never to be seen again. Others were executed with a head shot from a Luger before being dumped in a canal and many were beaten to death in a KL (*Konzentrationslager* or concentration camp) or tortured in a Gestapo cellar. Hitler personally ordered that the July 1944 bomb plotters should be hanged with piano wire from butchers' hooks. He ordered their death struggles to be recorded and enjoyed watching their drawn out and agonising deaths.

However the most common form of judicial execution was decapitation by guillotine. With typical Teutonic literal mindedness they called this device the *Fallbeil* which translates as 'drop axe'. Some were set up in town squares but most operated in sordid basements or gymnasia in a range of forbidding prisons. The German guillotines were not nearly as fancy as the earlier French guillotines but were low slung and built for efficiency rather than show. Quite a few alterations to the basic design were made in an attempt to make the guillotine even more efficient. They needed to be more efficient and robust given the heavy work schedule they were required to perform.

Firstly the Germans introduced a much heavier blade in order to allow shorter all metal uprights to be used. In addition they dispensed with the bascule, the movable tray to which the French victims were strapped. No doubt considering the feelings of the victim, the executioner could choose whether the condemned would be decapitated facing down away from the blade or facing up towards it. In addition the blade could be covered from sight and the victim would be backed towards the device while it was covered by a screen. Twenty of these machines were personally ordered by Adolf Hitler and approximately 16,000 people were executed between 1933 and 1945. This eclipsed the number killed in France during the height of the 'Terror' between 1789 and 1794.

With typical Teutonic efficiency the families of those executed had to pay a fee of 1.5 Reichsmarks for each day in custody, 300 Reichsmarks for the execution and 12 Pfennigs to cover postage expenses for the invoices. The executioner at Plotzenee prison, Roettger, could complete one guillotining every three minutes and was paid 60 Reichsmarks per job.

Adolph Hitler used his dominance in the Reichstag to legislate the reduction in the age of those who could be executed to 14 years old. Political opponents were the chief victims of the new improved guillotine which eventually saw 45 machines operating throughout the Reich. Offences such as expressing doubt that the Nazis would win the war or listening to Allied radio were capital crimes. In Plotzenee during one 11-hour period, 75 were executed using two guillotines at the same time. 1,400 were executed in Vienna alone.

Johann Reichhart has the dubious honour of being the most prolific modern executioner with 2,876 recorded victims during this period. He made many modifications to his *Fallbeil* to make it more efficient. Previously victims had been strapped to a bascule which was then slid forward so that their neck was under the blade. A *lunette* (semicircular hoop) was than locked down over the neck to hold the victim in place. Reichhart dispensed with this procedure and had his assistants slide the condemned prisoner into position and then hold them down until the blade was released. Disposal of blood from the decapitated corpses was an issue so Reichhart erected a guard surrounding the head which forced the blood to splash down into a funnel linked directly into the prison's drains. He was obviously something of a handyman.

The Allies did not prosecute Reichhart and he was responsible for preparing the gallows for the hanging by Pierrepoint of those war criminals convicted during various post war trials.

How was it possible for the Nazis to take such a dreadful toll of human life?

They created a police state almost unrivalled for the absolute control it exerted over its citizens. It was this legal apparatus that allowed the Nazis to keep the German people fighting until the entire country was overrun and Hitler committed suicide in May 1945.

The genesis of the police state

Once Hitler was appointed Chancellor on January 30th 1933 he moved quickly to consolidate power and eliminate his opposition. In the deal hammered out with President Hindenburg only three Nazis would be in the new Reich's Cabinet. Hitler was Chancellor. William Frick was Minister for the Interior and Hermann Göring was placed in charge of the police in Prussia and Berlin. It was this control of the police that allowed Hitler to terrorise his enemies and begin building his totalitarian state.

With the tacit cooperation of his coalition partners a wave of beatings and arrests swept through Germany. The SA (Storm Battalion) were given a free hand and communist or socialist activists were targeted as the first concentration camps, Dachau outside Munich and Oranienburg outside Berlin, were built to cater for the new flood of political prisoners. Aiding the Nazis were the national police controlled by Frick and the 90,000 strong Prussian police controlled by Göring. In February 50,000 auxiliary police were recruited from the SA to help with the bloody crackdown.

Also founded in early 1933 were the *Geheime Staatspolizei* who became known by their fearsome nickname, the *Gestapo*.

As the head of the Prussian police Göring stated his aims clearly.

> It is not my business to do justice, it is my business to annihilate and exterminate – that's all.

Eyewitness accounts abound of Nazi brutality. The most obvious violence was carried out by the SA. It was ignored by the majority of Germans as they went about their business. If you were not Jewish, Communist or homosexual you were largely unaffected by the Nazi crackdowns on undesirables. Foreign visitors to Germany found the new reality confronting. Christopher Isherwood wrote in his book *Goodbye to Berlin* describing the routine nature of violence in the Nazi state. Walking through what used to be the most civilized city in Europe Isherwood saw three SA men walking with Nazi banners on their shoulders, each banner was fully equipped with Swastika flag and arrowhead staves. Suddenly the SA men saw a Communist party member who they forced into a building's entrance alcove and proceeded to kick and stab with their banners;

> "Another passer-by and myself were the first to reach the doorway where the young man was lying. I got a sickening glimpse of his face – his left eye was poked half out and blood poured from the wound. Twenty yards away stood a group of heavily armed police who disregarded the whole affair."

> Christopher Isherwood, *Goodbye to Berlin*, Penguin Books, London, 1969, p 80.

Lina Haag was married to a communist and she experienced at first hand the unwelcome attentions of the SA as soon as Hitler became Chancellor.

Bursting into her apartment a large posse of SA came to make brutalize the young women and her family. Fully equipped with revolvers and truncheons they proceeded to destroy her possessions. Chairs were smashed, drawers emptied, clothes torn to pieces, smashed pictures and butted holes in the wall plaster looking for 'contraband.' Lina was forced to stand to attention in her petticoat while the SA men, many who used to be trusted neighbors, leered and gloated. Most intimidating to Lina and her husband, a member of the German Reichstag, were the loaded revolvers left on tables and cabinets, fully cocked and ready to be used at the smallest token of resistance by the SA men. Haag's husband was arrested, any legal protections given by the Weimar Constitution being totally ignored by the Nazis.

Things were only to get hotter for anyone opposing the Nazis, making these events seem mild in comparison. The Reichstag (National Parliament) fire on 27th February was a propaganda coup for Hitler. There are conflicting theories as to what started the fire that tore through the building in the heart of Berlin. It seems that Göring and some of his most trusted SA bullyboys used a tunnel connecting the Reichstag with the Reich Chancellery to gain access in the dead of night and set it alight with cans of gasoline and flares. Enjoying the luck of the devil, which Hitler certainly had at this time, a disturbed Dutch communist named Marinus van der Lubbe also put in an appearance with some lighter fluid and a match and set fire to the building at the same time.

Whoever lit the fire is not important. What is important were its consequences. Hitler persuaded a shaken von Hindenburg, the aged President of the Weimar Republic, to issue a decree 'For the Protection of People and State.' This was the basis for the totalitarian state which allowed Hitler to rule Germany with an iron fist for the next twelve years. Using Article 48, the Emergency Powers clause of the Weimar Constitution, Hindenburg suspended basic civil liberties.

No longer were Germans guaranteed a fair trial or freedom from arbitrary arrest. No longer could Germans trust that their mail would not be opened or presume that their personal possessions could not be seized. No longer could Germans express their opinions, join political parties or join trade unions without fear of persecution. No longer could Germans participate in the religion of their choice. No longer could a free and fair press safely express any opinions that were at odds with those of the regime.

Early concentration camps

Hitler's first reference to concentration camps was in 1921 when he promised to, 'stop the Jews from undermining our nation, if necessary by keeping their bacilli safely in concentration camps.' A small line in a crazed rant became a death sentence for millions and untold suffering for many more.

The first goal of the Nazi state was to break the organised working class. In 1926 Hitler declared there could be no peace until the last communist was converted or exterminated. Staring at the Reichstag fire an infuriated Hitler was reported to have said that there would be no mercy now – anyone who stood in his way would be mercilessly cut down. Whether his rage was confected or genuine, his henchmen took this as a cue for savage violence.

The Nazis smashed left-wing organisations' offices and targeted activists throughout industrialised German towns. Such was the speed with which the Nazis came to assume total power and destroy all human rights that no methodical planning had been put into place to organise lists of those who were to be arrested or places where the leftists could be incarcerated. No handbooks detailing how to interrogate prisoners, feed them or even restrain them were produced. It was up to individual SA cells to crack down on those they thought deserved *Schutzhaft* – protective custody.

Two hundred thousand political prisoners were detained in 1933 as the Nazis flexed their newly acquired police powers. Almost all were German and most were communists. The rapid development of political events meant that little consideration had been given to where the tidal wave of new prisoners could be housed. Arrest warrants weren't required.

A plethora of new sites sprang up and these were the earliest concentration camps. Most SA groups had a local pub, beer hall or town hall where they regularly met and often holding pens were extemporised out of beer cellars or gyms. Other sites were vacant or run down hotels, castles, sports grounds or even converted restaurants. In the past many of these were utilised by the SA as drinking halls before they sallied out to beat up opposition groups or terrorise Jews. In Berlin alone during early 1933 there were 170 concentration camps mostly confined to the working class districts colloquially known as 'Red Berlin'. This pattern was repeated across the industrial heartland of Germany, the Ruhr, and port towns such as Hamburg.

The advantage for the Nazis was they could grab somebody off the street and have them in custody in a matter of moments. There they could do as they wished. Even if the prisoners were not beaten conditions were often intolerable. Toilet facilities were overwhelmed, heating or bedding was not provided and only occasionally would food be issued. Straw thrown on the freezing floor of a beer cellar would not keep out the cold.

Well-known communists might earn regular beatings while lower-rung operatives or cardholding members could be totally ignored. The treatment of those confined was at the whim and predilection of their captors with no centralised supervision or guidelines. The local nature of the early places of protective custody meant that guards often had an intimate knowledge of their prisoner's past and frequently a final bloody reckoning was extracted to settle old scores.

Some state police forces allowed the use of empty wings of existing prisons and old workhouses, that were left empty after the end of the depression, were also ideally suited to confining prisoners. By April 1933, Bavarian prisons had twice as many political prisoners as criminal detainees. Those who were held in semi-autonomous protective custody were fortunate. They were protected to some extent from the full brutality of the SA. Reasonable rations and bedding were provided and, depending on the State's practices, prisoners were fairly well treated.

Most of these early camps lasted only for a short period of time. The Nazis still sought to maintain some veneer of legality and cavalier brutality enacted in thousands of semi-public venues was not the view of the 'New Germany' that they wanted the German public or the international press to see.

The Nazis rapidly decided to bring the situation under control, replacing these early, informal arrangements with several new and permanent camps. Oranienburg in Prussia and Dachau just outside of Munich were among the first of these institutions.

Journalists, communists, homosexuals, artists and any deemed to be dissidents were shipped off into protective custody in these concentration camps. Originally they were run by the worst of the SA sadists. Prisoners were routinely whipped with riding crops, pummelled by groups of guards, thrown against bars, kicked down stairs or 'shot while trying to escape'. By 1939, 200,000 German citizens had passed through the gates of the first concentration camps and those who were lucky enough to be released were thoroughly cowed. Originally meant for political prisoners, the early camps were used for confining convicted criminals from 1934 onwards. This allowed the Nazis to smear their opponents as criminals.

These criminal elements were often placed in a position of power, such as block warden, and they were allowed to terrorise those held for political reasons. Eventually all types of undesirables from German society were confined in the concentration camps springing up around the countryside. Patches affixed to their striped uniforms aided quick identification of their 'crimes.' Politicals wore red, professional criminals green. Blue was reserved for those who had tried to flee the country and Jehovah's Witnesses wore purple, homosexuals wore pink and social undesirables wore black. In a bid to clean up the German streets the Nazis instituted beggar's week. Homeless drifters throughout Germany were rounded up and sent to camps.

Soon the SS took over and Theodor Eicke, the director of the camp system, he had one simple guiding principle which would soon lead to unimaginable suffering; "Tolerance means weakness." Under this guideline even the smallest infraction would merit merciless punishment. Any prisoner questioning the Führer or the Father land would be beaten or even hung. This meant that any who discussed politics, agitated against the regime told 'atrocity stories,' read non Nazi political pamphlets, spread communist propaganda, or even discussed politics with other prisoners would be punished. Any who dared attack a guard or SS man would be immediately executed by shooting on the spot and those who shirked their designated labor could earn the same fate. Most importantly, in Eicke's mind, those who were fortunate enough to be released were not to discuss their experiences with any members of the public and, in particular, foreigners.

Theodor Eicke was one of the least-pleasant personages within the pantheon of top Nazis. Like many of his comrades he was a failure in civilian life and only managed to obtain success in a regime based on fear, loathing and violence. A notorious bullyboy, his bluff and burly exterior concealed his overbearing and vindictive nature. Determined to set an example to his men Eicke would brook no opposition and established a personal hold over the entire KL system.

Eicke left home in 1909 when he was seventeen before he completed school. Enlisting in the military he had an undistinguished military career and he was not deemed a good enough soldier to remain in the peacetime army despite 10 years service. The civilian police did not take to him and he spent most of the 1920s working in security for IG Farben. Finally falling under the Nazis' spell in the late twenties he became a fanatical supporter and had to flee the country after being arrested with a cache of home-made bombs. On returning to Germany in early 1933 he was imprisoned before being shipped off to a mental asylum. Fortunately for Eicke he had caught Himmler's eye and Eicke was released and appointed as commandant of Dachau. Realising that he had one more chance to make a fist of things Eicke gave total loyalty to Himmler and focused all of his energies on making the concentration camp system the apple of the Reichsführer's eye. Over the next years he built an empire of camps laid out along similar lines staffed with thousands of guards possessing the same brutal ethos.

Killed while engaged in battlefield reconnaissance on the Eastern Front in February 1943, Eicke did more than most to break political opposition and prepare the ground for the Holocaust.

Eicke developed the basic layout of the camp and Dachau became the model for all other KLs of which there were six by 1939. Eicke also instituted a training regime that was utilised throughout the Reich to desensitise the guards to prisoners' suffering. Guards were encouraged to be ill-disposed to all prisoners and treat them all as filthy criminals. They were encouraged to 'treat them rough' and root out all sympathy. 'Hate indoctrination' led to torture and ill treatment of German prisoners. Of course, this attitude escalated during the Holocaust.

Himmler Examines the model for Dachau concentration camp, 1935.

After the 'Night of the Long Knives' control of the camps fell to the SS. To administer the camps a new unit was set up within the SS structure, The Order of the Death's Head *Totenkopfverbände*. The number of men within this unit swelled exponentially and by 1939 they were staffing six major camps – Dachau, Sachsenhausen, Buchenwald, Flossenbürg, Mauthausen and Ravensbrück. Under Eicke's leadership a regiment composed of these troops was committed to some of the early *Blitzkrieg* campaigns where they proved to be an embarrassment to both the *Waffen SS* and the Wehrmacht.

New and old methods were used to torment prisoners. The basic aim was to break resistance as soon as possible. Arriving prisoners were often forced to run a gauntlet of baton wielding guards. Lined up on the camp square they would be 'welcomed' by the camp commandant. It was his role to scare the living daylights out of the prisoners by explaining the horrible consequences of any misdemeanors. They would be told in no uncertain terms that they were the scum of the earth and any who had worked against the new order could expect no mercy. Terms such as scum, dirty dogs, red swine, bloodthirsty schemers, crooks, seducers, swindlers of the people and Bolshevik murderers were among the more polite terms used.

To reinforce the point, up to 30 guards often set upon the new prisoners, beating them with truncheons or chains and kicking them mercilessly. Prisoners were not allowed to walk but would be harried by guards wherever they went. Pistols were waved in faces while they were called scum and swine. Individual identity was removed. Hair was shaved off and the striped uniform that became notorious in Holocaust images was given to each prisoner. Body searches were conducted, fingerprints taken and mug shots taken. Throughout this process the prisoners were mercilessly harried and the key message was instilled in the new arrivals – they were vermin and filth and their life meant nothing.

SS and SA guards didn't worry about inflicting damage. Whips, truncheons, boots, pistol grips, fists and open hands were all deployed ruthlessly. Skin was slashed, bones broken, organs ruptured and faces disfigured. Mock executions, whether in the solitude of a cell or on public display, were common. Men would plead for their lives in front of hundreds of inmates only for the firing squad to stand down or a pistol's firing pin to hit thin air, before they were hauled back, broken, to their cell. Two old prisoners in Sonnenburg were hauled from their cells and forced to dig two graves in the prison yard. They then stood in front of their handiwork waiting to be shot only for the SA firing squad to lower their rifles and burst out laughing.

Prisoners were spared no humiliation. They were shaven all over, forced to eat faeces or drink urine and made to masturbate in public or masturbate other inmates. Naked genitals were beaten and high pressure hoses were inserted into their rectums.

Women fared no better. Even before the enabling act many had been raped and beaten mercilessly in dank prison basements.

The 'Sachsenhausen salute' required prisoners to squat for hours with their arms outstretched. If they fell or dropped their arms guards were ready to beat them, often into unconsciousness before a hose was turned on them until they recovered and had to resume the position. Pointless tasks such as marching around the camp perimeter or shifting piles of rocks back and forth were used to break prisoners' spirits. Those who were found not to display the correct attitude were sent to the camp prison where they were kept in solitary confinement, subject to random beatings and given poor rations. Hard-core recidivists would be given the *strappado*. This was an ancient German torture technique that involved the wrists being tied behind the prisoner's back before they were suspended from a pole or a roof beam by this rope. Most experienced dislocated shoulders and blacked out with the excruciating pain.

One method favoured in all camps was the blitz attack. Truncheon wielding guards would descend on a new arrival and bash the living daylights out of him until he collapsed in a pool of blood. Any other inductees would quickly get the message. Alternatively the guards would burst into a cell where the prisoner had been placed in solitary and bash him with fists until he fell unconscious on the ground where they would continue to kick the living daylights out of him. There was no idea of a fair fight and up to nine SA or SS men would pounce on their victims.

Oranienburg was established at the same time as Dachau. Originally a brewery, its first commandant pioneered 'the standing cell' and built several in the basement of the camp. These were small closet like structures that held isolated prisoners in such close confines that they could only stand. Rations were limited to a couple of pieces of bread a day as well as water. It was recommended that prisoners be held for three days before being removed from the standing cell, given proper rations and allowed to sleep on a wooden cot. They would then be returned to the cell for another 72-hour stint.

This rule was not always adhered to. One prisoner was held for 192 hours without rest and was subsequently driven mad. Others were not allowed out for up to eight days and as a result developed acid burns on their legs and thighs from their accumulated urine and feces.

One victim of this torture wrote:

It was a terrible state, as I thought it was over for me, everything was so callous and distant for me. I couldn't lie down, couldn't crouch, the best was to stand, stand, six days and six nights. You touch the walls on both sides with your elbows, your back touches the wall behind you, your knees the wall in front of you. This is no punishment or pretrial detention, it is torture, straight forward. Middle Ages torture. I had bloodshot eyes, numb from bad air, I was just waiting for the end.

Karel Kasak, *Cesi v koncentracnim tabore Dachau*, in *Almanch Dachau. Kytice udalosti a vzpominek*, Prague, 1946. Cited in Zámečník, *Das war Dachau*, p. 349

In cases such as attempted escape, there would be a public hanging in front of the assembled prisoners.

Surprisingly few died in protective custody. However, those that did tended to be high-profile opponents of the regime or those who had made trouble in the early days of Hitler's rise to power. Many accounts from prisoners write of the excitement that guards would display when hearing that a particularly hated enemy was about to be delivered into their clutches. A 'welcoming' committee would often gather at the gates and as soon as the new prisoner arrived he would be hauled out of the police wagon and beaten even more brutally than usual. Once the unfortunate individual was placed in their cell they were often encouraged to commit suicide.

Hans Beilmer arrived at Dachau and was well known amongst the guards as a persistent agitator for the communist state. He had participated in the Red Republic of 1919 and had risen to become a KPD member of the Reichstag. On his arrival at Dachau he was savagely beaten and a placard reading 'Welcome' was placed around his neck. Taken to the block which was used for particularly despised prisoners, (a converted toilet block) Beilmer was regularly beaten. After each beating he was given a piece of material and his considerate guards explained how it could be fashioned into a noose. Others of his companions slit their wrists and Beilmer was shown their pathetic corpses before being given an ultimatum. If the communist politician refused to kill himself in the next 12 hours his SA captors would finish the job. Fortunately two sympathetic SA guards allowed him to escape, perhaps a demonstration of the informal structure and slack security of early camps.

Security was tightened afterwards but Beilmer had served his purpose. The SA and SS guards made no secret of the savage persecution and faked suicides of some prisoners. It effectively cowed the less high-profile prisoners who thanked their lucky stars they weren't in the Nazi sights.

Some prisoners were targeted because they were Jewish. Fritz Solmitz was also a centre left journalist. As far as the Hamburg *Gauleiter* was concerned, Solmitz was a perfect candidate for elimination. He was transferred from the relatively benign Hamburg prison to one of the new camps and placed in solitary confinement. Waiting for him in his cell were nine guards who whipped him even after he collapsed to the floor. A head wound ensured that his blood spattered over the guards. After days of beating Solmitz was discovered dead in his cell. It was ascribed to suicide but the journalist had outwitted his captor. He had written the torture and threats on a cigarette papers which he secreted in his watch. This was returned to his next of kin who were able to read how he had been urged by a succession of bullies to commit suicide.

The prominent politicians Friedrich Ebert and Ernst Heilmann had been beaten when they arrived at Oranienburg. When transferred to a SS-run camp the reception was even harsher. Pulled from the police van they were beaten with window slats and table legs. They were then tossed into a pit with three Jewish prisoners and almost buried alive. Ebert was told to bash his companions but refused. Although threatened with immediate execution with a Luger to the back of his head, he refused and was thereafter treated with a grudging respect. Guard dogs were set upon the prisoners and finally Heilmann could take it no longer. He stumbled over the free fire zone at the camp perimeter and was shot. In a grim irony the wound was not mortal and he survived.

Others inmates were just in the wrong place at the wrong time. Lina Haag was eventually arrested and sent to Dachau. She wrote how almost every morning a dead women would be found, battered and bruised, under their bed or under a table where they had sought to seek refuge from the deadly blows inflicted by the guards. Suffering 'extreme' rigor mortis, most of the nameless victims were frozen forever with terrified stares.

There could be some exaggeration in this account. Not many perished in the early days of the concentration camps. Oranienburg was shut down in 1936. It had held 3,000 inmates of whom 16 had died. Many undesirables were returned to society after comparatively short stints in the early camps and by no means all felt the full brutality of the SA and SS guards.

Nevertheless the camps fulfilled their function of cowing the elements of society who were likely to resist the new regime. Particularly in 1933, sentences for most prisoners rarely went beyond three months. The new regime felt that shock and awe tactics with a brief spell in a camp were sufficient to ensure future compliance and rapid turnover was the order of the day. Some were released after only a week or so while those detained for a longer period were transferred to the new permanent camps.

Those within the camps got the message. In the national election of November 12, 1933 almost 100 per cent of KL inmates voted to support the regime, just like the rest of the population.

Many emerged from custody with permanent physical scars. Returning to their community, a hobbling gait or sunken features reminded their neighbors of the consequences of going against the regime. Others had no physical injury but were broken internally. A once proud German citizen who had shat his pants in mortal terror or begged for mercy in front of hundreds of onlookers would look sideways if he witnessed Nazi injustice and would become a silent supporter of the regime, unwilling to risk its wrath again.

A sort of gallows humour evolved in German society. A popular joke ran:

Heinz opened his mouth too wide and as a result spent a few weeks of ideological training in a concentration camp. After his release a friend asked what life was like there.

'Excellent,' he replied. 'At 9am we were served a cooked breakfast in our bedrooms. Then there was light work for those who wanted to work and some sport for those who didn't. Lunch was plain but good, nobody ever went hungry, afterwards we did some more light work. For supper we were served some dumplings. In the evening we had lectures or a film. Or else played games.'

The questioner was much impressed. 'Incredible' he says. 'All those lies we hear about the concentration camps! The other day I spoke to Schmidl who had just been released from one. He told me rather different stories about his camp.'

'Yes,' said Heinz, 'That's why Schmidl is back in his camp.'

A popular ditty soon made its way into the German vernacular:

'Dear God make me dumb, so I may not to Dachau come.'

While this humour shows efforts to deal with the new horror that seemed to appear in German society out of nowhere, concrete steps were taken to prevent 'Atrocity Propaganda'. Camps close to large settlements were closed down. Residents from surrounding towns such as Dachau were warned to steer clear.

On March 23rd a new law 'The Decree Against Malicious Attacks' meant that anyone who reported or even discussed rumoured abuses could be sentenced to a stint in the very institutions that they had criticised. One man was sentenced to a year's imprisonment. The judges in their summation explained that such rumours had to be ruthlessly punished to stop others from committing similar deeds.

Hitler grabs total power

Nevertheless the powers of arrest and imprisonment were not enough for the budding dictator – he wanted total power within the German state. He obtained this with the Enabling Act. After seeing what happened to Hitler's political opponents, most of the remaining political parties almost fell over themselves in their haste to approve the act which required a two thirds majority in the relocated Reichstag to pass.

No dictator could have asked for more!

The Enabling Law, 24th March 1933

Article 1 –   The Reich Cabinet is authorised to enact laws.

Article 2 –   The laws enacted by the Reich Cabinet may deviate from the constitution.

Article 3 –   The laws enacted by the Reich Cabinet shall be prepared by the Chancellor. They come into effect, unless otherwise specified, upon the day following their publication.

Any decree by Hitler could become law immediately. The Enabling Law was meant to last until 23rd March 1937 but it was renewed, by decree the day before, and every four years thereafter.

The German Communist Party was already illegal and on June 22nd the Social Democratic Party was banned, its property confiscated and its seats in the Reichstag declared invalid. The other parties soon followed suit and some even abolished themselves! In November 1933 another Reichstag election was held. Not surprisingly the Nazis received all of the votes and all of the seats in the Reichstag. In January 1934 the State Parliaments were abolished.

Given the extraordinary powers of the Enabling Act, Hitler and the top Nazis began the process of *Gleichshaltung* (coordination or synchronisation). All aspects of social and economic life were bought under Nazi control. Political, social and cultural institutions were to be ideologically supportive of Nazi ideals and controlled by trusted party members. Any opposition within these institutions was to be eliminated through violence, threats or exclusion. It had the effect of persecuting some but the majority felt they were part of a united community committed to the well-being of the *Volk* (People). Those who were reluctant were to be coerced into accepting Nazi ideological requirements. Those who didn't cooperate had their personal safety, assets, right to work and freedoms stripped.

The 1.6 million strong civil service was brought under control in April 1933 with the 'Law for the Restoration of the Professional Civil Service.' Under this law civil servants of Jewish descent were removed. Suspect workers were removed 'because of their previous political activity' along with those whose qualifications were inadequate. Trade unions were next for the chop and on May 2nd 1933 all trade unions were banned. The police and SA raided union offices and arrested leaders. Dr Robert Ley was set up as the head of the *ersatz* (imitation) union, the German Labour Front.

In 1933 the judicial system became the tool of the Nazis and all judicial appointments had to meet strict criteria and interpret the law in a manner which suited the Nazis. In addition the People's Court was set up in April 1934 to deal with crimes against the state. There was no appeal against judgments from this court and show trials rivalling the worst Stalinist farces were staged. Most of those sentenced by the People's Court ended up on the guillotine – no appeals were allowed.

Members of the judiciary became enthusiastic supporters of the new regime. Politically unreliable officials were sacked, fundamental legal principles abandoned and punitive laws were interpreted more strictly. The prison population, not counting those in the 'protective custody' of the concentration camps, almost doubled between 1932 and 1935. In 1935 there were at least 100,000 permanent prisoners in jails compared with three thousand in the camp system. The judiciary were keen to show their support by treating prisoners more harshly. Rations were cut and brutal treatment escalated. This was particularly so after the SS took over the KL camps and many SA guards were transferred for employment in the criminal system.

Often judges recommended a suspect be transferred to a KL if the prisoner could not be found guilty of a criminal offence. Similarly, incorrigibles could be released once they had served their sentence but authorities would ensure that there were SS personnel ready to arrest them at the prison gates to continue confinement in a KL. The legal system soon acquiesced to the random killings in the concentration camps. Early attempts to investigate the circumstances of those who were 'shot while trying to escape' were stonewalled by uncommunicative guards and it was made clear that to pursue an investigation would be a waste of time and perhaps dangerous.

The informer state

Once official channels of freedom of speech were closed down and any informal criticism of the new regime was dealt with ruthlessly. A culture of spying grew and all communities were closely monitored by a network of official and unofficial informers. A prisoner in one of the early KLs wrote how new prisoners were bought in day and night for the smallest offence. One farmer was imprisoned for the possession of two useless rifles, a workman drunk in a pub earned arrest for saying Hitler couldn't help him. Even citizens who had been a member of the communist party years ago were not spared. While these individuals were no real threat to the new regime they all had one thing in common – an ex-lover, a disgruntled neighbor, or even a business rival had seen fit to inform upon them and report them to the Gestapo.

As individuals tried to ingratiate themselves with the Nazis any seemingly innocent event could be turned into a malevolent communist plot by a suspicious informer. Smoking chimneys aroused the suspicion that incriminating papers or books were being burnt, often leading to house searches where everything was trashed. People took to shredding paperwork and flushing it down the toilet. Not raising the arm in the Hitler salute, nor attending military parades or not showing sufficient enthusiasm when saying '*Heil* Hitler' could result in a visit from the Gestapo or a letter requesting the person attend the local lock up. Parades of SA troops became an almost daily occurrence in many major cities and towns. It was required that anybody in the vicinity or people passing by should drop everything and salute until the parade had passed. Domestic and international letters were closely monitored and a careless word to a stranger was all that was required for a black mark to be placed on a citizen's record.

These records were extensive. As well as having to prove one's Germanness and freedom from the Jewish 'taint', all had to register with the local '*Orpo*.' The *Ordnungspolizei* or 'Order Police' were the regular police force and maintained files on all in their district.

More important for monitoring the population's attitudes was the Nazi infrastructure that was imposed upon society and penetrated every aspect of German life. By 1938 the Nazi party had five million members and over half a million paid officials.

The lowest level official was the Block Leader. One was

appointed to every block of apartments, every street of houses or every small village. On average a block leader supervised forty households. They maintained a card system that had the pertinent details of each resident including political background, employment history and, most importantly for the Nazis, friends and associates. The block leader's role was to establish who was 'solid' and encourage others to inform on dubious characters. A small suggestions box was provided to facilitate anonymous accusations.

A cluster of five or six blocks was supervised by a *Zelle* (cell) leader who was in turn supervised by an *Ortsgruppe* leader equating to a town or suburb of 1,500 households. The *Ortsgruppe* were supervised by Nazi officials at the level of a *Kries* (district) of which there were 760 further grouped into *Gaue* (region). There were 32 *Gaue* in Germany and they were supervised by a top Nazi Party official, the *Gauleiter*. Known as 'Golden Pheasants' due to their bright brown uniforms, they had a reputation for sumptuous living and rampant cronyism.

It wasn't so pleasant for those being supervised by this informer network that reached into all levels of German society. Much was published by the Nazis on how a block leader could carry out his duties:

> It is the Block Leader's duty to find people spreading damaging rumors and to report them immediately to their superior so that the Political Police (Gestapo) may be informed. As well as reporting subversion the Block Leader must spread and defend Nationalist Socialist Ideology and remind party members of their responsibilities to the party and the state.
>
> In addition the Block Leader must maintain a card file on each individual and family within his zone which must be up to date, recording past and present political associations.
>
> It must be the block leaders' aim that the sons and daughters of families within his zone become members of the various formations of the Hitler Youth, SA, SS and the German

Labour Front, and that they visit National Socialist Meeting, rallies, celebrations, etc. Individuals who resist these goals must be reported.

Obviously the block leader was not somebody you would particularly want to ask over for dinner. Block leaders were trained to elicit information in innocent conversations and recruit informers, especially children, to find out what was said behind closed doors. Nazi fifth columnists would start conversations with strangers in pubs, clubs, sporting events or on public transport. They would introduce into a conversation a mild criticism of the regime and hope that the other participant would carry it further and condemn themselves with negative comments and sentiments.

Each office, government department, school or business had informers. Public servants would be considered to be acting against the state by refusing to inform upon a colleague who had criticised the party. Early Nazi decrees stated that the Nazi Party and the state were one. Any criticism of the party was thus treason.

The result of being denounced was arrest for questioning. Throughout Germany a new and disturbing pattern emerged. Late at night or early in the morning the Gestapo or *Kripo* would arrive at a suspect's door and demand entry. These times were chosen as it was most likely the victim would be undressed and vulnerable, or relaxed and unsuspecting. One or more members of the Gestapo, clad in their menacing ankle length leather coats and supported by heavily armed police, would then seize the suspect and hustle him down to the waiting car. Family members learnt not to interfere and knew that there was no point protesting or resisting, many looked on with glazed eyes as they saw their loved ones disappear, perhaps forever.

The blood purge

In a breathtakingly short period of time Hitler had assumed control of most aspects of society. There was one barrier to total control – his '*Alte Kameraden*' in the SA.

While the Western press dubbed the events of 30th June 1934 as 'The Night of The Long Knives', the Germans refer to it as the 'Blood Purge.' This is an appropriate name given the many bloody methods of execution used by the Nazis. Death squads operated throughout Germany, rounding up victims and executing them in a variety of ruthless and bloody ways.

A conflict between Hitler and the SA had been brewing for a long time. Although Hitler had destroyed organised opposition throughout much of Germany he had yet to deal with the paramilitary arm of the Nazi party.

By 1934 the SA numbered approximately three million men. They were a highly organised paramilitary with members in every town and village in Germany. The Army perceived the SA as a clear and present danger to their status partly due to the huge disparity in numbers and partly due to the aggressive posturing of the SA leadership, especially Ernst Röhm. The SA was made up of men who were predominantly from the lower-middle class and the unemployed. They represented the more radical element of the Nazi movement and still clung to socialist ideas which had been propounded by Gregor Strasser but had largely been abandoned by 1933.

Röhm and many in the top echelons of the SA believed the revolution had not gone far enough. The wealthy landlords, the industrialists and the Old Prussian Junker military still dominated much of German society. Hitler had come to power with the support of these groups and the constant rallies, marches and demands of the SA seemed to portend a second National Socialist Revolution.

The military felt particularly threatened. Many in the

army were sympathetic to the Nazi party and were aware of Hitler's desire for rearmament. Hitler thought that the SA had served its purpose enabling the Nazi rise to power. Neither he nor the High Command approved of Röhm's plan to incorporate the military into the ranks of the SA so that his organisation could become the main military force in Germany. While delusional in many respects, Hitler knew he needed the Wehrmacht if he was to carry out his future policy for the conquest of Europe.

Hitler still possessed his superb sense of timing. Aware that President Hindenburg was on deaths' door, Hitler wanted to combine the role of Chancellor and President so that he could be appointed Commander in Chief of the armed forces. He needed the army to transfer its loyalty from the president to himself. To do this he was more than willing to sacrifice the aspirations of the upstart SA.

The army leaders and Hindenburg made it clear that Hitler had to move decisively. On 20th June 1934 the Chancellor met the President who threatened to declare martial law and rule by decree if the situation was not resolved. Hitler had already met with leaders of the armed forces and negotiated their support by assuring them they would be the sole bearers of arms in the new Third Reich.

The day after the meeting with Hindenburg, Hitler gave the orders to move against his old comrades.

Operation *Hummingbird* was organised by Göring and Himmler. The SS was to carry out the purge. The army was able to keep their hands clean and General von Fritsch confined all operational units to barracks on the 25th of June. Himmler and Göring drew up lists of those who were to die. Hitler must have had some input as many obscure individuals who had earned his enmity years before the rise to power were included.

The 'Night of The Long Knives' began on June 30th 1934. Troops of the SS and Gestapo took the SA leadership by surprise in a coordinated series of raids and arrests. Hitler himself travelled to the Bavarian town of Bad Wiessee where Röhm was enjoying a homosexual free-for-all with some of his chosen SA favourites.

Towards five o'clock in the morning Hitler accompanied by members of the SS and Gestapo climbed into a convoy of trucks and sedans and made their way to the Hotel Hanselbauer. Preceding the convoy was an armoured car lent by the army, ready to shoot up any who sought to get in the way. As the convoy drew up in the hotel courtyard Röhm's aide-de-camp Graf Anton von Spreti was the first to wake up and investigate the cause of the disturbance. Known for his exceptional good looks he was set upon by Hitler who slashed him across the face with his riding crop.

Hitler then burst into Röhm's bedroom where he was seized by SS men after a rude awakening and berated by Hitler. Some SA personal caught in compromising positions were shot out of hand. Röhm was not immediately executed. Hitler himself tumbled his old comrade out of bed and chivvied him off to his arrest.

Many Brownshirts were taken along with other civilian victims to Dachau or a variety of prisons where swift execution by firing squad or pistol followed. Other executions were done much more publicly.

Quite a few were killed at their places of work or their homes.

Herbert von Bose who had acted as von Papen's secretary (von Papen was a rival who sought to manipulate Hitler) was gunned down at his desk in his government office.

Nobody told Anton von Freiherr that smoking was bad for his health and he was shot in the smoking room of his ancestral home.

Dr Erich Klausener was a devout Catholic. Shot by an SS officer he was able to call his priest to come and give the Last Rites but his killers didn't allow the priest access to the dying man as he slowly bled out.

General Kurt von Schleicher was relaxing with his wife

Elizabeth when six SS troopers burst into their lounge and gunned them down in a hail of pistol fire.

Several waiters and restaurateurs who were associated with Röhm's homosexual clique were gunned down while at work. Edmund Heines was shot when found in bed with his chauffeur. Gregor Strasser's lawyer Gerd Voss was shot when he objected to his office being searched.

Most unfortunate was the case of Dr Wilhelm Eduard Schmid. This peace-loving man was astounded when a group of black-clad SS troopers burst into his apartment and hauled him off into custody. He would have been even more astounded when he was shot in his cell several hours later. The good doctor was a victim of mistaken identity. A well-known political activist Ludwig Schmitt lived on a different floor of the apartment building and was the intended target. Able to take the hint, Ludwig fled soon after. Dr Schmid's widow received an apology from Rudolf Hess.

Ferdinand von Bredow reportedly had his head beaten in with truncheons while in a police van before his battered corpse was thrown into a ditch. Werner Engels paid for allegiance to Röhm by being driven into some woods outside of Breslau and executed by shotgun. Gustav Ritter von Kahr was hacked to death with axes and thrown into a swamp near Dachau. Emil Sembach was taken into the Bavarian mountains before being shot by a detachment of SS troopers. Father Bernhard Stempfle was a former associate of Hitler who maybe knew too much about Geli Raubal's (Hitler's niece and lover) death. He was found in a wood near Munich with three bullets in his heart and a broken neck.

Karl Ernst's status as a member of the Reichstag didn't protect him and he was arrested while fleeing to the docks at Bremen. He was flown to Berlin where he was shot by a *Leibstandarte* firing squad. His last words were 'Heil Hitler.' August Schneidhuber displayed remarkable sang-froid when he was executed. Shot a few hours after his arrest by Hitler's chauffeur Emil Maurice he declared, 'Well boys, I don't know what this is all about, but anyhow, shoot straight.'

Some unfortunate individuals placed their faith in Hitler and paid for it with their lives. Oskar Heines was a member of the SA who on hearing of the 'attempted Putsch' turned himself into Gestapo headquarters in Breslau to explain the situation but was executed immediately. SA Stabsführer Wilhelm Sander was in Berlin when he heard of the waves of arrests. Thinking that Göring, the Chief of Berlin Police, was acting without authority he flew to Munich to alert Hitler. Sander was arrested, flown back to Berlin and shot.

Ernst Röhm had risen in the Nazi hierarchy due to his willingness to use violence against real and perceived opponents. His executioner, Theodore Eicke, would take this violence further by a quantum leap as inspector of concentration camps. He was sent to kill Röhm to strengthen his credentials with Himmler. At 5.00am Eicke and a trusted subordinate, Michael Lippert, made their way to cell 474 in the newly built Stadelheim Prison complex in Munich. They had come straight from Dachau. Several prisoners had just been beaten to death at Dachau and some had been marched beyond the prison wires, in full view of the thousand or so prisoners, before being executed with rifles and pistols. These victims were small fry in the orgy of payback that constituted the Night of The Long Knives. Eicke and Lippert had a much bigger fish to fry.

At first the two SS men were denied access to Röhm by the prison governor. As the governor stalled a furious Eicke declared angrily that he was there on the personal orders of Adolf Hitler. The Führer had personally ordered Eicke to solve the Röhm 'problem'. Hitler wanted his old comrade to be given the opportunity to commit suicide as an honourable way out. If he didn't take that option Eicke was to resolve the issue with a couple of 9 mm slugs.

The governor made some frantic phone calls and eventually had to let the two SS men through. They stormed through the prison corridors which were lined with armed policemen until they got to cell 474. Here Eicke placed on Röhm's small table in the cramped cell a copy of the Nazi newspaper *Völkischer Beobachter* with details of the execution of six top SA men on the front cover. On the newspaper was placed a Luger with one shell in the breach. They delivered Hitler's message and gave the SA supremo ten minutes to make up his mind. Röhm blustered out a furious protest before the two assassins stepped out of cell closing the door behind them. After ten minutes had elapsed the cell door was opened again and the untouched pistol was retrieved by a policeman.

Eicke and Lippert aimed their pistols at Röhm who had stripped off his shirt and was standing against the cell wall. Both men pulled their triggers and Röhm stumbled backwards before sliding down the wall, bleeding heavily but still alive. Eicke was more of a theorist than a practitioner and he ordered the younger Lippert to finish the job. Lippert stepped forward and put another slug into Röhm's heart. Röhm's last words have variously been reported as '*Heil* Hitler' or 'Führer, my Führer.'

Gregor Strasser, who had at one time rivalled Hitler for popularity within the Nazi party, was shot on the 30th of June in a Berlin prison. It took two days for him to die and his demise was officially listed as suicide. No doubt the executioners found favour in Hitler's eyes for giving his rival such a long and painful death.

The Nazis ensured that the victims' relatives were not given the chance to arrange public shows of mourning. Many of the dead were cremated and their ashes put in cigar boxes or cheap urns before being forwarded to the next of kin. In some instances only personal effects were returned. The journalist Fritz Gerlich's widow received his glasses in a box, one lens had been shattered by a bullet and was encrusted with blood.

Some individuals had lucky escapes.

Hermann Ehrhardt fled into woods adjoining his estate when he saw two automobiles filled with Gestapo arrive at his front door. He took two shotguns with him and was later smuggled into Austria by friends. Paul Schulz was arrested in Berlin and taken out to a lonely stretch of woods near Potsdam. He bolted and was shot in the back. He played dead and as his captors went back to the car to find something to wrap his corpse in, he jumped up and ran off into the woods. He made his way to the house of retired admiral Lübbert where he hid while an amnesty was negotiated with Hitler through a third party.

SA-Gruppenführer Karl Schreyer was arrested in Berlin and taken to Columbia House. He was about to be shot at 4am, 2nd July 1934, when the order to stop all executions came from the Führer.

Ernst Udet was invited to Gauleiter Wagner's banquet in Munich 30 June 1934. He was the only one to escape from the banquet which was in fact a prearranged trap for Hitler's enemies. Although dazed and with a large gash on his forehead he ran into Hitler who took pity on the pilot and told him to leave immediately.

Otto Strasser's wife, Gertrude Strasser was arrested by the Gestapo and tortured for several weeks. She escaped while being taken to a concentration camp and fled to Prague.

Quite a few enemies of Hitler and his cronies were destroyed physiologically if not physically eliminated. Arrested along with their peers and held in detention while others were hauled out and shot, when they were eventually released they knew never to even think of defying Hitler again. Konrad Adenauer, the future chancellor of West Germany in the post-war period, was held for three days before being released.

The Night of The Long Knives cemented Hitler's control of the Nazi party and the Nazi control of Germany. Any potential dissidents would think twice before publicly questioning the regime. Official death lists put the number executed at 75 but it appears 260 would be a more accurate number. It is estimated that 200 to 400 lost their lives. The military didn't bat an eyelid when two of their top generals, von Shleicher and von Bredow were gunned down.

Many more arrests were made and it was estimated that as late as 1935 800 victims of the Röhm Purge were still being held in Dachau. In a few years' time the SA was a shell of its former self. From having four million men at the height of its strength it dwindled to 1.5 million thereafter.

Nevertheless the SA was not without some sting in its tail. During the latter months of 1934 and into 1935 nearly 150 SS leaders were assassinated by an unknown organisation. A little card was pinned to the corpses with the two letters 'RR' (*Rächer Röhm* – the avengers of Röhm). In one of the few failures of the Nazi security system, the Gestapo never managed to track down these assassins.

On 2nd of August 1934 President Von Hindenburg died at the age of 87. Using the powers given to him in the Enabling Act, Hitler prepared and published a new law which combined the office of President and Chancellor. Hitler was now head of state, head of the government and supreme commander of the armed forces. All members of the armed forces took an oath of loyalty, not to Germany but to Hitler personally. Hitler could embark on any scheme devised by him or his evil henchmen and none could challenge his actions except through violence. It took the combined forces of Russia, America and Britain to destroy the punitive legal system devised by the Nazis.

Gallows humour

Germans quickly learnt survival skills. Not speaking to strangers, looking away during arrests, trotting out trite Nazi catechisms, presuming that everybody was an informer – this was how you survived.

A black humour evolved. Jazz was banned in the new state

so bands would begin a musical number with a politically acceptable introduction from songs such as Horst Wessel before breaking out into some 'Negro Music.' The number would be finished not with the original jazz tune but with the end of the Nazi song tacked on to the climax.

Jokes were aimed at the Nazi leadership that used innuendo and metaphor, something that would not stand up in court should they be accused of subversive sentiments. Some examples of this subtle humour follow.

Can you imagine? I'm lucky enough to have got a brand new signed portrait of Adolf Hitler! Now I've got a dilemma. Should I put Hitler against the wall or hang him?

Do you know that in the future teeth will have to be pulled out through the nose? Why? Because in Germany nobody dares open their mouth.

It is 1933. A desperate looking Jew appears at a registry office with an urgent request to be allowed to change his name. The official is none too keen with the request but asks the Jew his name anyway. 'My name is Adolf Stinkarse.' The official agrees it is a pretty bad name and agrees to change it. He asks what name the Jew would like to adopt. 'I'd like to be known as Maurice Stinkarse' said the Jew.

A Jew was arrested during the war when he was denounced for killing a Nazi at 10.00am before eating the brain of his victim. This is his defense.

"I'm innocent on all charges. In the first place a Nazi hasn't got a brain, secondly Jews are forbidden by the Torah to eat pig and thirdly I couldn't have killed him at 10.00am because everybody, including myself, is listening to the BBC at that time of night.

Even these jokes had to be delivered to the right people,

people you could trust. The Germans developed what a quick furtive look around to see if anyone was listening, a look that was named the 'German glance'. The jokes were also called whisper jokes. They had to be delivered to a trusted friend and could not be overheard. Many took aim at the Nazi leadership.

What's the difference between Chamberlain and Hitler? Chamberlain takes his weekend in the country while Hitler takes a country in his weekend.

The ideal German. As blond as Hitler, as tall as Goebbels, as slim as Göring and as chaste as Röhm.

Hitler visits a lunatic asylum. The patients give the Hitler salute. As he passes down the line he comes across a man who isn't saluting.
    'Why aren't you saluting like the others?' Hitler barks.
    'Mein Führer, I'm the nurse,' comes the answer. 'I'm not crazy!'

Göring has attached an arrow to the row of medals on his tunic. It reads 'Continued on the back.'

One day while driving in the country Hitler and Göring ran over and killed a farmer's pig. Göring went into to the farmer's house to break the news, but doesn't return. Hitler is too terrified to move and sits in the car trembling with fear. Two hours later Göring reappears saying that the farmer had for some reason put on a three course meal complete with dumplings, Bratwurst sausages and wheat beer. 'I can't explain it,' said Göring 'All I said was "*Heil* Hitler! The pig is dead."'

Some jokes illustrated what it was like to live under the Nazis. A young girl is talking to her friend:

'My father is fortunate to be in the SA, my oldest brother is in the SS, my little brother is in the HJ (Hitler Youth), my mother is part of the NS women's organisation, and I'm in the BDM (Nazi girls group).'

'Sounds a lot, do you ever get to see each other?' asks the girl's friend.

'Oh yes, we meet every year at the party rally in Nuremberg!'

The Nazis passed laws in 1933 and 1934 banning comments that criticised the regime. But court cases usually resulted in just a warning or a fine, and alcohol was taken as a mitigating factor. Anti-Jewish jokes, of course, were welcome and they flourished in the 1930s, reflecting the anti-Semitism present in German society.

During the war, the regime tried to entertain the troops and distract the civilian population by promoting comedy films and harmless cabarets. Jokes about Italy's disorganised army also featured heavily.

The German army HQ receives news that Mussolini's Italy has joined the war.

'We'll have to put up 10 divisions to deal with him!' exclaims one general.

'But he's on our side,' says another.

'Oh, in that case we'll need 20 divisions.'

As it became clear that Germany was losing the war and Allied bombing started wiping out German cities, the country turned to bitter sarcasm.

'What will you do with yourself after this war?'

'I'll finally go on a holiday and take a trip round Greater Germany!'

'And what will you do in the evening?'

The authorities cracked down on defeatist jokes and Marianne Elise Kürchner, a Berlin munitions worker, was convicted and executed for dropping this bombshell:

> Hitler and Göring are standing on top of Berlin's radio tower. Hitler says he wants to do something to cheer up the people of Berlin. 'Why don't you just jump?' asks Göring.

A fellow worker overheard her telling the joke and reported to her local block leader. While it wasn't the best joke ever, it could hardly be called a hanging offence.

Priests were not spared the guillotine for telling bad jokes. In Prague a Catholic Professor of Religion, Karel Kratina, was executed for this 'continued malicious utterance':

> A man in a railway carriage who was reading *Mein Kampf* burst out laughing. His companion asked what was so funny. The man read out a quote from the Führer. 'Give me the government for ten years and you will not recognise the Reich.'

This was a clear reference to the Allied bombing campaign and earned the good professor a date with the executioner.

Another priest told a joke about a dying religious soldier who asked to see a picture of those he had sacrificed his life for. On the left he placed a picture of Göring, on the right was a picture of Hitler and in the middle was placed an image of Christ. This not so subtle allusion to the two criminals who died on the cross with Jesus was deemed to be treasonous and in November 1943 the priest was decapitated.

2

THE GESTAPO

Prinz-Albert Strasse

The heart of the Gestapo empire was 8 Prinz-Albert Strasse. This building in the centre of Berlin covered 62,000 square metres or 1.5 acres and it was here that the Gestapo perfected the methods of interrogation that would make the organisation a byword for terror throughout Germany and occupied Europe. Just as Dachau was the model concentration camp, the procedures in Prinz-Albert Strasse were replicated throughout the Reich and the mere mention of its name would strike fear into the heart of every German.

The imposing grey building had all of the required hardware to run a terror state. Large garages at the rear housed a multitude of black sedans that would stream out in the dead of night to pick up the next batch of suspects. Kennels housed vicious German Shepherds and Alsatians trained to maim and kill on command. Interrogation cells were equipped with all the hardware needed to break even the bravest man.

The upper floors were given over to administration. Some of the communications hardware given to the top SD and Gestapo officials made any James Bond fantasy look harmless by comparison. Walter Schellenberg had a large office luxuriously furnished with rich carpet and expensive sideboards. On these sideboards was an array of telephones with direct lines to the Reich chancellery and other Nazi leaders. Microphones were embedded in every surface so any innocent conversation could be analysed and recorded. They were concealed in lamps, under desks and even in chairs throughout the headquarters ensuring no subversive comment would go unheeded. Schellenberg's desk was his favourite item. Two machine guns were built into it and with a press of a button he could spray his whole office with bullets. Another button triggered a siren which summoned a troop of heavily armed SS guards to the office and sent other squads out to surround the building and block every exit. Schellenberg carried other insurance measures whenever he left his office. These included an artificial tooth laden with cyanide that would kill him in thirty seconds as well as a signet ring which had a gold capsule hidden under a large blue stone containing another dose.

Gestapo methods

The main business of 8 Prinz–Albrecht Strasse was interrogation of politically suspect individuals.

On the first floor communal cells held those recently rounded up. Other cramped cells in the basement held individuals who were being deprived of any human contact in order to break them down. These individual cells deep in the bowels of the building under the Berlin streets were closely guarded by SS men who ensured that none of their charges could communicate and handed all of their food in through a flap in the door. Dim lighting from weak light bulbs or referred from daylight filtering from street level grilles were the only brightness in their otherwise miserable existence. Sometimes the number of those arrested exceeded the cells in Gestapo headquarters and the overflow would be housed in Moabit prison until they could be bought for interrogation.

Many suspects were brought in and given a cursory questioning before being released back to their families. The point had been made to these more fortunate individuals – remain loyal to the regime or you're for it. To reinforce the message these temporary prisoners would spend one or two night in the cells where they were able to hear what happened to those who the Gestapo treated with greater rigour.

The methods of torture were as varied as the Gestapo imagination could make them. Often all that was required was two days of sensory deprivation. Some were interrogated without violence while next to them another prisoner was tortured mercilessly. The implied threat was enough to make even the bravest German spill the beans.

Many were greeted with violence. Beaten over the head, kicked in the testicles, stripped of their clothes and bucketed with freezing water, prisoners were abused and screamed at as they were hustled into their cells. As in the concentration camps, a blitz attack was frequently used where several men set upon a prisoner, often with barking dogs adding to the atmosphere. The first many knew of their future was when their teeth were knocked out by gloved fists or as they crashed to the concrete floor. New arrivals were often seized by four men, pinioned to a table and thrashed as a way of greeting.

Beatings could last for hours and hours. Thrown against the walls of the interrogation cells and hit many times prisoners would collapse and be left unconscious. An hour later a bucket of water would revive the prisoner and the beating would begin again. Many were summoned from their cells in the dead of night and beaten so badly so that blood leaked out of pores on their skin. Riding crops and coshes could be used. Often one or two parts of the body such as the soles of the feet or the kidneys were beaten time after time. The Gestapo worked in relays – when two men got tired another two would take over while the others put their feet up.

Bicycle chains with handles attached were diabolical instruments. They could be used to lacerate flesh like a whip or were squeezed like a garrotte around a limb or joint. With enough force the chains could break bones, tear cartilage

The Heart of the Terror State – 8 Prinz-Albrecht Strasse in Berlin, 1933

and lacerate flesh. Leather gloves were adapted by tying them to strips of wire and cutting away all but the portion for the thumb. Prisoners would be hung for hours with all of the weight of their body concentrated suspended by the thumb joint. Whips made from hippopotamus hide caused unbearable lacerations.

Those implicated in the July Bomb Plot (the 1944 bombing of Hitler's HQ in East Prussia) were tortured with a range of devices that seemed to hearken back to the Middle Ages. One plotter had his hands tied behind his back and a device filled with razor sharp needles was placed between his palms. A screw mechanism forced the needles out of their casing into his fingertips causing excruciating agony. When this didn't force a confession he was strapped to an old bed frame and metal cylinders were placed around his bare legs. Once again a screw was turned but in this instance nails emerged from the cylinder to lacerate his legs. Following this the victim was placed on a rack and stretched before being tightly bound in a bent position restricting all movement. While in this helpless pose he was set upon and beaten, regularly crashing to the floor.

Some tortures lasted for days at a time. Prisoners would be taken into a spare room occupied with two chairs a desk and a typewriter. One agent would sit opposite the seated prisoner asking repetitious questions for hours on end. Around the prisoner other agents would snarl and make threats, wearing down resistance. The interrogators would demand that the suspect sign confessions. Often these confessions were blank and the list of suspected crimes would be filled in once signed. Many signed just to be allowed to get back to their cot and sleep. Other tortures were designed to make suspects sleep by rendering them unconscious. Some interrogators favoured tying hands and feet together into a large bundle of blood–deprived flesh. A stick was then placed under the knees and used to suspend the person upside down between two chairs. After 15 minutes the interrupted circulation concentrating in the skull rendered the victim unconscious with blinding headaches. He would be revived and strung up again if he still held out.

In some prison yards the Gestapo would handcuff a prisoner with his hands behind his back, then with a pole thrust between his arms, lift him by his hands until his toes barely touched the ground. This was repeated time after time and the screams of pain would echo throughout the cells. Some courtyards had a wooden horse to which the prisoner was shackled before being whipped on the buttocks with a bullwhip.

Gestapo compounds in the centre of town, such as Prinz-Albrecht Strasse would use different means to cover their activities. Prisoners learned to be wary of multiple vehicles revving their engines in the drive or music being piped through the loudspeakers. These noises were used to cover particularly painful tortures or even executions by a shot in the back of the neck or a firing squad.

Brute force was not the only option. The fear of torture was often enough to get subjects to spill the beans. Some high-profile captives required more devious means. Determined to find out whether Johan George Elser had any accomplices when he tried to assassinate Hitler, Head of the Gestapo SS-Gruppenführer Muller summoned four famous hypnotists to delve into the assassin's subconscious. They didn't find much and as a result fell back to one of their other techniques. Elser was fed copious amounts of extremely salty herrings before being locked in a room with gas heaters cranked up to high. He was deprived of fluids and the resulting dreadful thirst was meant to convince him to confess. Promised liquid refreshment Elser still refused to spill the beans, mainly because he had no beans to spill. Even Himmler got into the Elser road show. Several times he burst into the bomber's cell and gave him a good kicking, all to no avail.

The Gestapo within Germany never numbered more than about 40,000 men. They weren't an all-powerful organisation monitoring every German. They relied on a network of informers and used cunning methods to get arrests.

The basis of the Terror state was in place well before the Nazi ascension to power. The SD (The Nazi Secret Police) and SS had been accumulating information on known political enemies since before the 1933 takeover. The enemies of the party had been carefully filed. Their dossiers were remarkably detailed. Professional and political activities were recorded, family, friends, housing, possible hideouts, friendships, strengths and weaknesses, especially vices, were all carefully filed away. Laws passed by Göring in June 1933 made it an offence for public servants not to denounce anyone who criticised the regime. Each factory and business had a party cell organised by the replacement organisation for trade unions

Listening to foreign broadcasts was forbidden to Reich

citizens. Newspaper ads were often placed to entrap would-be listeners. Adds selling powerful receivers complete with headphones were placed in many dailies. Any who answered were promptly placed on a register of suspected persons and were even paraded through the streets with the radios behind them.

The Gestapo didn't always follow protocol. Sometimes they set out to kill. In June 1934 a liberal intellectual who had written speeches for the Vice Chancellor Von Papen attracted admiration in German society at large as well as the antipathy of the Gestapo. Dr Edgar Jung was snatched from his apartment on June 21. When his wife came home she searched for her husband to no avail. The last trace of his existence was the hastily scrawled word 'Gestapo' on the bathroom wall. Jung had likely used this room as a hiding place before he was hauled off into custody. His wife finally found out what happened to him. On the 30th June his battered and bruised body was found in a ditch by the side of a rural road.

Heinrich Himmler

Ruling over this evil police empire was none other than Heinrich Himmler – an unpleasant dilettante who through a combination of factors became one of the most powerful people in Europe. In another life he may have grown up to be a sadistic teacher who humiliated children in his care or maybe a priest who used the protection of the church to abuse his ignorant parishioners. Instead he organised a police state equalled only by Stalinist Russia and Maoist China. He did have one skill – picking subordinates who were equally ruthless and could implement their master's crazy racial theories without conscience.

Despite his idealistic belief in Nazi doctrine Himmler was sickened by the sight of Russian prisoners and Jews being shot at close range. On one of his rare visits to a killing centre, blood spattered onto his uniform and the Reichsführer almost passed out.

Himmler was too young to fight in the Great War but relished the tales of returning soldiers, wishing he had of been able to fight for the Kaiser. After 1918 he became somewhat less idealistic and several police reports describe him as a pimp, earning a living off the immoral practices of several young women in Munich. The young Himmler couldn't make a go of this trade and after being chased out of Munich became a chicken farmer in 1921. Becoming attracted to politics he was involved in the Beer Hall Putsch of 1923 and this gave him an entry into Hitler's inner circle. Hitler recognised a fanatical crony when he saw one and in 1929 Himmler was placed in charge of the SS, Hitler's bodyguard troops who were set up as an insurance policy against Röhm's SA.

Himmler bought into Hitler's racial fantasies and made sure that the members of the SS were archetypal Aryans. Although small in number their fanatical loyalty allowed them to destroy the SA leadership and concentrate most of the security apparatus of the Reich in Himmler's hands. The SS, Gestapo, The SD (Nazi Intelligence organisation) and the civilian police all fell under his remit. Only the old military intelligence unit, the *Abwher* under Admiral Canaris, remained independent. Himmler managed to destroy the bulk of that organisation with ferocious reprisals after the July Bomb Plot in 1944.

Himmler's fanatical devotion and organisational genius, together with the laws enacted by Hitler's suppliant Reichstag, created an independent police state that went on to commit horrendous crimes throughout Europe.

Any photos of Himmler belie this evil nature. He had a weak chin, a narrow torso with large hips and fat legs. He was slightly above average height and muscular. He was prematurely bald and at the age of thirty three when he began his police career and outwardly he had the look of a servile accountant. He favoured a small moustache, perhaps to distract from his tiny chin and protruding ears. Himmler had a puffy face and flabby neck that even the immaculately tailored SS uniforms couldn't disguise. He always looked ill at ease in any photos, especially those where he was forced to smile. It's obvious that smiling was not one of his skills.

Thin metallic-rimmed eyeglasses covered his soulless eyes, a true indication of his lack of humanity. Hard, bluish-grey eyes were only matched by his very thin colourless lips. Needless to say no laughter lines creased his features.

His curious, unhealthy neck was one of the first things that struck his visitors, the skin was flabby and wrinkled and like an old man's neck. This stood in contrast to his rather youthful looking face. His hands were abnormally small and delicate, even feminine. They were white with transparent blue veins. Just as his face remained emotionless when he interacted with others, so his hands stayed inert before him, enigmatic and motionless.

Napoleon put in 18-hour days – so did Himmler. But rather than dealing with all measures of empire, Himmler made sure he knew everything that was going on in his police state network.

As with all aspects of the Nazi state many agencies performed the same task and there was considerable overlap as different groups competed for influence and resources. The RSHA (*Reichssicherheitshauptamt* – Central Security Office of the Reich) sought to bring as much of the police and intelligence network as possible under one umbrella organisation. It was initially run by Reinhard Heydrich and later by Ernst Kaltenbrunner, two of the regime's coldest killers. The structure of the RSHA was as follows.

Office 1   Recruitment and personnel allocation.

Office 2   Logistical support – exclusively for SD.

Office 3   The SD – the Nazi intelligence agency
                   concerned with domestic intelligence operations

which was used for information gathering and generally passed intelligence onto other agencies for action.

Office 4   The Gestapo – the political secret police with unquestioned powers of arrest and torture. They often referred cases to the People's court for sentencing and execution.

Office 5   The *Kripo* – the criminal police, concerned with ordinary police matters.

Office 6   The SD – concerned with foreign intelligence gathering.

The Gestapo in occupied Europe

The Gestapo and SD were responsible for keeping the occupied territories of Europe in an iron vice of fear. It is perhaps best to examine the methods used by these agencies by examining two individuals. Klaus Barbie, the butcher of Lyon, and the terror supremo Reinhard Heydrich.

Klaus Barbie and the Lyon Gestapo

Barbie was born on the 25th October 1913 in Bad Godesberg in the Rhineland. Ironically his family migrated from France to avoid persecution at the hands of Louis XIV. He had other reasons to hate the French. His father was permanently disabled by a wound inflicted by the French at Verdun and died prematurely at 45. His father joined the anti-French resistance when the Ruhr was occupied and instilled in his son an intense dislike of the French. When Klaus' father died in 1933 the family was left largely destitute at the height of the depression. Not being able to find paid employment and not in a position to fund further studies he enrolled in a Nazi Party voluntary work camp in Schleswig-Holstein. This experience had a powerful effect on the young man and he became a fanatical Nazi.

In 1935 he joined the SS and was assigned to the SD. During this time he met both Himmler and Heydrich. He was impressed with Himmler's humility and noted Heydrich's intellectual and aloof cast. His first posting was as an assistant in the Jewish Affairs department in the office of the SD before being posted to the *Kripo* Headquarters in Alexanderplatz where he gained a lifelong love of investigating and interrogating. After this he was posted to the vice squad. He and his associates went undercover in the seediest quarters of Berlin to arrest pimps, prostitutes and homosexuals. The latter would be brutally beaten before being locked away. During this period the Nazi persecution of homosexuals was swept under the carpet but all other undesirables were removed from public view for the Olympic Games. In 1937 he became member 4,583,085 of the Nazi party and in 1940 he graduated from the exclusive leadership course at Charlottenburg as a SS Untersturmführer (Second Lieutenant).

The German military has for several centuries encouraged initiative in its junior officers and non-coms. The SS training obviously reflected this and Barbie soon stood out as an inventive and imaginative persecutor of the enemies of the state. There was nothing he could not turn his hand to and he combined a deadly cunning with a willingness to use extreme violence to attain his objectives.

Barbie first showed his aptitude when transferred to Amsterdam where he was given the role of rounding up exiled Germans and Jews. Barbie proved to be a master of deception and he initially sought to reassure the Jewish population in Amsterdam which numbered around 100,000. One of his greatest ruses was when he politely approached the Jewish council and humbly asked for the addresses of 300 young men who had mistakenly been removed from their training camp and who the authorities wanted to return to their positions. Impressed by the polite German the council leaders had compiled the required list and handed it over to

Barbie. Next day a roundup of the young men was carried out and they were all shipped off to Mauthausen KL as a reprisal for a bombing attack. They were all dead within the year and many were used in the initial gassing experiments.

Dutch Fascists began to beat Jews in the street and attack their businesses and homes. One Dutch storm trooper was killed and harassment escalated to a full-scale battle. The Jewish quarter was sealed off by raising all but one of the bridges over the canals. Barbie and his troops were mobilised and on 22nd February and attacked the Jews with appalling ferocity. Resistors had their heads beaten in and 445 males were sent to Mauthausen. Some hard-core resistors were shot by firing squad. Barbie was in charge of the firing squad. He allowed one of the condemned to listen to an American hit record before they were all shot. Promoted to full lieutenant Klaus still had some shred of humanity and almost vomited when he saw the head wounds inflicted by the firing squads. Nevertheless, for his aptitude in bashing and killing Dutch civilians Barbie was awarded the Iron Cross second class.

After a brief sojourn in Russia the up and coming Gestapo man was given his first command. In November 1942 Barbie became the Gestapo head at Lyons, the second largest city in France.

Barbie was in charge of Office IV in the Lyons police apparatus – The Gestapo. He divided his department into six sub-sections dealing with resistance, communists, sabotage, Jews, false identity cards, counter intelligence and the intelligence archives. He proved to be an efficient leader whose initial compliment of 25 officers grew into the hundreds as branches were set up throughout the region. Barbie proved to be a workaholic and led operations in most of the branches. He was able to dedicate himself with a fanatical zeal as his family were back in Germany and he had an accommodating French mistress who didn't monopolise his time.

Klaus Barbie was a torture specialist. The activities of the sadistic head of the Gestapo in Lyon were limited only by his imagination. There were no legal restrictions on what he could get up to. He was in good company – many of the Gestapo's hardest men were sent to France to crack down on resistance. Just as Barbie was notorious in Lyon, Paul Blumenkamp was greatly feared in the Clermont-Ferrand region. Known as a ruthless interrogator, Blumenkamp was helped by his female assistant Ursula Brandt, known for her love of fur coats and blood spatter.

Lyon Gestapo headquarters was at the École de Sante Militaire (School of military health) previously used for training nurses. The organisation had been forced to move here when its earlier premises proved to be too small for the increasing workload and rapidly growing number of staff. The new location had purpose-built torture facilities and it was in these rooms that Barbie earned his nickname 'The Butcher of Lyon'. Pictures from the time show Barbie with a confident and knowing sneer. This was no doubt the brutal visage which hundreds of French saw as Barbie invented new and excruciating forms of punishment.

Barbie would maintain a veneer of civilisation before revealing his true nature. A young Jewish girl, Simone Legrange, witnessed both sides of his character he interrogated her and her parents about the location of her siblings.

Initially she was found him quite charming as he gently questioned her while stroking a dark long haired cat. He placed the cat down on his desk and complimented Simone on her good looks before stroking her long hair. Simone and her parents genuinely did not know the answer to his questions and when the desired response was not forthcoming they saw his true nature.

Barbie wrenched her hair as hard as he could and began yelling the same question, time after time, interspersing each query with a savage yank that seemed likely to rip her scalp off. He then began beating the teenager, slapping her to the floor before forcing her up with the toe of his boot.

"… He knocked me about all day. My face was completely torn to pieces. My lip was split. I was covered in blood, and I hadn't eaten. He took me to my mother's cell. He had the door opened and called to my mother, 'Well there you are, you can be proud of yourself.' The beatings continued for five days."*

The family was then shipped to Auschwitz.

Prisoners were routinely beaten while within custody. When they returned to their cells they were often a mass of open wounds and purpling bruises. Many were going to end up shipped to a KL or with a bullet in the head so Barbie and his crew were not fussed if they caused permanent damage.

One trick was to bury a shovel and only allow the cutting edge to protrude from the ground. Prisoners then lay with their spine against the edge before they were whipped on the stomach, chest and lungs. The prisoners would then fracture their backbone as they thrashed around during the painful lashing.

After an initial questioning prisoners were taken to the specially equipped rooms designed by Barbie and his henchmen. Each room had one or two baths, a table with leather straps to hold the prisoner in position, iron pokers and pincers, a gas oven to warm the irons and crude electrical prongs. The baths were filled with freezing or boiling water. Prisoners were hogtied and a broom handle was thrust under their arms while they were immersed in the hot or cold water. They were repeatedly plunged into the water until they lost consciousness and were hauled out and revived with kicks and blows while they lay soaking on the stone floor. Barbie and his crew often had classical music playing while they tortured their victims – not to try and conceal what they were doing but as a warning to other captives as to what was about to happen. Many prisoners felt

* Tom Bower, *Klaus Barbie: Butcher of Lyons*, Michael Joseph, London 1984, p 59.

their guts churn with fear as the gramophone started up and steel nailed jack boots clattered along a corridor as the Nazis came to grab another unfortunate individual.

Barbie's other favourite device was the cosh. He would beat prisoners for days on end, thrashing every part of the body causing external and internal wounds. This was combined with dunking as well as acid injections into the bladder.

Hooks were installed onto the ceilings and suspects were suspended by their wrists and bashed while their shoulders became dislocated. Four agents at a time would bash the hanging prisoner, rendering that unfortunate unconscious. A doctor was sometimes on hand to revive the prisoner, who would wake to find the Gestapo knocking back some schnapps and laughing. Sometimes they would be offered a slug before being taken back to their cells, all as if it was a gigantic game. Beatings could last for weeks and at other times they would be hauled up to the fourth floor to witness a friend or family member being bashed. Mock executions were used to try and elicit information. After one such event a young woman was tied stomach down onto an upturned chair and thrashed with a spiked ball attached to a cosh. One women was ravaged by Barbie's dog.

Mario Blandon was a resistance assassin and was on the way to another job when arrested at a roadblock. Hauled before Barbie he was assured that all his compatriots were dead and that he would soon follow. On the second day of his custody Barbie had Blandon stripped and burnt him with cigarettes, pushed him under the bath water and pushed three-inch needles through his rib cage into his lungs. When Blandon passed out others would be hauled in for treatment. Once he witnessed an execution.

One night there was a lot of noise and Barbie came down the stairs pushing someone ahead of him. He kept three steps behind him ... you see I was watching this with the eye of a professional killer and I knew exactly what was going to happen. Barbie shot the man in the back of the head. The head split apart while the man somersaulted to the bottom of the stairs like a rabbit.'*

Barbie often enjoyed looking on while his men did the bashing. Erich Bartelmus worked under him as the head of Sub Office IVC in charge of Jewish affairs. He enjoyed the brutal tortures and often did the heavy lifting while his boss enjoyed a sandwich and a beer. Victims would be savaged by police dogs or hung from hooks upside down until they began to bleed from their nose, ears and mouth. Suspects had their heads immersed in a bucket filled with soapy water or acid could be injected into kidneys or up the urethra. Fingers and toes were severed with blunt knives, breasts and nipples cut off and often limbs were scorched before being severed. One fellow was scalped before his eyes were gouged out.

Sometimes Barbie got a bit enthusiastic and beat top resistance operatives to death before they spilled the beans. His superiors let these mishaps go. 'The Butcher of Lyon' kept his assigned territory's population on a tight leash through terror, violence and covert operations.

Whether members of the Gestapo would have become sadistic psychopaths in a non-police state regime without on-the-job training and Nazi ideology permeating their existence is open to question. Nevertheless many sadists thrived in their position. Not many prisoners survived Barbie and his henchmen's ministrations but those that did remember the joy their abusers took in their daily work.

One of the top resistance leaders who was beaten to death on Barbie's orders was the Alsatian Joseph Kemmler. A witness to his interrogation saw how a simple beating could kill a prisoner in short order.

* Tom Bower, ibid, p 63.

Barbie began questioning Kemmler in French. His captive merely repeated 'never' to all of the questions. Barbie hit Kemmler with his gloved hands each time that response was given. The interrogation was being held in a requisitioned house during a partisan roundup and incongruously in the corner of the room was a piano. During pauses in the questioning Barbie would go to the piano and play the song 'Speak to me of Love' with his bloodied, gloved hands before returning to the task in hand.

The following day Barbie got serious. Kemmler was taken to an upstairs room and was stood up against a glass partition. Two Frenchmen armed with a thick rope which had a hook fixed to the end continually beat the resistance leader between the shoulder blades, on his midriff and down to his thighs. Barbie would ask questions and the beating would resume. After ninety minutes Kemmler could no longer stand and his inquisitors sat him on a chair before leaving the room. Fellow captives saw the beaten man shudder and lean forward. Five minutes later a puddle of urine formed under his chair as he died and lost control of his bladder.

A study of Barbie and his actions is instructive as many Gestapo departments in Office IV burnt their records. Post war testimony of the goings on in Lyon has given us a chance to see how these departments used different methods to hold down captive populations.

Gestapo districts were set up throughout the occupied territories. These mirrored the organisation of Gestapo departments in Germany. However they were given authority from Department D which divided up occupied territory into zones and allocated personnel to staff them.

Department A targeted political opponents and dealt with communists, sabotage, reactionaries and liberals and assassinations while Department B was chiefly concerned with persecuting Jews.

Throughout the occupied territories the Gestapo

established a reputation for hard-handed methods and terrorism. While Gestapo units in Germany had to deal with domestic threats which had been all but eliminated by the outbreak of war, Gestapo agencies in occupied territories combatted increasing armed opposition to the regime through increasingly violent means as the war began to turn against the Nazis. Violence escalated as the Allied dropped supplies to partisan bands and resistance cells.

The Gestapo showed no mercy and torture, massacres, reprisal shootings and mass executions became the order of the day. Most Gestapo bureaus relied on auxiliaries recruited from the native population to aid them in their activities and often these groups exceeded the Germans in their savagery. The *Milice* in Occupied France were feared more than their Nazi counterparts, especially by the communist resistance fighters who expected no mercy. The *Hlinka* Guard in Slovakia fulfilled a similar role and organised the massed deportation of Slovak Jews as well as concentration camps in the region. They represented right-wing Catholic organisations much like the *Milice* in France.

As the German fronts collapsed and districts were evacuated the Gestapo tried to cover their tracks with typical German efficiency. Paper work and files were burnt and suspects or people who had witnessed torture were executed. Often collaborators who had been crucial to the Gestapo's clandestine activities were shot en-masse to ensure that they could not be used in post war trials.

So efficient was this scorched-earth strategy that many members of the Gestapo were able to melt seamlessly back into society after the war and never paid for the horrendous crimes that they committed. Often they were anti-communist specialists and as a result were employed by the occupying Allies in a similar role in the post-war reconstruction of West Germany. Many trapped behind the iron curtain were helped to escape from the Soviet authorities or earned large amounts of money as spies.

Barbie was hired by the Americans and proved adept at sharing his skills honed during his rule in Lyon. He was an efficient gatherer of intelligence and developed a network throughput his region

Before the Gestapo could torture prisoners they had to be apprehended. Informers and collaborators were essential for identifying suspects. As soon as he arrived in Lyon Barbie was offered the assistance of the Lyon police chief and the German quickly identified a cadre of trustworthy Frenchmen whose right-wing, anti-communist and anti-Semitic credentials could be proven. Additionally a flood of French poured into Gestapo headquarters to launch denunciations against possible resistance targets and the Gestapo had to sort the wheat from the chaff and recruit long-term collaborators. Barbie was able to recognise those who were particularly vicious characters and soon he had picked a core of 50 who formed his 'personal army'. Many were members of the French Nazi party (the PPF) and they launched a reign of terror throughout Lyons. François Andre was a particularly vicious ex-communist whose maimed face hinted at the beast within.

Andre led a fascist gang that robbed and murdered any suspected resistance supporters as well as wealthy Jews. They took gold, jewels and property and divided it up among themselves and the Germans. They essentially used the power Barbie gave them to run a criminal gang. Most of their leads were obtained by Office VI of Barbie's outfit who had Frenchmen form queues every day at special denunciation kiosks scattered around the region. Unable to follow every lead the details were given to Andre's 'Movement for National Anti-Terrorism' (MNAT) who would pick and choose the most profitable investigations. The MNAT moved into the Gestapo headquarters in 1944.

Some collaborators proved to be double agents. Barbie had a special way of checking loyalty. He would kit them up in German uniform and take them out on anti-partisan raids where they were encouraged to shoot captured French. This did not always work and one Frenchwomen led some of the Nazi police into an ambush which resulted in four casualties. Under interrogation she confessed her true loyalty, was executed and thrown into the Rhone.

The most ardent supporters of German rule were the *Milice*. This was the French version of the Gestapo and they were known as the 'Black Terror.' Dressed in khaki uniforms, black ties and black berets the approximately 35,000 *Milice* were led by the fanatically anti-communist Joseph Darnand who believed in 'destroying Bolshevism, for nationalism, against Jewish leprosy, for French Purity, against pagan freemasonry, for Christian civilisation'.

The primary task of the *Milice* was to take on and defeat the French resistance. They worked within the locality they resided in and as such their knowledge of suspect identities was far greater than the Germans. This made them a dangerous opponent to the resistance particularly as there were few rules governing their behaviour. The Germans were only interested in results and torture was commonly used. Often whole families would be rounded up and interrogated. As a result many *Milice* were assassinated which led to escalating violence as Frenchman killed Frenchman throughout France.

Barbie and his Lyon Gestapo were involved in large and small expeditions to round up Jewish fugitives and young men to provide forced labour for the Reich. They also cooperated with the military to hunt down partisans.

When Barbie and his henchmen arrived in Lyon in November 1942, approximately 42,000 Jews had been deported from German occupied France. Many had fled to the illusory safety of Vichy France and it was the Gestapo's role to round up as many of these remnant populations as possible. Raids were launched almost immediately and Sub Office IVC under Hans Welt had rounded up about 150 by early January.

But Barbie had bigger fish to fry. Using his characteristic guile on 9th of February he rounded up the key Jewish personnel in of all the Jewish organisations throughout France. By happenstance the headquarters of the Federation of Jewish Societies was located in the Rue St Catherine in Lyon. Barbie and his crew arrived very early in the morning with his men in plainclothes and arrested all within. They kept them under guard within the building ensuring that they did not draw attention to themselves. Throughout the day people seeking advice on how to escape the Nazi clutches arrived at the building only to be snapped up by the waiting Gestapo. Many were looking for false papers or financial aid and some were even recruiting for resistance groups. Approximately 100 were rounded up that day and 86 were immediately dispatched to Auschwitz. Barbie signed a telex to Paris headquarters describing his successful ruse and thereby firmly placed himself in the centre of the Holocaust.

It's estimated that approximately 8000 Jews were sent to concentration camps on Barbie's watch. Originally they were housed in the cells of the fortress of Montluc but such was the enthusiasm of the *Milice* that the cells soon filled up and temporary accommodation had to be found for those soon to be deported. They were placed in jerry-built wooden huts in the central courtyard of the fortress. Even these uncomfortable, poorly-made barracks soon became overcrowded and every two weeks the inmates were hauled out and put in cattle trucks for transit to a KL in Germany.

The horror experienced by 41 children who had been protected from the terrors of war in the extremely isolated town of Izieu as they were dragged down from the mountains and placed in this way station to damnation can only be imagined. Welt had heard rumours for months that the village's biggest house was being used as a school and a refuge for orphaned Jewish youths ranging from three to 24 years of age. None of the occupation troops had been in the vicinity and the entire area was untouched by the war.

This all changed on the morning of 6th April when two trucks full of Gestapo and *Milice* ground their way up to the village and disgorged their deadly cargo in front of the refuge. The Germans assured the principal that the 41 children were to be evacuated for their own safety. Despite protests the children gathered their possession and were brutally tossed onto the waiting lorries. Suddenly aware of their deadly new reality they began crying and singing out for assistance. One boy, Theo Reiss, made a break for it but he was brought to the ground and savagely beaten with rifle butts before being tossed back onto the truck like a sack of potatoes.

Barbie's sent a telegraph to his superiors in Berlin. This document spelt out his 'achievements.'; the home closed, 41 children aged 3 to 13 transported along with ten adults including five women. This signed and dated document ties Barbie to the holocaust, one minor functionary among thousands.

Most were shipped to Paris then Auschwitz where they were gassed. Only one of the young adults survived.

The Gestapo's other main role was rounding up insurgents and using their intelligence to help the military attack partisan groups hiding in the countryside. Informants were crucial to this process and so successful was Barbie in making agents turn that three out of four British-led operations in the region were compromised and broken up while French resistance organisations were thrown into disarray and disbanded. Jena Moulin became the head of resistance in the Lyon area uniting all groups, except the communists, under his control. When captured and tortured the network was infiltrated and as soon as the Gestapo began turning up and arresting operatives the remaining resistance fighters knew the game was up and had to head into the hills to avoid capture. Barbie knew that only one traitor was required and entire cells would be destroyed.

Himmler himself sent a letter of commendation to the

Lyon Gestapo, highlighting Barbie's role as commander and awarding him the Iron Cross, First Class, with sword – a significant honour. However, as a good Gestapo man Barbie should have been having more children and there was a negative comment placed in his file. He explained to his superiors that he did not have enough time for leave and was too busy bashing up the French in Lyon.

A similar coup occurred in March 1944 when 'Chatoux', a local resistance leader, was captured. Taken straight to headquarters he soon confessed and gave up his whole underground network. 101 resistance members, including the regional chief were picked up. Key supporters in the police, medical profession and post office were rounded up. False documents and propaganda could no longer be published leading to a dramatic drop in resistance activity.

Much of the region around Lyon was perfect *Maquis* (French guerrillas) country, combining hills, mountains and wooded territory interspersed with fertile farmlands and a many small villages. Much of the land was quite inaccessible and perfect for airdrops from the Allies. These were stepped up during the latter half of 1943 and 1944 as Allied forces moved closer to southern France and continued to assert their domination of the air. Railways were attacked, power stations destroyed, industry attacked and patrols of Germans were ambushed with increasing frequency.

The Germans responded to these attacks with reprisals and military actions. Although most of the German troops were second-line reserve formations they were still able to make a good fist of terrorising the local population. The citizens of the town of Nantua humiliated some German collaborators by stripping them naked before painting swastikas on their bodies and parading the men and women through town. Eight days later in December 1943, a troop train carrying 500 infantry plus Gestapo agents arrived and sealed off the exits to Nantua. Sweeps were then conducted and 120 men were deported to KLs in Germany. The

Gestapo took it a bit further and drove to a nearby town where a *Maquis* unit had earlier held a parade. Three leading citizens including the mayor were arrested and decapitated, their bodies left on the outskirts of town to serve as warning to others.

Barbie responded to the execution of two German soldiers by setting up a machine gun at the head of the stairs leading down to the cells at Gestapo headquarters. Several cell doors were left unlocked and when the air raid alarm was set off that evening 22 resistance fighters made a bolt for freedom. They were all shot down as they emerged onto the ground floor. 'Shot while trying to escape' in Nazi parlance.

One of Barbie's worst atrocities occurred during sweep of the highlands to the North of Lyon. In the vast snow-covered hilly region a rigid curfew was imposed and anyone out between 8.00am and 6.00am was shot on sight. Cars, bicycles, and trains could not be used and all telephone lines were cut ensuring *Maquis* groups could not coordinate a response or flee the region. Pitched battles were fought and any *Maquis* who fled could easily be followed by the paths they left in the snow. Artillery and air support ensured that the Wehrmacht had the upper hand and the remnants of the French resistance fighters fought a deadly game of cat and mouse with the Germans.

Enter Barbie. Acting on tip offs from collaborators he led a convoy packed with German infantry, *Milice*, collaborators and Gestapo agents and began a reign of terror. One village saw families of resistance fighters rounded up and several Jews shot for 'resisting arrest'. The convoy then proceeded to Evosges, a town of a couple of hundred people that had not yet been impacted by the war. Conducting a search operation some flour bags with the Swastika printed on them were revealed, evidence that stolen German supplies were there. The owner of the house, Jean Carrel, was dragged out of bed and shot by Barbie, no questions asked. As the rest of the villagers were herded to the centre of town some young men who were trying to avoid compulsory labour in Germany made an escape attempt but were captured by the German cordon, beaten and dragged back to the village. Barbie walked up to Jean Brun, a local resistance fighter who was nominated by a collaborator. He asked where the *Maquis* hideout was. When no answer was supplied, Brun was shot by Barbie.

Frustrated by lack of progress the Germans pulled the mayor out of his house with his wife and daughters. Seeing the Germans setting the house alight the mayor urged his family to flee. They did so but their father was shot in the stomach. Holding out his hands as the Germans cocked their rifles his fingers were shot off before a final head shot put him out of his agony. Houses of suspected resistance supporters were burned and those who had given supplies or fed *Maquis* were shot. Under Gestapo orders they were not to be buried for eight days but lay where they fell, a warning to all. Other villages followed in the murderous rampage and isolated farmhouses were destroyed.

It was all counter-productive. The meaningless atrocities led hundreds to join the *Maquis* units which were rapidly resupplied with parachuted supplies.

As the German military situation deteriorated in France after the Normandy landings, so too did their moral compass. Resistance attacks increased and it was obvious that the Germans would soon have to quit Lyon. The scorched-earth approach, common in Russia, was tried in France as the Gestapo tried to cover their tracks.

Barbie and his crew had frequently organised massed deportations to concentration camps. This no longer became feasible, as what rolling stock remained had to be used for military purposes while the front line crumbled under incessant allied air attacks. The rail lines were also routinely cut by insurgent sabotage. Barbie decided to dispose of his problems closer to home.

Groups of prisoners were routinely told to come out of

their cells leaving any remaining belongings behind. Loaded onto trucks guarded by Gestapo and SS they were driven out into isolated parts of the countryside. The Germans had the decency to remove their handcuffs before the mute prisoners walked single file into hidden copses and hedgerows where they were lined up and executed. With some twisted irony the weapons used were captured Sten guns or Thompson submachine guns seized from intercepted airdrops. No attempt was made to bury the bodies and they were left where they fell. Some prisoners saw the writing on the wall and wrote letters to their loved ones but these were seized and burnt.

On the night of 26th July the war came to Lyon when a bomb was thrown into a restaurant frequented by the Gestapo. No one was injured but a reprisal was carried out immediately. Five prisoners were dragged from Gestapo cells at noon the next day and shot in front of the damaged café. This shocked the locals who so far had escaped the mass shootings which were common in the countryside.

On 15th August 1944 the landings of American forces on the southern coast of France took place. The only force between the experienced American forces and Lyon was a few understrength German formations. They were ordered to begin a fighting withdrawal and on 17th August the final clearing operation was ordered by Barbie in Montluc prison. One hundred and nine prisoners, mainly Jewish, were taken to Bron airport on the outskirts of Lyon. Here they were shot and buried in bomb craters that covered the field. Two days later 110 prisoners were taken to a disused fort. Thirty five *Milice* were present and the prisoners had their hands tied behind their backs before being led up to the first floor and shot. As they arrived they had to walk over the bodies of their comrades and blood started leaking through the floorboards onto those waiting below.

Once the job had been done the bodies were covered in petrol and set alight before the building was destroyed with dynamite.

At Gestapo HQ prisoners were executed in their cells. But this was not enough for Barbie. All documents were burnt and 20 of his most trusted informants were murdered by hit squads specially organised by the Gestapo chief. He was 'cleaning up the mess' and making sure that none could reveal his crimes from the previous 21 months. He even ordered his French girlfriend to be liquidated. On the 22nd of August Barbie left Lyon for the last time, limping from a self-inflicted wound incurred when he was shooting prisoners in one of the final massacres.

As the Reich collapsed thousands of other Gestapo agents proved that Barbie was not alone in delighting in tormenting his prisoners. Some specialised in physical torture while others delighted in inflicting mental pain.

Gestapo Sturmbannführer Johannes Post was one of the latter. During his trial after the war he was proud to discuss how he had ensured that each condemned prisoner he was put in charge of knew exactly what was going to happen to them. Squadron Leader James Catanach was one of the 70 or so airmen who escaped from Stalag Luft III in the so-called Great Escape. As an airman he expected that if recaptured he would be returned to his POW cage where he would be put in the hole (solitary confinement) for a week or two.

However with the terror raids increasing Hitler had ordered Himmler and his Gestapo to execute all of the recaptured airmen. This number was modified to 50 and Catanach was one of the unfortunate ones. Catanach was bundled into a car travelling through Kiel towards the site of his execution with the smug Gestapo executioner sitting next to him. Post pointed out interesting landmarks before casually remarking, 'We must get on, I have to shoot you.' The incredulous airmen didn't believe what he had heard so Post repeated himself. Thinking that the Gestapo officer was pulling his leg Catanach responded with his own joke, 'Another time. I have an appointment in the cooler at Stalag

Luft III. I've done nothing wrong except go under the wire.'

The car reached a field and stopped. Catanach was dragged out and now knew that it was not a joke. Post said he had orders to shoot the airman. The Australian's last word was 'Why?'

Others were shot in batches. Six airmen were hauled out of Gorlitz prison and told by the Gestapo officers Sharpinkel and Lux who used more official procedures. They told the prisoners that they had been sentenced to death by the Supreme Military Commander (Hitler) before taking them in a light truck to the edge of a nearby forest. The men, who remained remarkably calm, were then lined up and shot. In broad daylight.

Acting against the Geneva Convention the airmen's remains were cremated before being sent in primitive urns back to Stalag Luft III. The news of the killings got back to Allied newspapers and added a little bit more to the ferocity of the air war then raging across Germany.

Reinhard Heydrich and the Czech Gestapo

Just as Barbie's role as a Gestapo enforcer is well documented, so are the Gestapo's actions in the Czech protectorate. The best way to examine this is to look at the murderous career of Himmler's Deputy Reinhard Heydrich. While Barbie was a minor functionary, Heydrich rose to become one of the main architects of the police state throughout the occupied territories, as well as one of the key architects of the Final Solution.

Feared by all around him, including Himmler, he was a perfectionist who achieved mastery of everything he turned his hand to, whether it was fencing at the Olympic Games or terrorising and brutalising a conquered people.

Heydrich was born in Saxony in 1904. Brought up in an upper-middle class household devoted to music and culture there was nothing in his ancestry to suggest that he might

Reinhard Heydrich, The Spider at the Heart of the Police Web. The Final Solution was named in his honour – Operation *Reinhard*.

develop into a psychopathic, cold-blooded mass murderer.

However, he was badly treated by his peers. The gangly child with a huge protruding shark fin nose was teased for being Catholic, for having Jewish ancestry and for his funny high-pitched voice which persisted into his later years. His mother was a martinet who believed in harsh discipline enforced through frequent floggings. The product of this upbringing became a driven individual who found it difficult to relate to his fellows.

His vicious nature was first revealed when at the age of 16 he joined the local *Freikorps* organisation and participated in the brutal crackdown on left-wing groups. He also became obsessed with the German Volk movement and convinced himself that his blue-eyed blonde-haired racial heritage conferred a supremacy over his fellow man. Perhaps to compensate for the persistent rumours regarding his supposed Jewish heritage he became rabidly anti-Semitic. He also became a hater of the new Republic when his wealthy family was reduced to penury with the fallout from the war. Becoming a cadet in the navy Heydrich was still teased but this did not dent his growing arrogance.

Heydrich also developed great interest in women and pursued sex with the same self-driven desire for achievement he applied to everything else. He had many sexual relationships and in 1930 was accused of having sex with the unmarried daughter of a shipyard director. According to popular Nazi legend, as a result of his refusal to marry her, Heydrich was forced by Admiral Erich Raeder to resign his naval commission in 1931 for conduct unbecoming an officer and a gentleman.

His Aryan features allowed him to join the SS and Himmler interviewed him for the job of building up a SS intelligence service. So impressed was Himmler that he gave him the job and Heydrich began organising the SD (*Sicherheitsdienst* – SS Security Service). This one-man operation soon developed into a huge organisation with informers at all levels of society and dossiers on any individuals who might be likely to challenge the state and Hitler's supremacy including top Nazis such as the SA leaders. Files were even kept on 'good Nazis' and folders full of gossip and rumours about the sexual activities or finances of the top Nazis were maintained ensuring the Heydrich and Himmler were feared by all. Hidden microphones and cameras ensured that no secrets were kept. Many top Nazis even feared meeting Heydrich or being in his presence during the few official gatherings he attended. With his murderous glare, Heydrich could frighten even the most hardened Nazis.

Heydrich's ruthless diligence and the rapid success of the SD earned him a quick rise through the SS ranks. He was appointed SS Major by December 1931, then SS Colonel with sole control of the SD by July of 1932. In March of 1933, he was promoted to SS Brigadier General, though not yet 30 years old.

Heydrich was a member of the elite Aryan order but was haunted by the persistent rumours about his supposed Jewish ancestry. As a result he developed tremendous hostility toward Jews. Heydrich also suffered great insecurity and some degree of self-loathing, exemplified by an incident in which he returned home to his apartment after a night of drinking, turned on a light and saw his own reflection in a wall mirror. He took out his pistol and fired two shots at himself in the mirror, muttering 'Die, you dirty Jew.'

By April 1934, amid much Nazi infighting and backstabbing, Himmler assumed control of the Gestapo with Heydrich as his second in command actually running the organisation.

Heydrich was instrumental in drawing up the list of those who were to be assassinated in the Night of The Long Knives.

Heydrich did not court the media and preferred to pull strings from behind the scenes. Despite cultivating a low profile Heydrich had a huge impact both domestically and internationally. He fabricated evidence against Soviet generals and this may have led to Stalin's purge of his top military brass. This in itself was a tremendous boost to the German war effort in 1941.

He may have been responsible for Germany ultimately losing the war. By blackmailing the Commander in Chief of the Army and the Minister of War he forced them to resign allowing Hitler to become the Commander In Chief of the German military.

German nationalists in Czechoslovakia were supported by Heydrich and in March 1938 he established the Gestapo Office of Jewish Emigration. This was headed by Adolf Eichmann and laid the foundations for the Final Solution. Heydrich was responsible for smashing organised resistance in Austria after the 1938 *Anschluss*.

So successful was Heydrich that the SD, Gestapo and *Kripo* were all placed under his control with the umbrella organisation Reich Main Security Office (RSHA) in 1939. With almost total power within the Reich Heydrich was allowed to begin to transform his masters' racial visions into reality. Poland was the first country to feel his evil touch.

Heydrich formed five *Einsatzgruppen* led by some of his cronies in the SD to systematically round up and shoot Polish politicians, leading citizens, professionals, aristocracy, and the clergy. German-occupied Poland had an enormous Jewish population of over two million persons. On Heydrich's orders, Jews who were not shot outright were crammed into ghettos in places such as Warsaw, Cracow, and Łódź. Overcrowding and lack of food within these walled-in ghettos led to starvation, disease, and the resulting deaths of half a million Jews by mid-1941. Heydrich declared, 'We have had to be hard. We have had to shoot thousands of leading Poles to show how hard we can be.'

'The Führer has ordered the physical extermination of the Jews,' Heydrich told his subordinate Adolf Eichmann, who later reported that statement during his trial after the war. In furtherance of this aim four even larger *Einsatzgruppen* were formed to take the war into the conquered territory of the Soviet Union.

Unsatisfied with the messy nature of the *Einsatzgruppen* killings Heydrich was ordered to organise the 'Final Solution of the Jewish question' by Göring. This he did when he convened the Wannsee conference on January 20th 1942. Heydrich bluntly stated that Europe would be combed of Jews from east to west, and the fate of an estimated 11,000,000 Jews living in Europe and the Soviet Union was decided.

Before this in September of 1941 Heydrich was given another task. This would prove to be his downfall and would also lead to hundreds of innocent deaths in the town of Lidice. He was appointed Deputy Reich Protector of Bohemia and Moravia in former Czechoslovakia and he set up his headquarters in Prague.

Heydrich was a great believer in the carrot and the stick method of ruling. He established a successful policy of offering incentives to Czech workers, rewarding them with food and privileges if they filled Nazi production quotas and displayed loyalty to the Reich. Any dissidents were ruthlessly tracked down and confined in the Small Fortress just outside Prague.

This was a fortification built in the late seventeen hundreds which was converted to a prison soon afterwards. Prior to WWII its main claim to fame was that it was the place where Gavrilo Princip, Archduke Franz Ferdinand's assassin, remained chained to the wall until he died of neglect and tuberculosis. The Gestapo took it over and it became notorious as a place of torture, starvation, disease and execution.

As captives entered the prison they passed under a sign at the main gate which read 'Work Makes You Free'. Few inmates had the chance to prove this as they entered dreadful conditions of captivity. Communists, Jews, resistance fighters and other political prisoners were confined, and from 1940 to 1945, 32,000 prisoners were held captive. The relatives of resistance fighters were also rounded up and treated as badly as resistors. In cramped ancient cells the inmates were forced to live three or four to a bunk with no heating in winter and excruciating heat in summer. Food was poor and there was little hygiene leading to severe outbreaks of typhus and spotted fever, particularly during the hot weather. Two thousand five hundred died of 'natural causes' at least 700 were executed on the firing range and most of the others perished after being deported east to be liquidated. Torture and interrogation cells were close to the main prison blocks ensuring that the sound of every breaking bone or fist hitting flesh would be heard by all.

Heydrich paid particular attention to the Czech Jews and established a ghetto at Theresienstadt (Terezin to the Czechs) adjacent to the Small Fortress. Jews from Austria, Germany, Denmark and the Netherlands were concentrated here along with those from Prague. One hundred and fifty thousand transited through here during the war and the crowded living conditions, malnutrition and disease ensured that 33,000 people died here even though it was not an extermination camp.

Anyone who tried to escape from the ghetto or was not sufficiently pliable was hauled up to the prison for confinement in one of the two cells reserved for Jews. These were small cells designed for one or two inmates but up to 60 would be crammed in with no fresh air, light or toilet facilities. Heinrich Jockel, the camp commandant was confined here prior to his execution in 1946. The Jews, along with the Russian prisoners, did not receive any medical aid when sick.

Heydrich's assassination led to Kurt Daluege becoming the new 'Protector' and thousands were herded into custody. When the Soviets liberated the fortress 17,000 starving lice-covered inmates were found within. One thousand died despite the best efforts of Russian medical teams.

Obergruppenführer Heydrich always drove to his Prague headquarters in an open-topped Mercedes without armed outriders, usually with the hood retracted. This was to demonstrate the power he had over his subjects. He continued this practice against advice from his colleagues.

On May 27th 1942 as the vehicle turned a bend it came under attack from British-trained Czech patriots. Wounded by bullets and shrapnel he died after four days. Upholstery from the car's seats and bits of his uniform were lodged in his intestines where they turned septic and led to blood poisoning.

The Nazi reckoning was savage. The Gestapo and SS hunted down and murdered the Czech agents, resistance members, and anyone suspected of being involved in Heydrich's death, totalling over 1000 persons. In addition, 3000 Jews were deported from the ghetto at Theresienstadt for extermination. Inmates at Sachsenhausen concentration camp were charged with conspiracy and shot on the spot. In Berlin 500 Jews were arrested, with 152 executed as a reprisal on the day of Heydrich's death.

Hitler was furious and broke into an apocalyptic fit. He demanded that 30,000 Czechs be immediately executed as a reprisal. Heydrich's successor talked Hitler out of it, not on any humanitarian grounds but by arguing it would harm the already strained labour force in the Reich Protectorate. Hitler relented and ordered the arrest of 10,000, especially intellectuals. In the days that followed 3,188 were arrested. Of these 1,357 were liquidated while another 657 died while being interrogated in Gestapo basements and in the Small Fortress.

These 2000 brutal deaths were not enough to satisfy Hitler. Karl Hermann Frank, the Sudeten German Secretary of State received an instruction to carry out a special reprisal action that would be trumpeted throughout the Reich and teach the Czechs exactly what it meant to defy the new regime. Frank was to choose a small community and wipe it out. Frank didn't need any extra urging and he selected the small town of Lidice. There were several links to a village and some captured resistance documents implicated some residents in the assassination plot. That these links were actually related to another town did not bother Frank. The orders to destroy the settlement were issued and the Gestapo pounced on its inhabitants on June 9th. Realising the error, Berlin did have the good grace to send a couple of Gestapo men to arrange for the necessary evidence to be found.

The convoy carrying the Gestapo and a police battalion arrived at 9.30am when most inhabitants of the sleepy rural town were in bed. The police set up roadblocks and a cordon while SS and Gestapo men drove into the town square and proceeded to assemble the terrified population. Men and boys over 15 were forced to line up on one side of the square while women and children lined up on the other. Horak farm with its large stone barns was chosen to pen the males in while the rest of the population was forced into the village school.

While this was happening the police battalion went through the village collecting anything of value and destroying furniture, doors and windows. Livestock was herded off and farming implements were carted away. Any mattresses were collected and used to line the exterior wall of Horak farm.

At 5.00am the next morning the women and children were dragged out of the school and placed in a waiting convoy of lorries. Forced in at the point of bayonets they were driven off to an uncertain future. The 198 women and 99 children were separated soon after. The women were sent to Ravensbrück KL where 35 were immediately selected to go to Auschwitz. Six survived the war, the others had perished, mainly in medical experiments. Of the 99 children 17 survived by being raised as *Volksdeutch* (foreign Germans) while the others were sent to Chemnitz to be gassed.

As their families were being driven from Lidice the men

were bought out of the barn in groups of ten and lined up against the mattresses. A specialist extermination squad had been bought out from Prague and experience had taught them that bullets fired against Czech stone barns caused nasty ricochets, hence the mattresses. From ten in the morning until three in the afternoon the killings continued. Some of the town's men were at work during the initial round up. No matter, the Gestapo visited their places of work and grabbed them too. In all 192 were slaughtered.

The Gestapo still had a point to make. Demolition squads burnt the buildings before blowing them up with explosive charges. In 48 hours Lidice was reduced to an unsightly blackened stain on the ground. A barbed wire fence was erected around the site warning that any who were found there would be shot. Several other towns were destroyed on dubious evidence of involvement in Heydrich's death. Propaganda newsreels were not present for these events. Two thousand villagers were estimated to have died in these *Aktions*.

However, Himmler had only begun his revenge. In honour of his acolyte one of the worst crimes against humanity, the liquidation of the Polish Jews, was named Operation *Reinhard*.

The man who had done so much to set up the Gestapo and developed its ruthless practices had his name given to the worst aspects of the Final Solution.

3

STERILISATION
AND EUTHANASIA

Lebensunwertes leben (life unworthy of life)

The German medical fraternity became willing participants
in the mass murder of countless victims in the Third Reich.
Medical theorists laid the foundations of murder with
philosophical treatises describing those who were no longer
acceptable to live on the face of the earth. Under the pretext
of healing, the first euthanasia program – T4 – began.
Involving the entire medical community it maintained an
illusion of correct medical practices with stringent record
keeping and peer reviews. Nevertheless this could not
conceal the true nature of the program – killing innocent
citizens of the Reich.

Those who were disabled and mentally unsound were the
victims. T4 was expanded under the new guise of 'Special
Action 14f13'. This allowed German doctors to embark
on the first mass killings of concentration camp inmates.
Still concealed under a cloak of legality and best medical
practice, respected doctors and professors condemned weak
prisoners to death in the early gas chambers. As the rate of
killing escalated even these pretences of medical correctness
disappeared as a new medical conveyor belt of death began.
While hundreds of thousands died in the gas chambers
throughout the concentration camp system, doctors
engaged in their own Holocaust. A phenol injection into
the heart was the final solution for many cast-off inmates in
the factories of death.

Throughout the entire process all the medical practitioners

involved maintained the illusion that their charges were being looked after. It was best to lull their victims into a false sense of security rather than having riots in the killing centres.

Gleichschaltung, or coordination and synchronisation meant a new deadly norm was initiated throughout the Reich. This of course was applied to the legal fraternity, unions and police forces. But it also extended to the field of medicine, perhaps its most lethal incarnation in the new Reich.

The entire medical community, from professorial teachers, surgeons, medical universities and the mental health system all became accomplices in Hitler's sick racial fantasies. Violent crimes were carried out by thousands of doctors, nurses and medical orderlies. Those who signed the paper work condemning a mentally sick patient to a tortuous death in an early gas chamber were equally guilty of murder as those who killed with a needle filled with a combination of toxins and morphine. Not as well-known as the Nuremberg Trials of the Nazi bigwigs, the Doctors' Trial in 1946 exposed an entire profession that facilitated countless deaths through forced starvation, poison injections, morphine overdoses and gassing by carbon monoxide in purpose-built chambers or converted buses.

Starting with those with physical or mental impairments it eventually extended to those who were socially undesirable or of Jewish origins. Paperwork was the structure upon which policies of euthanasia were based and each death required from four to seven signatories or inspectors who would each add their little increment leading to the killing of the victim. The experience and methodology developed by the medical profession was to morph into the mass killings of the Holocaust. The first KL-organised killings were carried out by the same teams who organised the euthanasia.

The *Gleichschaltung* of the medical profession was completed through the Nazi dominated 'Reich Physician's

A bus used in T4 and 14t13 ... its harmless appearance conceals its deadly purpose.

Chamber.' All practicing physicians had to belong to this and all pre-1933 medical organisations were either subsumed or disbanded. Doctors deemed unworthy of joining this establishment were banned from practicing and politically unreliable or Jewish doctors were gradually denied their livelihood. In 1939 they were stripped of their licenses. It is estimated that 350 German doctors actually committed some type of medical crime but this represents the tip of the iceberg. Thousands acquiesced to referring patients to the euthanasia or sterilisation commissions when required, knowingly starting their patients on the road to an ethically unsound death. They also actively slandered and discriminated against their Jewish colleagues and adopted suspect racist ideologies.

Sterilisation

As early as 1924 Adolf Hitler took great delight in banging on about the purity of the German race. Those who were disabled mentally or physically were one group who earned his disfavour. These ravings of a madman, ravings that could not be considered as realistic in a normal society, became part of his blueprint once in power. Hitler wrote in *Mein Kampf*:

> Those who are physically and mentally unhealthy and unfit must not perpetuate their own suffering in the bodies of their children.
>
> If for a period of 600 years those individuals would be sterilised who are physically degenerate of mentally diseases humanity would not only be delivered from an immense misfortune but also restored to a state of general health such as we at present can hardly imagine, a race from which all those germs would be eliminated, the causes of our moral and physical decadence.

It is representative of Hitler's tenuous grasp on reality that he thought that any regime would spend 600 years destroying the weak and unsound. Nevertheless as soon as the Nazis gained power these crackpot ideas were put into action. Hitler created a medical fraternity within Germany which had the aim of destroying all 'unworthy' Germans.

He was influenced by the theory of eugenics which was partly a result of Darwinian theories of evolution. Eugenics was a social theory popular with many scientists, philosophers, academics and writers in the early 20th century before gene theory was developed.

The fundamental belief of these ideologists was that the physical and mental characteristics of human populations could be improved through manipulation of their genetic make-up. In other words, a society could achieve positive outcomes – like increased productivity, intelligence, health, or reductions in crime – if it removed unhealthy or 'undesirable' genetic elements.

Hitler, other Nazis and some German academics were avid believers in eugenic pseudo-science. Hitler thought of German society as a sick organism, its bloodstream contaminated by degenerate and undesirable elements. Those 'contaminating' Germany were the racially impure, the physically disabled, the mentally infirm, the criminally minded and the sexually aberrant. The high crime rate of the depression and the excesses of the artistic scene during the Weimar republic were the most obvious signs of a 'degenerate' society, as was the 'gay' scene in Hamburg where up to 10 per cent of the population were considered to be homosexual.

Because of his ideas about racial struggle and the survival of the fittest Hitler believed that radical, sustained and violent actions had to be taken against the undesirables. Birth certificates and government records could identify those who were racially suspect, but the medical community was required to identify those who were mentally and physically disabled. They were then required to solve the problem. Forced sterilisation and euthanasia were the preferred methods. Just as the police force fell on supposed enemies of the state, and the legal fraternity threw away all principles to clamp down on political undesirables, so did the medical fraternity adopt violent and inhumane methods at the bidding of their new masters.

The first Nazi eugenics policy, the Law for the Prevention of Hereditarily-Diseased Offspring, was passed in July 1933, six months after Hitler became chancellor. It gave German doctors open slather to condemn any person with questionable habits as suffering from genetically related illnesses. Examples of reportable cases were mental retardation, schizophrenia, manic-depression, blindness and deafness, or other severe physical deformities. Chronic alcoholism or the abuse of narcotics could be considered a genetic disorder at the doctor's discretion. Even those who occasionally had epileptic fits were suspect.

When Wilhelm Frick, Minister of the Interior, introduced the measures in late June he declared that the

German people were in danger of *Volkstod* 'racial extinction.'
Early estimates provided to Frick of those who needed
sterilisation were as follows:
Congenital feeble-mindedness: 200,000
Schizophrenia: 80,000
Manic depression: 20,000
Epilepsy: 60,000
Chorea: 600
Hereditary blindness: 4,000
Hereditary deafness: 16,000
Bodily malformation: 20,000
Hereditary alcoholism: 10,000.

Bodily malformation included crippled states such as
clubfoot, harelip or a cleft palate. These numbers covered
only those held in institutions. It was presumed at least twice
as many were in the community who would also require
forced sterilisation.

Up to 360,000 Germans were sterilised using these laws.

The law also set up Hereditary Health Courts, comprised
of two physicians and a lawyer. These courts examined
individual cases and ruled whether patients should be
'rendered incapable of procreation' by being sterilised.
When the law came into effect on the first day of 1934,
the Hereditary Health Courts were swamped with cases.
In their first three years these institutions ruled on almost
225,000 patients, ordering compulsory sterilisation for
around 90 per cent. Sterilisation orders were handed down
so rapidly that state hospitals did not have the operating
theatres or staff to keep up.

The vast majority of sterilised patients were suffering
from mental illness or deformity. Of the patients sterilised
in 1934, 53 per cent were intellectually disabled or feeble-
minded, 25 per cent schizophrenics and 14 per cent
epileptics. The panel did not have to meet the patients they
were passing judgment on and would usually go on a simple

referral. The referral did not always come from a health professional although all doctors were required by law to submit any possible names. Ninety per cent of petitions taken to the courts were acted on and only five per cent of appeals against sterilisation were upheld.

Once one of the 200 Hereditary Health Courts had decided upon sterilisation, a letter was sent to the subject explaining that they had no choice in the matter and that there would be no adverse health effects. The usual method of sterilisation was vasectomy for men and ligation of ovarian tubes for women. Many patients had to be restrained while undergoing the operation and several thousand Germans died during or as a result of the operation, mainly women due to the increased danger of tubal ligation.

School children were educated by the Nazi state. A textbook explained that while it cost the state ½ of a Reichsmark for the state to educate and support a normal pupil a 'backward pupil' cost three times as much while a blind of deaf pupil cost the state 4 Reichsmarks. It was also explained to the students that retired person on a pension was able to get by on 433 Reichsmarks but a mentally ill individual cost the state 1944 Reichsmarks to be cared for. The students were invited to draw their own conclusions as to the best fate for those less fortunate individuals.

In the 1920s Algerian troops in the French army were stationed in the Rhineland. Five hundred teenagers of mixed African and 'Aryan' descent were a byproduct of this Versailles treaty-approved occupation and a secret order ensured that they were all forcibly sterilised.

Euthanasia – T4

While forced sterilisation was no doubt extremely unpleasant to those who suffered it, they probably would have preferred it to the next development of Nazi racial eugenics – euthanasia.

Once again this was a body of radical thinking which the Nazis adopted as policy – usually such ideas would have been seen as belonging to the lunatic fringe of academia. One of the most influential treatises was written by Adolf Jost in 1895. Entitled, The Right To Death, it argued that just as in war the state sacrificed the young to strengthen the state, so it could kill those unworthy of life.

This point was taken further in the painfully titled 'The Permission to Destroy Life Unworthy of Life' written by two professors Karl Binding and Alfred Hoche. Hoche was interested in anatomy and took part in autopsies. He preferred people who had been guillotined as they were the freshest possible 'material' for his research. Hoche detailed how he had taken part in at least one illegal experiment on such a person. Smuggling himself into an autopsy as an assistant to investigate the effects of electricity on the human central nervous system, Hoche connected a hidden motor to the body to see if he could make it move. Eventually, after the state prosecution gave him special permission, Hoche was able to experiment on bodies within two minutes of their execution by guillotine.

He obviously had something of a warped ethical sense and as such he was able to reverse the fundamental goals of a physician. It was argued in the text that to kill the disabled was to cure them. Death was the ultimate therapy and he characterised it as 'healing therapy' and 'healing work'. The people who earned his particular ire were the 'human ballast' Ballastexistenz, empty shells, subjects so disadvantaged or retarded that to destroy them was in fact not killing as they were already dead.

At least Hoche had the decency to commit suicide when his ideas were seized upon and exploited by the Nazis, but not before they became the moral justification for unbridled killing.

Using the ethical blueprint built by Hoche the German medical fraternity quickly began killing their genetic chaff.

From 1934 mental hospitals began to develop euthanasia mindsets. As funding dropped patients were put on starvation diets and neglected by the staff.

These attitudes were formally encouraged by Hitler. While there is no smoking gun directly linking him to the Holocaust there is direct evidence that he encouraged the 'mercy death' of children.

As early as 1935 Hitler was heard to explain that during times of war the population would be desensitised to mass death so that it was an ideal time to kill disabled children. By 1938 decisive steps were taken and members of Hitler's staff 'encouraged' parents of disabled children to beg Hitler for permission to euthanise them. One individual stood out. An infant called Knauer was born blind and was missing all of his limbs except for half an arm. Hitler ordered his personal physician Karl Brandt to visit the unfortunate family and if the case was as dire as reported he was to give the physicians permission to terminate the unfortunate individual with Hitler's authorisation. Hitler also guaranteed that he would use his power as Führer to quash any legal proceeding that might be launched against them.

Little Knauer became a medical Rubicon. Once the line had been crossed German physicians began killing disabled children on a mass scale. Initially only newborns were drawn into the deadly web but eventually toddlers, teens and even adults were killed. As if to hide their shame under the guise of respectability, an impossibly long named organisation was set up to kill these innocents. The *Reichsausschuss zur wissenschaftlichen Erfassung von erb- und anlagebedingten schweren Leiden* (loosely translated as 'Organization for the scientific recording of unregistered genetic ailments and suffering') was tasked with compiling a registry of all children under three who had any disease such as spasticism or mongolism and sent out questionnaires to all medical practitioners. Midwives and doctors were required to report any such children. Initially they presumed that any information provided was for compiling statistics and willingly filled in the required forms.

Not so. Once a baby was identified three experts filled in another form. This form had three columns under the word 'treatment.' A+ written in the first column meant death. A− in the second column meant life and the word 'observation' was written in the third column if no decision was reached. No medical examination of the subject was carried out by the three experts nor were medical records examined. The questionnaires filled in by the doctors and nurses were the only resource used to determine life or death.

Those marked for death were dispatched to selected pediatric institutions. Staffed by politically reliable doctors they were often kept in isolated wards until they could be dealt with. Eventually 30 killing centres were set up in Germany, Austria and Poland. This large number allowed parents to bring their offspring to a relatively close institution. On dropping off their children the parents were assured that the most modern techniques would be used to try and cure their babies.

Doctors could convince themselves that they had tried to save the child but they also needed the parents to acquiesce. Parents were told that they should be grateful that the state was seeking to cure their children. Those who were reluctant to hand over their children were threatened with withdrawal of guardianship. Some were called up for special labour duty.

Before being killed the children were kept for a couple of weeks to maintain the fiction that some attempt at a therapeutic cure was being sought. Once the window dressing was complete the institution's director, with a wink or a nod, would instruct as junior practitioner to solve the problem and kill the child. The sedative Luminal was the weapon of choice in this war against hereditary weakness. Dissolved in tea it would be given over a period of one or two days until the child lapsed into a coma and died.

Many developed resistance to this drug and in these cases a hot shot of morphine was administered. Even those who had been given a reprieve and kept under 'observation' were usually upgraded to '+'.

At least 5,000 children were killed using these methods before 1941. Seeking to absolve their conscience the doctor's adopted doublespeak to cover their crimes. Many recorded how 'excitable' children needed extra sedation. Pneumonia or complications from surgery were given as the cause of death.

These children were lucky. Others were starved to death. One Doctor, Hermann Pfannmuller, was so devoted to Nazi ideals that his institution at Eglfing-Haar gradually reduced the rations of the children committed to his care so that they slowly died a painful whimpering death, too emaciated even to cry. Justifying his actions by describing how they saved the Reich medication costs, he was also proud to announce that not only disabled children were killed using this method, but also the offspring of Jewish couples. This was in 1939.

As early as 1940 the methods that would be used on masses of Jews and Gypsies in the East were already being trialled in medical institutions throughout the Reich. Seeking a more efficient method than individual injections, mass gassings were trialled. The patients were largely docile as they trusted the health professionals who were charged with looking after their wellbeing. One experiment took place in the Brandenburg Asylum on January 4th 1940 and was witnessed by Doctor August Becker of the Criminal Technical Institute (KTI) of the German police.

For this first gassing about 18–20 people were led into this 'shower room' by the nursing staff. These men had to undress in an anteroom until they were completely naked. The doors were shut behind them. These people went quietly into the room and showed no signs of being upset. Dr Widmann operated the gas. I could see through the peephole that after about a minute the people had collapsed or lay on the benches. There were no scenes and no disorder.*

Letters were sent home to those who were unfortunate enough to lose a loved one. An example might read:

Dear Herr Schmidt.

As you are no doubt aware, your daughter Fraulein Hanna Schmidt was transferred to our institution on ministerial orders. It is our sad duty to be required to inform you that she died here on 07/08/1940 of influenza. Unfortunately all of the sterling attempts by the doctors to keep the patient alive were not successful. We wish to express our condolences for your loss and hope that you will find some comfort in the knowledge that the death of your daughter has at least her from her incurable suffering. In accordance with health department and police guidelines it was necessary to cremate your daughter's corpse immediately. Please inform us if you wish the urn to be sent to you – free of charge.'

As with the gassing of children, the forced euthanasia of adults had Hitler's grubby finger prints all over it.

Hitler issued a 'Führer Decree' in October 1939 announcing that the new official policy of killing children was to extend to adults. Informing this ideal was his typically simple understanding of those faced with disability. His caricatured understanding of the mentally ill was that they were reduced to living on sand or sawdust as they continually sprayed uncontrolled excrement. Others ate their own filth as a matter of course.

The Decree was issued in October but backdated to 1st September, the date of the invasion of Poland. No doubt this was so Hitler could claim it was a wartime measure.

* The Gas Chamber at Brandenburg

http://www.deathcamps.org/gas_chambers/gas_chambers_brandenburg.html

Not only would he be exterminating the Slavic hordes to the east, but the genetic enemies within. The decree places Hitler and his entourage fair and square in the middle of massed killings.

> Reich leader Bouhler and Dr Brandt are charged with the responsibility for expanding the authority of physicians to be designated by name, to the end that patients considered incurable according to the best available judgment of their state of health, can be granted a mercy death.*

This pronouncement gives new meaning to the term 'killing with kindness.' This decree was written on Hitler's own private stationary, something rarely done and displaying to his subordinates the import of his intentions.

The T4 program got its name from its headquarters at Tiergarten 4 in the Chancellery district, Berlin. Once again questionnaires were sent out to medical practitioners in psychiatric wards and hospitals. No doubt those who filled them in knew the exact purpose of the forms even though they were once again designed to appear as innocent data collection forms. There was one key difference to the forms sent out to pediatric institutions. A description of the adult's ability to contribute to society by working ability was emphasised.

Once again a panel of three experts appraised the forms. But rather than being able to see their colleague's recommendations they each received an individual copy for each patient which were then collated at T4. Once again a red '+' meant death.

A new organisation dubbed, with typical Nazi double-speak, 'The Common Welfare Ambulance Service Ltd' was created to collect those who got the deadly cross. Transport

* Robert Jay Lifton, *The Nazi Doctors – Medical Killing and the Psychology of Genocide*, Basic Books, USA, 1986, p 63.

Bernburg sanatorium where almost 10,000 victims of T4 were gassed with carbon monoxide.

lists were sent to hospitals with a pick up date and a request that the prisoners be loaded onto the purpose built buses complete with personal possessions, medical records and any valuables that had been held for them. These buses were driven and staffed by SS men in white coats covering their black uniforms. Observant individuals noted the leather jackboots peeking out from under the reassuring medical gowns. The buses had windows painted over or permanently drawn blinds. No destination was announced and special passes were issued to the driver allowing him to proceed through any checkpoints without interruptions. Initially the patients were taken directly to one of the killing centres springing up around Germany but it was decided to take them to an institution for observation for a couple of weeks to help build a picture of legitimate medical practice.

There were six main killing centres. Most were ex-asylums and prisons and all had high walls while being located away from urban centres. This allowed prisoners to be unloaded, killed and cremated with a minimum of fuss. Almost all were killed within 24 hours of arrival. Originally doctors used injections to 'mercy kill' their charges using combinations of curare, morphine and cyanide. This proved to be problematical as some patients required more than one injection and needed to be restrained.

Hitler's advisor Doctor Brandt initiated an experimental gas chamber at the killing centre in Brandenburg while it was being converted from a prison. Setting the scene for the Holocaust to come it was planned by Christian Wirth of the SD. Patients were led naked into a fake shower room complete with benches and shower nozzles. Carbon monoxide was pumped through the nozzles after an SS doctor opened the gas cock. It was important that doctors performed the actual killing, maintaining the myth of beneficial mercy killings. Brandt reported the satisfactory results to Hitler who then approved the building of similar chambers in the other five facilities at Hartheim, Sonnenstein, Grafeneck, Bernburg and Hadamar.

Patients were deceived. Senior doctors delegated junior physicians to do a thorough external check, complete with officious-looking clipboard, stethoscope and white gown, on the victims as they stripped off and made their way to the 'shower'. Of course there was no beneficial health outcome from this procedure and it was merely a way of camouflaging the real aim of the procedure. They also ensured that the correct person was in fact being euthanised and looked for past health complaints that could perhaps be used on the faked death certificate. Most of the time the patients were, it appears, deceived. Few resisted and those who did were subdued by brute force – not an uncommon occurrence in many psychiatric wards.

Once within the chamber a strict protocol was followed. The junior doctor allowed the gas to enter the chamber and observed the progress of the poisoning through a small window in the chamber's door. As soon as he believed that the patients were dead the gas was turned off and fresh air was pumped into the chamber. The doors were opened and patients destined for an autopsy were taken to the morgue while the remainder were taken by SS orderlies straight to the crematoria.

The deception practiced on the patients was extended to the next of kin. The first that many families heard of their loved one's involvement in the T4 program was a letter explaining that due to the exigencies of a wartime economy it was necessary to move the patient to a specialised treatment centre. A subsequent letter would be received two weeks later explaining that it was impossible to visit the relative although all possible medical therapies were being employed for their welfare. The final letter was a death certificate. Aware that news travelled quickly within the German community despite the rigid controls of the totalitarian state, each certificate had to have a falsified cause of death.

Many options were open to the doctors who not only had to carry out the killing but write the certificate. Infectious diseases, pneumonia, heart disease, lung cancer and a range of other complaints were used. It was important the doctor tied the cause of death to preexisting complaints and the Nazi state was kind enough to provide the young doctors with guides on how to come up with a plausible cause. One such guide focused on septicaemia, a poisoned bloodstream. This was deemed appropriate for patients who used to smear themselves or their surroundings with fecal matter but it was not recommended for patients with a reputation for cleanliness. Families were also informed that due to the need for rapid disposal of the corpses in the interests in public health their loved ones were cremated and the ashes were available if requested.

Of course although the main goal of the T4 was to exterminate individuals in a clean and clinical manner, things went wrong. One family received two urns. One patient's death certificate recorded the cause of death as appendicitis even though this organ had been removed years before. The sheer coincidence of multiple patients shipped off by the 'Common Welfare Ambulance' service all dying at the same time was too much for many to swallow, especially if those who had died were in robust good health before their transport. Occasionally a patient would return home even though his family had received a death certificate.

The killing also took a toll on those who were involved. One young doctor experienced recurring nightmares where he continually saw the patients gradually collapsing and falling over each other. The orderlies found it difficult to get the stench out of their noses as the patients voided themselves within the chamber. Many of the orderlies took to drinking heavily at local bars, letting slip their grisly occupation. The unsworn members of the institutions including laundresses and cooks quickly cottoned on to the real purpose of these centres and spread the word.

Most telling of all was the relationship between buses arriving with patients, soon to be followed by foul acrid smoke spewing forth from the crematoria chimney. The burning process was not always perfect, locks of hair and greasy smoke often settled on local streets, especially if it was a still day.

By the time T4 closed down in late 1942 approximately

80,000 civilians had been killed. Aspects of the program were ceased due to public pressure, one of the few instances of Hitler and the Nazis having to restrict their murderous impulses.

Hitler's cousin euthanised

The program wasn't closed down before it led to the death of a distant cousin of Hitler. The Viet family were related through Hitler's paternal grandmother to the Schicklgruber clan. Adolf's distant cousin Aloisia Viet was born on 18th July 1891 in the small town of Polz, Austria. In January 1932 at the age of 41 she was committed to a psych ward in Vienna. Previous to this she had spent six years working as a chambermaid in a Vienna hotel but for one week she had been displaying schizoid behaviour. After committal her condition deteriorated. She was convinced that she was visited by Jesus Christ and she developed deranged, scatty behaviour with hallucinations, depression and delusions. Her aggressive behaviour resulted in Aloisia being strapped to her cot and by 1935 she was only being kept alive by being fed through a tube. A doctor's report suggested that mental illness was hereditary. Aloisia's mother, father and sister had all had episodes and all suffered from varying degrees of schizophrenia.

On 28th November 1940 Aloisia was transported to an appraisal centre on the Danube before being referred to an unknown institution. After this she is heard of no longer.

BEGINNINGS OF THE HOLOCAUST – 14F13

The other major referral was to the KPs, concentration camps. It was here that any pretense of medical practice became entirely hollow. All of Germany knew of the beatings and deprivation faced by inmates within these camps. It fell to the medical fraternity to kill those who were wasting away under the terrible conditions. These were victims of human cruelty, not hereditary problems or unstoppable illness. The doctors were to aid and abet the full brutality of the regime. 14f13 was the title given to the new program. With typical Nazi code-speak, any concentration camp administrator would have immediately recognized the true goals of the process, the number 14 identified the outcome as death.

As with all of the T4 program, these killings were carried out with the pretense of benign care. It began when two Nazi doctors, Mennecke and Steinmeyer, presented themselves at the Sachsenhausen infirmary in April 1941 and began to examine 400 prisoners selected by the camp authorities. Most of these cases were unable to work, had suppurating wounds from beatings and malnutrition and were more skin and bone than flesh. Some were in reasonable health but were referred due to minor deformities. The key reason the doctors were asked to examine these hapless individuals was because they were no longer able to work.

The examinations were not cursory and the doctors took two days of intense work, only breaking for lunch at the SS officers' canteen, to question the patients about their health and study their records. Treating their patients amicably, rumors and suspicions in camp soon dissipated and the story that they might be transported to Dachau for light duties began to gain currency.

The Germans had a much grimmer fate in store. Mennecke and Steinmeyer were veterans of the T4 action. Two months after the visit a final list was sent to Sachsenhausen of those who were deemed *Lebensunwertes Leben*. In batches of 90 to 100 the inmates were summoned to the camp infirmary where they were given an intravenous sedative before being bundled onto large lorries. Taken to nearby Sonnenstein in Saxony they were all gassed on arrival.

There was no lull in the two months between the Doctors' visits and the transports. In that time they also visited Auschwitz, Buchenwald, Ravensbruck, Gross-Rosen and Dachau to name a few. From each camp they made their deadly selections. Eventually twelve doctors were regularly travelling to the main camps to inspect weakened inmates.

The program escalated. Before KLs got their own death apparatus the burgeoning number of sick and incapacitated prisoners required a drastic solution. The inspections became more cursory. Often a prisoner would be paraded naked in front of the doctors, the red cross on the paperwork was then made before the prisoner was hustled out without any questions being addressed to the inmate. Many were too weak to walk and were carried into the infirmary and carried out without being put down. Occasionally a question would be asked and one or two were even reprieved. Usually they had been decorated at the front in the Great War.

Once the conveyor belt inspection was finished the paperwork received a final review at K4 headquarters before the inmates' final marching orders were dispatched. As 1942 progressed and the killing stepped up most inmates knew of their likely destination. Each batch was accompanied by their KL SS guards who were clearly under no illusion what was happening. Each camp arranged their own transport and Mauthausen employed bright yellow postal buses to dispatch their inmates. Nevertheless most held out some hope that they were being transported to lighter duties until the arrival at their designated killing centre. Here any lingering doubts would have evaporated upon seeing the crematoria chimneys which were by late 1942 in full swing.

Handed into the care of T4 personnel many tried to impress upon the medical staff how healthy they were hoping for a last minute reprieve. Too late. The prisoners were herded into the gas chambers. Now fully aware of what was happening many screamed, collapsed or vomited with fear. Brute force was required for these later executions and many had to be herded violently into the chamber before the doors were forced shut. Time after time the cylinders of Carbon Monoxide gas supplied by IG Farben was pumped

Operation *Reinhard* in action ... victims are transported to one of the death camps.

into the lungs of the former concentration camp prisoners before they collapsed in unruly piles on the floor of the 'showers.' The T4 staff extracted gold fillings from specially marked prisoners before hauling the inmates straight to the incinerators. No pretence of autopsies that characterised the medical 'mercy killing' of the earlier program were carried out, the medical profession acknowledged that they were engaged in callous murder.

The 14f13 continued into 1944 and was used by concentration camps to clear out unwanted ill inmates. Those with advanced medical facilities abandoned the programme all together and adopted a more direct means of killing inmates. Phenol injections to the heart.

Outwardly Phenol killings were like a regular medical procedure. A doctor or his assistant attired in a white coat would wait in a treatment room for the patient to be bought to him. The patient would be seated, the site of the injection swabbed and the needle's deadly cargo delivered directly into the circulatory system. In any cases this was more convenient than 14f13 as paperwork was not required and the inmates did not have to be transported.

Patients would be summoned to the camp surgery under the pretext of an inoculation of some kind. Entering the surgery they would see a metal table with an array of syringes, somehow comforting in their number. Surely, a patient might think, there is no way so many could be used for anything but benign purposes. A bottle of alcohol and cotton wool were on the table along with a well-used rubber tourniquet. The subject would be asked to be seated by a polite orderly who would then position his or her right arm on a metallic support table. Uttering kind words the physician, would apply the tourniquet and apply pressure to make the veins become visible. The modern day problem of having too much flesh so that veins could not be found would not have been a problem with the malnourished camp inmates. The doctor then rubbed alcohol just below the elbow like a normal procedure and injected the phenol.

Phenol, also known as carbolic acid, is a toxic compound. One gram is sufficient to cause blackouts, spasms, and the paralysis of the central nervous system and, with prolonged exposure, multiple organ failure. In the camp jargon such injections were known as *spritzen* and those in the know also referred to it as 'phenoling'. These civilised almost gentle styles of executions had one major problem. They were not quick enough.

Maybe suitable if a doctor had to kill of one or two individuals, once the horror of liquidation gained pace coarser methods were required. Children died fairly quickly once injected but adults could take up to an hour to die as the poison slowly wound through the system. There was also the danger that the needle could penetrate right through the vein and inject the lethal agent into the flesh. This led to painful subcutaneous acid burns as the patient dropped in and out of consciousness.

120 Auschwitz children were killed in one large batch in early 1943. As orphans they had been doted on by other inmates and bought a small glimpse of happiness as they played. The two doctors charged with their murder bought them into a washroom at the end of the barracks. One by one they were injected and were heard to fall to the floor and spasm with a death rattle amid plaintive cries for mercy. The two doctors who performed the 'procedure' emerged shaken and pale. A more efficient means was required. One which did not require a doctor to perform it and which guaranteed a quicker death.

The procedure was changed to injecting the 'concentrated aqueous solution of phenol' directly into the heart. It was determined to be inexpensive, easy to use and guaranteed to cause death in 10 to 15 seconds when injected into the heart ventricle. A large syringe and a long needle were used. The solution was poured out of a thermos like device into a bowl into which the needle would be placed, the plunger pulled back and the syringe would be filled. The subject was then ushered into a small room where two assistants bade them sit on a small footstool. The right arm was used to cover the eyes while the left arm was extended horizontally and pulled gently back to expose the chest and rib cage. Sometimes the right arm was used as a gag, placed across the victim's mouth to stifle any cry. The needle was then thrust directly into the heart through the space between the fourth and fifth rib and the prisoner usually crumpled forward, unconscious, then dead. With no time to waste, even as they were in their death throes, the victim would be seized under the armpits by the two orderlies and thrown into an adjacent room onto the pile of corpses from previous 'inoculation' and another subject would be ushered calmly into the clinic. Different practitioners boasted of their efforts, three in one minute or a hundred in an hour.

The still warm corpses took on a pinkish livid colour as small haemorrhages took place under the skin. The open eyes of the surprised inmates were bloodshot and for some reason the Phenol delayed the onset of rigor mortis for a couple hours. No doubt the incinerator *Kommandos* would have welcomed this as the bodies were hauled out of the death rooms and taken to the crematorium.

This was no small part of the holocaust. Hospitals in camps throughout the Reich were converted into institutions of murder. It is estimated that in Auschwitz alone during 1941 and 1943 an average of 45 were killed using this method each day. Sometimes up to two hundred could be murdered during 'consultation hours.' Injections were not given on Sundays.

JOSEF MENGELE

The best-known doctor from the Nazi era is undoubtedly Doctor Josef Mengele. Notorious is a better description. Other doctors limited themselves to one or two areas of

Joseph Mengele at Auschwitz between two of the camp commanders, Baer and Hoess.

medical investigation, not so Mengele. His appetite for experimentation was equaled only by his sadism.

Mengele was a driven scientist. Any crackpot idea gave him license to kill with an injection, the gas chamber or even an NCO willing to 'dispense' a 9mm slug to the brain. Dwarfs and twins were his special interest and many were saved from the selections on the ramp at Auschwitz and for a short time enjoyed the protection of the Nazi doctor. As a test subject a prisoner would be shielded from the full horror of Auschwitz and receive rations above the starvation level issued to the less fortunate. Those under Mengele's protection were not allowed to be 'damaged' by guards or *kapos* (prisoners given administrative or disciplinary roles).

This protection lasted as long as Mengele was concerned with studying the external physical characteristics of his charges. If a more intimate examination was required 'Pepe Mengele', as some of the children called him, moved calmly to the next stage of his clinical investigations; autopsy. Coldly and unemotionally he would administer a killing shot of phenol or else get an SS guard to kill the subject.

Mengele often saved Jewish doctors from the gas chambers and employed them as research assistants. Many of these doctors and researchers told how Mengele could be seen laughing and smiling with his subjects, have them killed and then cut them up on an autopsy table, all within half an hour. One family of six dwarfs thought themselves safe. Taken to Auschwitz hospital as soon as they arrived from Hungary, Mengele and his assistants spent several hours measuring them in meticulous detail. One hour later the family were being de-fleshed in a large boiling vat and eight hours later the bones were packaged and on their way to a Berlin University for further study. Mengele performed a last service for many of his subjects. If an internal examination was not required but an 'action' in one of Auschwitz's gas chambers was proceeding he was quite happy to load the un-needed subjects into his car and drive them personally to the 'shower block.'

Mengele was one of the few decorated Nazi doctors. Having spent several years in the cauldron of the Eastern Front with the 5th SS Panzer grenadier Division Viking he was wounded before being transferred to Auschwitz. When he arrived in May 1943 the camp had grown far beyond its original size and housed upward of 140,000 prisoners. It had two roles. The first and most notorious was as one of the killing centres for Operation *Reinhard*. Numbers are impossible to determine but at least 1,700,000 million Jews from the General government (Poland) and Hungary were killed in the biggest of all death factories. It was also a massive holding pen for a mass of diseased and starved humanity forced to work until they dropped in major industrial concerns located in sub camps around the main camp.

The camp doctors performed a crucial role in this institution. They were asked to 'select' between those who could be employed by the likes of Bayer and IG Farben and those who were to be sent immediately to the death chamber.

It was on the rail platform at Auschwitz where Mengele made the biggest impression and earned the nickname 'The Angel of Death.' Mengele was, it seems, something of a workaholic. This combined with his desire to ensure that no twins or dwarfs went straight to the gas chambers meant that whether assigned to selection duty or not, he usually made his presence felt. Survivors remarked upon his immaculate presentation. Dressed in full SS rig with his Iron Cross First Class pinned proudly to his breast Mengele seemed far removed from the straggling bewildered humanity upon which he was able to pass the sentence of death.

Women found him quite handsome with his polished boots; his tight fitting uniform, white gloves and polished cane. He often viewed the arrivals with a faintly sardonic air and was given to whistling operatic airs from Puccini as he pointed them either left or right with a casual wave. Jews were hustled out of the cattle cars they had been transported in. Forced by baying dogs and SS guards wielding whips into columns they were lined up and approached the SS doctors carrying out the selections. A casual nod or a flick of a riding crop would send healthy men and women to the left before being herded off to large barrack blocks and assigned a job. The old, sick and young would be sent to the right. These unfortunates were not deemed by the SS doctors to be healthy enough to perform useful work in the war industries surrounding the camp. Their destiny was to be sent for 'delousing.' Any disabled, deformed or weak were inevitably sent to what was in reality the gas chamber. Mengele was a 'nice looking man' who would look at their bodies and faces for a couple of seconds before saying 'Rechts' (right) or 'Links' (left).

It seems that this is the reason Mengele ensured he was present at as many selections as he could attend. It was important to his research that as many twins as possible were rounded up and he often waded through the struggling mass of humanity '… shrieking in a loud voice "Twins out, twins out!"' He was usually more composed and seemed to take a sadistic pleasure in deluding those about to be reduced to ash. One witness claimed that he would tell women to take care of their children with a smiling friendly manner. As he separated children from their mothers he would smilingly explain that they would be reunited with their babies in the nursery once they had been showered. One young woman was sent into the survivors' column but repeatedly sought to sneak back to her elderly mother's side in the row destined for the crematorium. When a Ukrainian guard hauled her back to the women's original column Mengele stepped in. 'Be reasonable', he said smiling,' let the poor women join her mother.' He waved them off as both women thanked him profusely.

In post war interviews Mengele claimed to be the good guy. He argued that he saved as many as possible, maybe two thousand by sending them into the work camps even though they were weak. The others, the sick and starving, or those covered in lice, they could not survive so he was merely sending them to a merciful end rather than a slow death in the camps.

Even Mengele's SS colleagues dismiss this idea. He had a reputation as a ruthless cynic who consigned a far greater percentage of arrivals to the gas chambers. Most SS doctors hated the work and many had to get drunk before appearing on the ramp and would use any excuse to avoid the task of sentencing tens of thousands to death. Mengele was one of the few who did not need artificial stimulants of any kind. The 'Canada Kommando' was the work detail of Jewish prisoners required to unload prisoner transports. As well as herding the living from the cattle trucks it was their job to throw out any who had died onto the platform as well as collecting any left luggage. During the Frankfurt

Auschwitz trial some who had survived this task testified that Mengele was always present. Like a shadow of death it was he who was the 'chief provider for the gas chamber and the crematory ovens.'

However it seems that maybe there was something of a myth built about Mengele. While he was often there looking for twins and dwarfs, records indicate he took his turn paired with a colleague like the other SS doctors on staff. Many survivors described him as a typical Aryan, tall blonde and blue eyed. That he was not very tall while being relatively swarthy, or even Mediterranean in appearance was not observed by many who swore that it was Mengele who had sent them to the work details while consigning their loved ones to execution. The myth of Mengele may have grown with the retelling.

What is not in doubt was his propensity for furious outbreaks of destructive anger. There was a case when an elderly Jew was selected for the gas chamber but repeatedly tried to go to his son in the work group. A furious Mengele hit the old man over the head with an iron bar, splitting the skull and dropping him dead. Another time Mengele drew his pistol and shot a *kapo* dead on the spot when the inmate allowed prisoners destined to die to join those of a work detail. Those who did not follow his instruction to go left or right would earn a crack over the head with the riding whip, if they were lucky.

Disobedience on the ramp could have much more dire consequences. In one case a mother did not want to be separated from her teenage daughter. She bit and scratched the face of the SS guard who tried to force her into the other line. Mengele drew his pistol and shot the mother and daughter. He then made an executive decision. The whole transport was sent to the gas chamber, even those who had previously been selected for work. "Away with this shit." was his last comment on the doomed people. One teenager, sent to the right while her mother and younger sisters were sent to the left begged and wept to stay with her family. Mengele grabbed her by the hair and dragged her to the ground before administering a fearful beating. The teenager's mother came to her rescue only to beaten in turn. He used his crop for other purposes. Elderly women had their wigs stripped off them and if a Jewish woman took his fancy he played the riding crop across her breasts and told them to undress, in full view of laughing *kapos*.

Auschwitz doctors were not only responsible for selecting prisoners who were able to work as forced labour, they also had to select those who were too weak to continue working or so sick that they posed a danger to the health of other inmates. Just as Mengele delighted in selecting those who were to die at selections, he displayed a ruthless enthusiasm in clearing out the sick. He often visited the hospital barracks at Birkenau and delighted in the terror that he caused. Those who were likely to need three weeks or more of treatment were most likely to be selected. Their names were given to the block warder and whoever was so named was handed a death sentence. He bought this process to a fine art of sadism. He would turn up at all hours of the day or night as the fancy took him. Sometimes a whole ward would be consigned to the gas chambers or shooting while at other times none would be selected. Surprise selections were his specialty. He would show up at the infirmary or the hospital at his whim, whistling operatic airs, and indifferently order women to the right or left. Sometimes it was not possible to tell which was the condemned group until Mengele made his final pronouncement.

One particularly loathsome character often carried out mass shootings at the behest of Mengele. Sergeant Eric Muhsfeldt with his pointed lined and scowling face and pointy ears chest could easily have been mistaken as a mythological Goblin. One Hungarian doctor who was forced to help Mengele with autopsies described one incident when Muhsfeldt came to him for a routine check-up after shooting 80 prisoners in the back of the head prior to their cremation. Dr Nyiszli commented that Muhsfeldt's blood pressure was high, and inquired as to whether this could be related to the recent increase in "traffic", as the mass murder of newly arrived victims was euphemistically called. Muhsfeldt replied angrily that it made no difference to him, whether he shot one person or eighty. If his blood pressure was too high, it was because he drank too much!

In late 1943 there was a severe outbreak of typhus in the women's camp at Birkenau, a sub camp at Auschwitz which was then under Mengele's control. Over a third of the 20,000 half-starved women were seriously ill with the disease. This dreadful bacteria is carried in the gut of infected lice living in clothes. As soon as one person becomes infected by being bitten they develop a fever. This creates an environment which is too hot for the lice so they migrate onto another person thus spreading the disease. Typhus has historically been known as ships fever, barracks fever or jail fever due to its lethal nature when present among dense masses of people in confided unhygienic conditions.

Mengele decided on a radical solution to the problem. One barracks had all 600 women shipped to the gas chamber whether they were healthy or sick. He then had the empty barracks scrubbed and disinfected from top to bottom. Women were cleared from an unclean block, scrubbed and given new clothes and their old filthy block was cleaned in turn before the process was repeated until the whole camp was cleaned. The 600 women who were gassed were merely collateral damage.

On another occasion Mengele sent 1100 suspected typhus cases in the Gypsy camp to be liquidated. Towards the end of 1944 the women of camp C were faced with another crisis. Deteriorating conditions at the front had led to a lack of transport to Auschwitz resulting in severe food shortages. By now there were 40,000 women in Mengele's care. There was not enough food to even provide the stipulated 700 calories a day. Mengele declared that since he could not feed all of the prisoners they would have to be liquidated. Every night for ten nights 4000 women were loaded into trucks and conveyed in a huge circular conveyor belt to the gas chambers. These women knew the fate that awaited them, having spent so long in the camp, and their shrieks and moans as they were carried to their fate can only be imagined. Each truck was loaded up with 80 emaciated women who either 'filled the air with their screams or sat mute, paralysed with fear.' Mengele was also charged with clearing out ill hospital patients. He asked his Jewish doctors to prepare lists of their patients and the likely date that they could return to the camp community as an active worker. Any who required longer than three weeks were destined for immediate execution. Mengele too would conduct ward inspections, something which bought terror to the bedridden patients. Those who had skin infections or unsightly lesions caused by malnutrition and scurvy were most likely to be selected by the doctor. With these smaller numbers, a phenol shot to the heart was his preferred method of 'treatment.'

Mengele had a dislike for gypsies. Maybe his slightly swarthy complexion gave him something of an inferiority complex but whatever the reason he treated them particularly harshly. At the doctor's insistence the entire Gypsy family camp of more than 4000 individuals was liquidated between July 31st and August 2nd 1944. Mengele personally supervised the operation. When a 4 year old girl pleaded with 'Uncle Doctor' to be spared Mengele instructed a German *kapo* to deal with her immediately. The young girl was seized and had her skull smashed against a lorry wheel.

Mengele's diligence was noted by his superiors. A report recommending him for promotion noted his "prudence, perseverance and energy" and noted "his performance can be called outstanding" despite the "very difficult conditions."

A by-product of this human suffering on an epic scale was doctor's such as Mengele were able to use the huge store of human cattle which was destined to be destroyed and reduced to nothing but ash as fodder for a range of gruesome experiments. He could pick and choose any people for his experiments and do anything he wanted. Mengele had obtained his peacetime doctorate with papers that seemed fairly harmless. His theses examined how various facial features differed between different ethnic groups. Seen as fairly dry and unremarkable they were published with barely a ripple of notice.

Auschwitz allowed him to take his research to an entirely new level. While he investigated many areas his obsession with twins seems to indicate that, following Nazi ideals of eugenics, Mengele was determined to find a way of producing super breeders, Aryan mothers who could knock out more than one child on a regular basis. Concurrent with that research were his experiments to try and alter eye colour. It was also noticed among his peers that dwarfism was a particular interest. Much of this is speculation. Mengele took his papers in a battered briefcase as he fled to South America to a life of friendless exile and loneliness. Sometime between when he fled the advancing Russians and his sad death by drowning on a beach in South America these papers have gone missing. Some tables and lists of numbers, with nothing to put them in context, are all that remain of his studies. That and eyewitness accounts of his crazed experiments.

Mengele was not lacking in subjects and the Nazi state was happy to provide him with specialised medical equipment to aid him in his 'studies.' The German Research Council (*Deutsche Forschungsgemeinschaft*) provided a state of the art pathology laboratory so that he could carry out his genetic research. With particularly Teutonic efficiency this facility was built into the main structure of Birkenau Crematorium number two. This allowed recently gassed victims to be dissected followed by immediate cremation. No expense was spared and the laboratory had a red concrete floor supporting a large marble-dissecting table complete with several sinks. Shelves lined the walls with specimen bottles waiting to be filled with interesting body parts that could then be shipped off to research institutions in Berlin and Leipzig. One Jewish doctor was horrified when she entered the laboratory and saw hundreds of eyes, bottled, pickled or pinned to the wall. Similar collections were in all of Mengele's labs scattered around the several sub camps. One female Jewish doctor, assisting Mengele in some experiments, almost came around to see him as human. That was until she peered into a package he was dispatching to Berlin and saw a multitude of eyes, blue, brown and green, peering up at her.

Being a good Nazi Mengele decided that for the greater good it was important to make as many people as possible look Aryan. Thirty-six children were selected form the Birkenau children's camp and a variety of substances were injected into their eyeballs to see if they could be made to turn blue. Many went blind or developed dreadful infections. Once they were of no use the children were shipped off to be gassed.

Twin children suffered particularly horribly. Initially they were well treated, bought up to acceptable weight with good food and housed in clean barracks with plenty of bedding. This allowed Mengele to ensure that each twin was in robust god health so that he could begin his comparative studies. After this initial phase they were moved from what was called 'the zoo' to the hospital in Camp B2F. Here truly mind boggling experiments with little or no scientific outcome were performed. One pair of twins were sowed together back to back and wrist to wrist. A crude incision had been made where the two were to be united and their flesh was so poorly stitched that gangrene set in soon after. The two lived for several weeks in this condition, sobbing all night as they tried to sleep. Sets of twins were given blood transfusions from twins with a different blood type. Mengele then observed the fevers and blinding headaches which followed. Amputations were performed without anaesthesia, lumbar punctures, typhus injections and a whole range of cuts or stabbings were carried out on the children and they were then observed to see how their body reacted to these assaults.

Mengele would then kill the twins and carry out autopsies to see if the internal organs had reacted in the same way for each child. There are reports that he got SS guards to carry out these killing but more commonly he took matters into his own hands. The preferred manner was to inject the children with a needle filled with chloroform into the heart. This coagulated the blood and caused heart failure but didn't not interfere with other bodily systems allowing a thorough examination of the organs. If one twin died of natural causes, the other would be killed and both could be examined together.

He electrocuted women, seeing how long they could survive. One woman with a baby had her breasts cut off so that Mengele could ascertain how long the baby would survive without feeding. He dissected a one year old child while it was still alive. He stood on the bellies of pregnant women until the foetus was ejected. With the Auschwitz Commandant Hoess and other officers he ordered 300 Polish children to be thrown onto a large blazing fire started in a deep pit. Any child who sought to crawl out was pushed back into the inferno with a stick.

Mengele was perhaps the worst of the Nazi doctors. But only by degrees. While he took Nazi eugenics to their extreme, much of the German medical profession was complicit in similar crimes.

4

DEATH SQUADS

Mobile killing – *Einsatzgruppen* and police battalions

In a warm summer evening in mid-1942 the men of Police Battalion 101 trundled in a convoy towards the town of Józefów. This small rural community was situated in the south of the Lublin district within occupied Poland. The day before the officers had attended a briefing and received their orders from the battalion commander, Major Trapp. The battalion was to liquidate the Jews who were concentrated in the town ghetto. As well as giving instructions to the officers, Tripp had seen to the issuing of leather whips to his men. Many enlisted troopers realised that this meant that they would soon be engaged in an *Aktion*.

Upon arriving at the outskirts of Józefów, Trapp had his men form up on three sides of a square. He addressed the entire battalion and explained that they would be clearing the town's ghetto and shooting its inhabitants. The Major explained that the task was not entirely to his tastes but that he had received orders for the task from above and the battalion would carry out its duty. Trapp exhorted his men by saying that in Germany women and children were being killed by Allied bombers and that they had to harden their hearts and understand that civilians were often casualties in war. He then made the link between partisan actions and the Jews.

Józefów was Police Battalion 101's genocidal baptism. While they had participated in rounding up Jews from Hamburg, their home territory, none of the men had carried out a mass execution. Strict instructions were given by the commander. They were given explicit orders to shoot the most helpless Jews. The young, females, the old and the sick were all to get a bullet in the back of the head. The only ones to be spared were working age males who would be dragooned into slave labour and sent to the Reich.

'Papa' Trapp then did something extraordinary. He explained to his 500 strong command that any who felt they were unable to carry out the action could step forward to be excused. Twelve stepped forward, including a young lieutenant.

The remaining Order-Police prepared for the action.

At company and platoon level the men were instructed what was required of them. Third company was to form a cordon and ensure that none escaped. Second company was to clear the ghetto moving from door to door and assemble the Jews at the specified assembly point, Józefów's town square. Any individuals who could not be readily bought to the collection area were to be immediately dispatched. The old and infirm were to be killed in their beds while infants could be bayoneted or shot. First company's task was to corral the captives before forming execution squads. These squads were given detailed instructions on how to kill their victims by the battalion medico Doctor Schoenfelder. This medical practitioner gathered the men around him and drew on the ground the outline of an upper torso, neck and head. He pointed at the spot where the neck joins the head and suggested that was the best place as it would minimise the amount of brain splatter but terminate life instantly. One soldier suggested that it was best to keep the bayonet on as that allowed the shooter to discharge at an appropriate distance from the victim's head, further reducing the mess created.

Those who had not taken up Trapp's offer to withdraw set to their task with a brutal will. When dawn arrived the Germans began rounding up the unwary inhabitants.

Working in subsections of two or three men they went purposefully throughout the ghetto. Any who resisted or couldn't move quickly enough were killed. Eyewitnesses walking through the streets after the action saw dozens of corpses, hanging out of windows, slumped in doorways and discarded on the pavement. All the patients of a Jewish hospital were killed. Babies were often killed while in their mother's arms, one bullet was all that was needed to finish them both off. Other infants were held at arm's length by the leg and shot with a pistol. Those who could move were harried to the town square with rifle butts and the leather whips issued the day before.

Second company delivered their charges to the assembly point but then returned to the ghetto to finish the job. By this time the rest of the town had woken up to what was happening and many Poles came to help the Germans as they conducted a second sweep. By 1942 rumours had swept through Jewish communities as to their likely fate. Many had sought to protect themselves by constructing ingenious hiding places. Doors were covered over with false walls, small alcoves were prepared as hiding places, as were false ceilings or cellars. Polish collaborators were particularly efficient at uncovering these hiding places. They would turn out fugitives and were allowed to loot any remaining personal possessions as a reward. Sometimes these hidden 'resisters' were shot on the spot, sometimes they too were bought to the collection point.

Once Trapp believed the ghetto was clear the killing began. Second company joined first company as the major was considerate of his men's feelings. He wanted the job done by nightfall so that they could all return to barracks for a good night's sleep.

The roundup of the Jews was done efficiently – 101 had performed that type of action often enough. The killing was frightfully botched and drawn out.

First and Second company were divided into killing

squads of about eight men. A squad would approach a group of Jews as they sat huddled in the town square and each man would collect one victim. A forest was adjacent to the town and each squad would walk in parallel single file with their victim next to them until they found an undisturbed location. Pushing their charge onto the ground each policeman positioned himself with his rifle and aimed at the head of his victim until the order to fire was given. Despite all of the Nazi efforts at dehumanising Jews, it would have been near impossible for all but the most fanatical of Nazis not to realise that the small child or wailing mother walking next to them was a person deserving of some degree of mercy.

But no mercy was given. Despite the pleas of the adults and the whimpering of frightened children, the men of Police Battalion 101 aimed their rifles at the heads of their victims and shot them in cold blood. Sometimes victims thrashed around in their death throes requiring another shot. At other times they merely shivered before lying still. The close-in nature of the procedure meant Germans were spattered with human gore. Brain matter, blood and bone splinters soiled their uniforms but time after time they emerged from the woods and seized another group of victims before taking them for execution. Each batch required another location and considerable initiative must have been needed to find an appropriate spot for liquidation.

Each man shot between five and ten Jews that day. Most of the victims were women, children and the elderly. One thousand four hundred Jews were killed. Many were exiles from Northern Germany, the same area 101 was recruited from, and would have been able to plead with their executioners in their native tongue.

It might be suspected that the men who carried out these horrible acts were all card carrying Nazis thugs. In fact a low proportion were members of the party. They were drawn from all walks of life. Professionals were recruited along with tradesmen and labourers. At least 39 Police Battalions took part in actions of these kinds and they were largely recruited from the older, less athletic sections of the German middle class. They were in fact drawn from sections of German society who were not engaged in essential war work, were not members of the Nazi elite and were not fit enough to be called up by the armed forces.

How was it that of the approximately 550 men of Police Battalion 101 only 12 refused to kill Jews when they were all given the option to withdraw? Although part of Operation *Reinhard* (The Final solution), Police Battalions were equally as active throughout the Soviet Union as the *Einsatzgruppen* and all organisations used similar techniques.

The actions of the *Einsatzgruppen* in 1941 are well known.

Following behind the armoured spearheads of the Wehrmacht as they penetrated into the heart of European Russia, these four 'Special Action Commandos' gained a fearsome reputation for killing Russian Commissars and Jewish civilians. It is a commonly reported belief that Himmler's decision to create the Operation *Reinhard* camps was taken to allow mass exterminations to take place without exposing Germans to the traumatic and emotionally debilitating experience of close up killing as described above. What is less known is that even after the disbanding of the *Einsatzgruppen* and concurrent with the slaughter of Jews in Operation *Reinhard* at least 31 police battalions roamed behind the front lines exterminating whole populations of Jews.

Operation *Reinhard*, the extermination of the Jews discussed and formalised during the Wannsee conference, utilised the four killing camps at Treblinka, Sobibór, Balzac and Auschwitz to wipe out Jewish communities who were located in population centres close to railheads. Police Battalions had two tasks in this operation. The first responsibility was to round up and deport those close to railway stations. The other was to exterminate those Jewish populations that could not be readily shipped to the killing camps. This mass slaughter continued through all of 1942 and well into 1943.

The actions of the 101 Police battalion display how they continued the murderous tasks of the *Einsatzgruppen* as well as organising transports for Operation *Reinhard*. Between July 1942 and November 1943 they were responsible for shooting at least 30,000 Jews and rounding up for transport to a death camp at least 30,000 more.★

In this the police were aided and abetted by at least 100,000 auxiliaries from various captured territories including the Baltic States and the Ukraine. These auxiliaries were distinguished from their German employers by their simpler uniforms and lack of insignia. They were also set apart from the Germans, if possible, by their fanatical hatred of anything communist. Many had seen their communities devastated in man-made famines and the ruthless political killings bought about by 20 years of soviet rule. The population was already brutalised in many ways and it was a simple matter of expediency to turn this violent mind set onto new victims while acting in the employ of new masters.

The Germans of the police battalions didn't have this factor influencing their actions so why were they so ready to follow such horrific orders? Centuries of anti-Semitism combined with nine years of Nazi propaganda are the explanation.

Nazi anti-Semitism

In their efforts to demonise the Jews, the Nazis pulled no punches. A 1938 schoolbook *The Poison Mushroom* describes a Jewish doctor raping and 'disgracing' a young child before trying to rape another blonde haired and blue eyed virgin.

★ Daniel Jonah Goldhagen, *Hitler's Willing Executioners: Ordinary Germans and the Holocaust*, Abacus United States, 1997, p 233.

Inge sits patiently in the Jew Doctor's reception room. She has to wait a long time. Again and again she remembers her talk with her mother and how her mother forced her to go to the doctor despite the warnings of her BDM (Nazi girl Guides) leader who said, 'A German must not consult a Jew doctor! And particularly not a German girl! There lies ruination and disgrace.'

While in the waiting room she had a disturbing experience. From the doctor's consulting room she hear another young girl pleading with the doctor asking her to be left alone. 'Doctor, Doctor, leave me alone' then crying – then silence.

After waiting another hour the door opens and Inge is confronted by The Jew. She jumps up in terror and drops a magazine. Her eyes take in the doctor's face, the face of a devil! He has a huge crooked nose; behind his dirty spectacles are two criminal gimlet like eyes while he licks his thick lips in criminal anticipation, anticipation that says 'Now I have you little German girl.'

The Jew approaches Inge his fleshy fingers reaching out to grab her. Inge slaps the fat Jewish doctor's face and flees down the stairs into the fresh air.'

Ernst Hiemer, *The Poisonous Mushroom*, Julius Streicher, 1938.

Not only is the Jew a rapist, he makes his patients wait for an hour after the appointment time. It is obvious that the author of this anti-Semitic tripe was paid a bonus for every exclamation mark. What else is obvious is that many Germans were so thoroughly brainwashed by the Nazis that they could read this stuff and take it seriously.

It was this level of brainwashing that permeated all sectors of the German media that allowed such outrages as the Holocaust to occur.

Hitler made his hatred of the Jews clear in a speech made in 1939 just before the outbreak of the war. He also stated his aim of eliminating the Jews from Europe.

Europe cannot find peace until the Jewish question has been
solved....... If the international Jewish financiers in and
outside Europe succeed in plunging the nations once more
into a world war, then the result will not be the Bolshevising of
the earth, and thus the victory of Jewry, but the annihilation of
the Jewish race in Europe.*

By examining such statements it could be argued that the
entire reason for starting the war was to kill Jews. Behind
the first columns pouring into Poland, *Einsatzgruppen* were
there to do their dirty work.

It took many years of excluding the Jews from German
life that allowed such things to happen. Between 1933 and
1935 laws were passed that removed Jews from most aspects
of daily life. Jewish students were removed from schools
and all were expelled in 1938. All adult Jews were removed
from positions in the civil service and universities. They
were forbidden to join sporting clubs, practice medicine or
law, and Jewish businesses had to register all their assets and
wealth. Regulations excluded the Jewish population from
theatres, concert halls, cinemas, parks, restaurants, holiday
resorts and they were not allowed to keep pets. They were
stripped of their driving licenses, were 'given the right' to
wear a yellow star and had to add either Sarah or Israel to
their names.

In 1938 the casual beatings dealt out to individuals by SA
bullyboys escalated to wide scale physical persecution. The
'June Action' led to 1500 Jews with a police record, (including
traffic violations) being arrested and sent to concentration
camps. This was minor compared to *Kristallnacht*, The Night
of Broken Glass.

On November 9 1938, in response to the murder of a

Jeremy Noakes and G Pridham, eds, *Nazism 1919–1945, Volume 3: Foreign
Policy, War and Racial Extermination: A Documentary Reader,* University of Exeter
Press, Exeter 1988, p 1049.

Nazi diplomat in Paris by a Jewish student, the Nazis began a systematic attack on Jews in Germany. The event was named *Kristallnacht* after all of the broken glass that littered the German streets after thousands of shops and houses belonging to Jews had their windows broken. SA and SS troops in plain clothes and with the approval of the Nazi leadership embarked on an orgy of destruction and looting. Jewish property was systematically smashed and burnt. Over 90 people were killed, 1000 Jewish shops and businesses were looted and 191 synagogues were burnt down. During the next week over 20,000 Jewish men and boys were rounded up and placed in concentration camps. Organised warfare against the Jewish population had begun.

Foreign observers were shocked by the naked hatred displayed by many Germans. Michael Bruce, an Englishman hurried out into the street where he was shocked to see what seemed to be the entire German community destroying a synagogue before turning their attentions to burning and looting Jewish shops. The street became ' a chaos of screaming bloodthirsty people' who set upon an elderly Jewess who was fortunate to be saved by Bruce. But all of this was eclipsed when the mob attacked a hospital for sick Jewish children.

> In minutes the windows had been smashed and the doors forced. When we arrived, the swine were driving the wee mites out over the broken glass, bare-footed and wearing nothing but their nightshirts. The nurses, doctors, and attendants were being kicked and beaten by the mob leaders, most of whom were women.*

By 1939 the Nazi state had effectively made their Jewish citizens into socially dead beings, separated from the rest of

* *Kristallnacht Eyewitness Accounts and Reminiscences*
http://motlc.wiesenthal.com/site/pp.asp?c=gvKVLcMVIuG&b=394831

society by laws, regulations and propaganda. Lacking all basic rights they could be targeted and victimised by any who took an active dislike to them. Many Jews sought to flee. Of the 525,000 living in Germany in 1933, 248,000 managed to flee by 1939. Another 30,000 managed to escape during the war. Those who remained were sent eastwards from 1939 to 1941, packed into ghettos with Poles throughout the General Government (occupied Poland). Others were sent to KLs where they were the first to feel the blows from their SA or SS guards, or dragged into the killing chambers of T4 and 14f13.

Those who were deported from Germany in the initial roundups were only given a brief stay of execution. The *Einsatzgruppen* and Operation *Reinhard* would ensure their extinction.

Einsatzgruppen campaigns

As operational units of the SD, *Sipo* (Criminal Police) and SS, the *Einsatzgruppen*'s role was to follow the front line troops arresting and eliminating political or racial enemies of the Third Reich. Initially deployed in small groups during the occupation of Austria and Czechoslovakia, by the invasion of Poland they were well organised and killed any undesirables they got their hands on. While the sensibilities of the Czechoslovakian and Austrian population meant that many of their actions in these countries were hidden from view, the wartime situation of the invasion of Poland meant that there was no need to conceal their deadly actions.

In September 1939, six *Einsatzgruppen* in Poland murdered about 15,000 Poles and Jews. Intelligentsia, politicians and military commanders were particularly targeted along with the Jews in order to lop off the intellectual head of the Polish state and allow the Germans to rule an ill-educated leaderless work force as they sought to Germanise the General Government. The 2,700 men for this campaign were drawn from security organisations and included many who had experience in the *Freikorps*. These ideological warriors relished the opportunity to decapitate Polish society. Nobles, priests, teachers, landowners, industrialists and university professors were among those targeted. This was no random killing spree, the list of those to be executed had been drawn up as early as May 1939 and was entitled *Sonderfahndungliste-Poland*.

The Germans drew up a similar death list of prominent Britons to be used after the completion of Operation *Sea Lion*, the invasion of England. Hitler believed that the best way to subdue the British would be to remove its leaders and prominent citizens. Two thousand three hundred were on this list, including Winston Churchill, his entire cabinet, Charles de Gaulle and Sigmund Freud. The list was entitled *Sonderfahndungliste GB*.

Poles attacked Germans that lived in their communities, further escalating the violence and justifying the massacres perpetrated by the Nazis. As the Wehrmacht marched into Poland, Polish organisations butchered many ethnic Germans leaving them in the streets of towns such as Danzig to rot.

German paramilitary groups, in particular the *Volks-deutscher Selbstschutz* (German self-defense battalions) were determined to avenge these attacks and teamed up with the *Einsatzgruppen* before engaging in an orgy of violence. Many small concentration camps were set up by these paramilitaries just as the SA had in 1933. Most of the inmates in these temporary camps were brutally murdered and by spring 1940 it is estimated 80,000 Poles had been executed.

The *Einsatzgruppen* were divided into *Einsatzkommandos* of company strength. While formally under the command of the Heer (army), the *Einsatzgruppen* received their orders directly from Heydrich. While some Wehrmacht commanders protested against the unauthorised shootings, massacres and looting going on in their rear areas they were powerless to stop them and had to supply the murderous gangs with ammunition, petrol and rations. General Blaskowitz sent a memorandum of complaint to Hitler which was dismissed as 'childish'. The general was dismissed soon after. After this any ambitious German officer knew not to make waves or quote the Geneva Convention.

The final task of these Kommandos was to force the two million or so Polish Jews into ghettos or register them in their place of residence. Many were chased into Soviet occupied territory after the partition of Poland. The killing of almost two million innocent citizens was not a realistic goal at this early stage of the German quest for a thousand-year empire. The Germans only sought to realise this objective in 1942 with Operation *Reinhard*.

No such sensibilities were displayed in the invasion of the Soviet Union. The Nazi leaders and Wehrmacht top brass considered that the approaching war would be a battle of annihilation where any rules of warfare or humanity would be ignored. The infamous Commissar Order issued by Hitler on June 6th 1941 called for the immediate execution of any Soviet Commissars or any prisoners displaying the incorrect attitude.

While all Wehrmacht units were tasked with carrying out this order, new *Einsatzgruppen* were tasked with eliminating Jewish elements. As they followed the fast moving military columns Jewish males were rounded up and executed. After several months women and children became valid targets too.

During preparations for invading the Soviet Union, four *Einsatzgruppen* were charged with eliminating political and ideological opponents. Each *Gruppe* was divided into smaller units called *Einsatzkommandos* and *Sonderkommandos*. Before the campaign began the personnel of all four *Einsatzgruppen* were concentrated in Pretzch and Heydrich personally instructed the officers of their function in the upcoming campaign. The assembled officers were told their targets in no uncertain terms. Any members of the Communist regime, anyone who might foment resistance and any Jews were to be killed.

At this early stage many of the commanders were unsure their charges had the stomach for the task. For this reason in the opening months of the campaign it was adult males who experienced the brunt of Nazi violence before it escalated to include females, the young and the old. Also there was no need to hurry as far as the SS hierarchy was concerned. The USSR would fall in fairly short order so it was presumed there would be plenty of time to do the job properly in the future.

As a result the initial actions were small in comparison to the horrors that would occur later. The first killing operation of Barbarossa took place in Garsden, Lithuania, when a Kommando of Einsatzgruppen A killed 201 people on the third day of the campaign. The first large scale killing actually took place in Białystok on June 27th by Police Battalion 309. Only on July 2nd were an *Einsatzgruppen* involved in a mass slaughter. Here they killed 1,100 Jews in the Ukrainian city of Lutsk. During many of these early actions the Germans were amazed at the anti-Semitic ferocity of their erstwhile conquered peoples who often led the way in attacking and killing their neighbors, particularly in the Baltic States and the Ukraine.

Initial reports from these early actions convinced Himmler that his men were coping well with the pressures of their task. In mid-July orders came from on high ordering the slaughter to expand to whole communities. Women, children, the elderly and the sick. No-one was to be spared.

The numbers killed were staggering; 23,000 killed in Kamenets-Podolski in August 1941, 19,000 in Minsk in November, 21,000 in Rovno, also in November, 20,000 in Kharkov in January 1942 and the largest and most notorious massacre of more than 33,000 over two days at Babi Yar on the outskirts of Kiev in September 1941.

Einsatzgruppen A was commanded first by Dr Franz Walter Stahlecker, attached to Army Group North, and operated from the Baltic States to the Leningrad area. It numbered about 1,000 men. Einsatzgruppen B, headed by Arthur Nebe (chief of Kripo, the criminal police), was attached to Army Group Centre, which operated between Belorussia and Moscow. For such a vast area it only had approximately 655 men. Einsatzgruppen C, commanded by Dr Otto Emil Rasch, was attached to Army Group Centre in northern and central Ukraine and numbered approximately 750 cold blooded killers. Einsatzgruppen D, headed by Professor Otto Ohlendorf, was attached to the Eleventh Army in southern Ukraine Crimea and Ciscaucasia. It had about 600 men.

Attached to each *Einsatzgruppen* were the men of Police Battalion 9 who were allocated at one company per *Gruppen*. The companies were further subdivided a so that each *Sonderkommando* had at least a platoon of policemen attached. In December 1941 Police Battalion 9 was withdrawn and replaced by the 3rd battalion.

Despite the bloody task assigned to these groups their commanders were not ill-educated thugs. Nine of the officers within Einsatzgruppen A held doctorates and three of the four *Gruppen* were commanded by doctors. Attached to their academic credentials were many years of anti-Semitic and anti-Bolshevik propaganda. This allowed them to be convinced in an intellectual way of the correctness of their actions.

And just as the perverted world view of the Nazis grew out of control so did the *Einsatzgruppen*. As the Nazi empire grew local killing battalions were set up to eliminate opposition. Einsatzgruppen E was created in Croatia after the conquest of Yugoslavia and targeted Jews and communists along with the Serbian intelligentsia. Einsatzgruppen G and H operated in Romania and Slovakia respectively. Einsatzgruppen Greichland terrorised the inhabitants of

Greece. Carinthia, Luxembourg, Norway and even Tunis all had their own mobile killing groups.

As the German columns drove into the Soviet Union the *Einsatzgruppen* also targeted soviet Commissars. The Commissars, attached to each Red Army unit to enforce correct communist ideology and ensure that orders from the Kremlin were followed, were regarded as particularly dangerous by the Germans. The Nazi High Command believed that it was subversive actions of captured Russian Bolsheviks which had started much of the revolutionary activity in late 1918 and early 1919 in Germany. It was imperative, in their view, that they be removed from the rest of the captured Russians to ensure that no similar incitements to rebellion could be practiced.

Commissars were easy to pick. Certain badges on their caps and uniforms indicated their status and many tore them off after capture. The outline of the insignia remained on the faded uniforms leading to rapid identification and death. Captured soviet soldiers were often keen to inform on the commissars who had earned the hatred of their fellow solders by enforcing draconian discipline and enjoying privileged status and superior rations.

As partisan attacks began in the rear area of the German lines orders were issued that all Jews were to be treated as bandits and executed on the spot. Methods also changed. Initially there was a semblance of legality given to the killings with trumped up charges (such as arson, sabotage or black market dealings) being read out before execution by firing squad. But given the huge amount of territory and the large number of victims these methods proved too slow and cumbersome. The method for which the *Einsatzkommandos* became renowned was developed.

Otto Ohlendorf, commander of Einsatzgruppen D, described the method. Firstly the unit would enter their allocated town and order the prominent Jewish citizens to assemble the rest of the community to allow them to be 'resettled.' Once the victims were assembled they were ordered to hand over their valuables and marched towards the place of execution. Once there they were divided into smaller groups and marched to the grave site which was usually an anti-tank ditch. Told to strip they were then told to kneel or stand in front of the ditch before being shot in the head.

Einsatzgruppen leaders kept highly detailed records including the daily numbers of Jews murdered. Competition even arose as to who posted the highest numbers.

In the first year of the Nazi occupation of Soviet territory, over 300,000 Jews were murdered. By March of 1943, over 600,000 and by the end of the war, an estimated 1,300,000.

One eyewitness account details the murderous actions of an *Einsatzgruppen* on October 5th 1942.

Accompanied by Moennikes, I went to the work area. I saw great mounds of earth about 30 metres long and two metres high. Several trucks were parked nearby. Armed Ukrainian militia were forcing people out, under the surveillance of SS soldiers. The same militia men were responsible for guard duty and driving the trucks. The people in the trucks wore the regulation yellow pieces of cloth that identified them as Jews on the front and back of their clothing.

Moennikes and I went straight toward the ditches without being stopped. When we neared the mound, I heard a series of rifle shots close by. The people from the trucks – men, women and children – were forced to undress under the supervision of an SS soldier with a whip in his hand. They were obliged to put their effects in certain areas: shoes, clothing, and underwear separately. I saw a pile of shoes, thousands of pairs, great heaps of underwear and clothing. Without weeping or crying out, these people undressed and stood together in family groups, embracing each other and saying goodbye while waiting for a sign from the SS soldier, who stood on the edge of the ditch.

During the fifteen minutes I stayed there, I did not hear a single complaint or plea for mercy. I watched a family of about eight: a man and woman about fifty years old, surrounded by their children aged about one, eight, and ten, and two older girls about 20 and 24. An old lady, her hair completely white, held the baby in her arms, rocking it and singing it a song. The infant was crying aloud with delight. The parents watched the groups with tears in their eyes. The father held the ten-year-old boy by the hand, speaking softly to him, the child struggled to hold back his tears. Then the father pointed a finger to the sky and, stroking the child's head, seemed to be explaining something.

At this moment, the SS man near the ditch called something to his comrade. The latter counted off some twenty people and ordered them behind the mound. The family of which I have just spoken was in the group. I still remember the young girl, slender and dark, who, passing near me, pointed at herself, saying, '23.' I walked around the mound and faced a frightful common grave. Tightly packed corpses were heaped so close together that only the heads showed. Most were wounded in the head and the blood flowed over their shoulders. Some still moved. Others raised their hands and turned their heads to show that they were still alive. The ditch was two-thirds full. I estimate that it held a thousand bodies.

I turned my eyes toward the man who had carried out the execution. He was an SS man. He was seated, legs swinging, on the narrow edge of the ditch, an automatic rifle rested on his knees and he was smoking a cigarette. The people, completely naked, climbed down a few steps cut in the clay wall and stopped at the place indicated by the SS man. Facing the dead and wounded, they spoke softly to them. Then I heard a series of rifle shots. I looked in the ditch and saw their bodies contorting, their heads, already inert, sinking on the corpses beneath. The blood flowed from the nape of their necks. I was astonished not to be ordered away, but then I noticed two or three uniformed postmen nearby. A new batch

of victims approached the place. They climbed down into the
ditch, lined up in front of the previous victims and were shot.

Hermann Graebe testimony at IMT Nuremberg on 10 November
1945 and 13 November 1945, *Nuremberg Document PS – 2992.*

Killing on such a massive scale inevitably led to some survivors.
On the evening of 14th August 1942 the SS surrounded the
ghetto in the village of Zagrodski, near Pinsk in Belorussia,
home to five hundred Jewish families. On Saturday morning
15 August 1942, the Germans entered the ghetto, ordering
the Jews to leave their houses for a roll call. All day, the Jews
were kept standing, waiting. Towards sunrise, the children
screamed, demanding food and water. But the Germans
would allow no one back into their homes.

That evening trucks arrived at the ghetto gates. The Jews
were ordered on board and driven out of the ghetto. Those
for whom there had been no room on the trucks were
ordered to run after them. Gathering their children and
encircled by a cordon made up of auxiliaries and police the
frightened women had to run with their children after the
trucks. Those who fell were immediately shot. On reaching
the destination, Rivka Yosselevska, a rare survivor, saw that
the people from the truck had already been taken off the
trucks and were undressed in front of a ditch some three
kilometres from the village by a low hill. Those who were
unwilling to strip naked were beaten and shot while those
who would not surrender their children were executed
immediately. Rivka saw friends and family butchered
mercilessly and when her time came a German auxiliary
seized her by the hair, positioned her above the death pit
and fired his revolver at her. She fell into the pit among
the hundreds of dead before other victims fell on top of
her. Swimming in and out of consciousness she eventually
managed to extricate herself from the cloying pit of corpses,
covered in human waste and blood.

A farmer took pity on Rivka Yosselevska, hid her and

fed her. Later, he helped her join a group of Jews hiding in the forest. There she survived until the Soviet army came in the summer of 1944.

Albert Bronowski, manager of the Rumbuli railway station near Riga, Latvia, witnessed the murder of thousands of Jews. In this instance the Germans lined them up ready for execution and had them place valuables such as rings, watches and necklaces as they moved single fire towards the trench. Machine guns and rifles kept up an incessant barrage and any who tried to flee were gunned down by the cordon of guards.

Yosef Weingartner from Kerch survived a murder action near the village of Bagrowo, approximately four kilometres west of Kerch and testified how the Jews were herded into the town prison before being told that they were all to be shipped to collective farms the following day. When five large trucks drove into the prison courtyard the following morning there was a great deal of pushing and shoving as all of the people wanted to get out and to the farms as soon as possible. All day the trucks came back collecting loads and moving off. Later in the day, in a moment of shocked realisation one of Yosef's companions realised that the trucks were only taking 25 minutes for a round trip, there was no way they could be hauling so many people any distance.

But this horrified realisation came too late and the last inmates, including Yosef were bundled into the trucks and after a short journey came upon a veritable mountain of clothing and a series of anti-tank trenches. Yosef and his wife were herded to the pit and as they embraced a rifle bullet tore open her head covering him with her blood and brains, the two collapsed into the trench and the Germans, thinking him dead, left Yosef among the corpses. He escaped after night had fallen.

Heydrich also sought to involve the local populations in the Nazis deadly work. In Poland the ethnic Germans had willingly turned to the bloody task and in many of the conquered territories pogroms broke out against the Jewish residents. In some areas it was necessary to incite the locals but, particularly in the Baltic States and the Ukraine, the locals willingly leapt upon their Jewish neighbors. Within weeks of Operation *Barbarossa* 40 pogroms were recorded and by the end of 1941 at least 24,000 Jews were killed in these 'spontaneous' outbursts.

One of the most notorious episodes occurred in Kovno, Lithuania. Jews were hauled out of their residences and before an appreciative crowd were beaten to death in a garage courtyard with iron bars. Such was the ferocity that German observers were sickened by what they saw. William Gunsilius described how 40 or 50 Jews were herded into a yard and kept under guard by armed Lithuanian civilians. The guards had only armbands to identify themselves as members of a paramilitary group. They watched on as one by one a well-built young man with his sleeves rolled up and armed with a crowbar selected one victim at a time, marched him into the yard and proceeded to beat him to death with ferocious blows to the head. Within 45 minutes all of the prisoners were dead and their killer grabbed his accordion and played the Lithuanian national anthem while standing on the mound of corpses he had created. The crowd, including women and children clapped and sang along.

There are several reason why local populations embarked on such carnage, beyond anti-Semitism. Many had been brutalised during the Russian civil war and by the collectivisation of the early Stalinist era. Many had come to see conformity with a totalitarian regime as socially acceptable behavior. Many simply transferred their allegiance to the German regime when it arrived. Some who had collaborated with the Soviet regime sought to divert attention from themselves by naming Jews as collaborators and killing them.

The German Order Police and local collaborators

provided the extra manpower needed to perform all the shootings. The Germans could not have killed so many Jews so quickly without local help. The police battalions often merely coordinated actions. The ratio of Order Police to auxiliaries was one to ten in Ukraine and Belarus. In rural areas the proportion was one to 20. This meant that most Ukrainian and Belarusian Jews were killed by fellow Ukrainians and Belarusians commanded by German officers.

The Wehrmacht was no passive bystander as it had been in Poland. German officers were encouraged to aid the killing squads and even perpetrate executions. Guidelines in the Operation *Barbarossa* Directive number 21 were intended to prevent friction between the SS and the *Heer* (army) in the upcoming operation. The Army was ordered not to interfere with special tasks given the SS but had to give supplies and full cooperation when requested and register all Jews in areas that were occupied and forward these lists onto the respective *Einsatzgruppen* operating in their rear area. The directive also specified that any killings of civilians perpetrated by members of the Wehrmacht could not be prosecuted by military courts ensuring that any atrocities would go unpunished. Hitler believed even before the campaign that Barbarossa was 'a fight to the finish. In the East harshness now means mildness for the future.' Himmler made it known that the party's aim was to reduce the population in the conquered areas of the Soviet Union by at least 20 to million souls.

Hiding the evidence

The *Einsatzgruppen* were disbanded in 1943. They, the police and the auxiliary battalions were responsible for the death of about 3 million Soviet Jews, including Jewish prisoners of war from the Red Army. However Ernest Kaltenbrunner, Heydrich's successor, was confronted with an entirely new problem. As the tide of war began to turn against the Axis forces in Russia it became necessary to cover up evidence of the massacres. Action commandos were utilised to exhume and burn the bodies.

This operation was named *Aktion 1005* and was coordinated by SS Colonel Blobel. He developed efficient disposal techniques such as alternating layers of bodies with firewood on a frame of iron rails. Blobel acted as a consultant for the extermination camps and was considered to be an expert in his field.

Often Jewish prisoners were required to carry out these disposals but the killing and sadism had by no means come to an end. Adolf Riba, a German who was in charge of the prisoners in Sonderkommando 1005 Mitte at Maly Trostinets testified to events there during November 1943. Firstly he described how thousands of bodies were exhumed from their graves and stacked ready for burning. Soon some trucks came from Minsk containing Jewish prisoners. Some were executed immediately while others were tied to stakes above the mound of desiccated bodies, doused with gasoline and set alight.

Throughout the east Jewish working parties toiled to cremate the remains of the victims of the *Einsatzgruppen*. Working parties were tasked with burning hundreds each day. The usual procedure was to place a row of dead bodies on a wooden pyre before placing branches on top of this layer followed by more interspersed copses and foliage. Sometimes these 'pyramids' contained thousands of victims and burned for three days. Once the working parties had finished they too were executed and cremated.

Another effect of the *Einsatzgruppen* was the deleterious effect it had on SS men.

In the city of Minsk, Heinrich Himmler witnessed Einsatzgruppen B conduct an execution of 100 persons, including women, and became visibly ill. After nearly fainting, he frantically yelled out for the firing squad to quickly finish off those who were only wounded.

After this Himmler ordered the commanders to employ a more humane method of extermination by using mobile gas vans. These trucks fed their exhaust into a sealed rear compartment containing 15 to 25 persons, usually Jewish women and children. However this method was judged unsatisfactory due to the small numbers killed and the subsequent unpleasant task of having to remove the bodies. It was these problems, as well as escalating alcohol related issues with SS personnel that led to the Wannsee conference where a more efficient means of disposal was organised. But even as Operation *Reinhard* established murder on an industrial scale, killing parties still roamed the East exterminating whole populations of Jews.

5

OPERATION REINHARD

Auschwitz – experiments in death

Operation *Reinhard* was the Nazi Final Solution to the Jewish question. Organised by Reinhard Heydrich at the Wannsee Conference it was the definitive plan to kill the Jews in Europe.

Four extermination camps would carry out this function, Auschwitz, Bełżec, Sobibór and Treblinka. Auschwitz began its life as a labour camp and gradually developed into an extermination facility. The other three were purpose built for *Reinhard* and were destroyed once they had fulfilled their purpose.

T4 had proven that gassing could be used to kill groups of people with a minimum of fuss. The opening up of the Eastern territories resulted in millions of Jews, gypsies, Russian POWs and other groups who were not compatible with the Nazi world view needing to be dealt with. The small scale operations in clinics within German mental facilities were clearly not adequate to deal with the vast numbers needing annihilation.

The *Einsatzgruppen* and Police battalions were roaming the occupied territories but their bloody and public methods were not what the Nazi leadership were after. Especially not in the General Government or Central Europe where heinous crimes of that nature could not be concealed from the local population or the international press.

Two methods were experimented with but both proved unsuitable. Arthur Nebe, a commander of an *Einsatzgruppen* who was originally from the Berlin police, came up with the idea of blowing Jews up with dynamite. How he thought this could be efficient and tidy is to be wondered at and the experiments were spectacularly unsuccessful. Groups were tied down with explosive packed under them. The resulting explosion led to body parts cascading down around the official observers' ears, landing in trees or bushes where they had to be gathered for burial. Quite a few of the subjects survived, complicating the whole procedure. Similar experiments were tried in captured Russian bunkers but unforeseen problems occurred. It was impossible to clear out the structure for successive groups to be executed and many survived the initial blast.

Another solution was the use of mobile killing vans where the exhaust was diverted into the cargo body at the rear.

One eyewitness records:

> There were two gas vans in use. I saw them myself. They were driven into the prison yard and the Jews – men, women and children – had to get into the van directly from the cell. I also saw inside the gas vans. They were lined with metal and there was a wooden grille on the floor. The exhaust gases were fed into the inside of the van. I can still today hear the Jews knocking and shouting, 'Dear Germans, let us out.'*

Nebe had some success with this method. Being chief of police in Berlin he got the workshop at Criminal Police headquarters to convert a clutch of trucks by diverting the exhausts and lining the interiors with sealed sheet metal to make them airtight. The modified trucks were then driven through to Minsk where his *Einsatzgruppen* was acting. They were used for several years transporting Jews from railheads to grave pits. The unsuspecting victims were asked to get

* Anton Lauer, Police Reserve Battalion 9. Quoted in *The Good Old Days: The Holocaust as Seen by Its Perpetrators and Bystanders*, E. Klee, W. Dressen, V. Riess (eds), The Free Press, NY, 1988, p. 73.

in the trucks to be driven to their new accommodation. After twenty minutes or so they were all dead and could be transferred straight to the already dug pits.

However these measures were costly and too high profile. Civilians and victims quickly cottoned on to these truck's true purpose. The key problem was that these vans took too long to kill small groups.

Auschwitz was the first KL to see experimental large-scale gassing. Commandant Rudolf Höss decided not to use the carbon monoxide method of T4 as it was too complicated setting up faux shower heads and the like. He instead chose prussic acid as his killing method. Originally used to fumigate barracks and clothing he believed the chemical, known as Zyklon B, would be the perfect method to exterminate humans. Pipes and imitation shower heads were not required, it was enough to toss the lethal pellets into a mass of struggling humanity and the job was done. In August 1941 it had been tested on a small group of POWs by an enterprising SS man, Karl Fritzsch, and Höss agreed to expand the trials. Fritzsch later claimed to have been the inventor of the Auschwitz death camp, not something that most people would want on their résumé.

Block 11 was chosen for these early experiments. Auschwitz prisoners were terrified of this bunker. It was regularly used by the SS to torture and murder inmates and was known as the death block. Russian prisoners who arrived in early September 1941 were the first batch to be killed and millions would follow. Windows and doors into the cellars of this large brick block were sealed. Two hundred and fifty sick prisoners were forced into the block's maze of corridors and rooms to be followed by hundreds of Soviet POWs. Once the prisoners were confined in the subterranean warren the SS tossed deadly prussic acid crystals into the confined space. As soon as these lethal packages came into contact with warm flesh or the warmer air they began to give off their deadly gas. The gas tore into the prisoner's mucus membranes before entering their bloodstream and stopping them from breathing.

The initial reaction to noxious gas, honed over millions of years of mammalian evolution, is that once a creature or person is exposed to a foul smelling scent they stop inhaling before moving away from the foul air. In an enclosed gas chamber, whether in an American penitentiary or in a KL, that option was not possible. Eventually the victim had to commit suicide and take a breath. This could take up to 15 to 20 seconds.

Once the deadly gas Prussic acid is inhaled, immediate unconsciousness does not occur. Symptoms similar to a heart attack or an epileptic fit are reported. Hyperventilation can occur resulting in dizziness. What's more, the prisoner is usually conscious for two or three minutes before the gas finally causes him to black out. Before losing awareness the prisoners begin to drool and look as if they are being strangled to death. The eyes bulge and the skin turns purple. Hypoxia follows, an excruciatingly painful condition where the entire body reacts to the lack of oxygen and shuts down the extremities such as the arms and legs, leading to violent spasms. Patients usually lose control of their bladder and bowels. Once blessed unconsciousness is reached, it can take up to 12 minutes for vital signs to terminate. The screams of the distressed victims of the early gassing experiments echoed around the camp laying another level of horror to the Auschwitz experience. Some dying prisoners tried to stuff their mouth with cloth to keep the lethal toxins out, but to no avail.

Höss was pleased with the result. Hundreds had been killed and not one SS man had to pull a trigger. There were obvious problems. Gas let loose in a confined space without adequate ventilation leads to the fumes taking a long time to dissipate. By the time Polish prisoners were ordered below Block 1 to clear out the corpses the dead had already started to decompose in the warm summer conditions. The corpses' limbs were intertwined and in their final spasms they had bit and clawed at each other leading to a bloody congealed mass of blood, flesh and shit. The bodies had to be carted through the entire camp to a primitive crematorium beyond the wire.

Undaunted, Höss relocated the gassings to the morgue that was built into this crematoria. It could hold hundreds of prisoners, was immediately adjacent to disposal facilities, was already sealed and was sufficiently removed from the main camp so gassings would not alarm prisoners. Höss observed the proceedings and described them in his memoirs as he awaited his own execution at the end of a rope. The Russians were first ordered to undress in an anteroom. Having no idea of their likely fate and under the impression that they were to be deloused the entire transport of prisoners moved quietly into the mortuary until it was filled to capacity. The doors were then sealed and gas was shaken down through the holes in the roof.

> I do not know how long this killing took. For a little while a humming sound could be heard. When the powder was thrown in there were cries of 'Gas!' then a great bellowing, and the trapped prisoners hurled themselves against both the doors. But the doors held. They were opened several hours later, so that the place might be aired. It was then that I saw, for the first time, gassed bodies in the mass.*

Auschwitz was peripheral to the main actions of Operation *Reinhard* but their killing facilities were continually upgraded. The sub-camp Birkenau became the chief extermination centre and nearby was located the 'Little Red House'. This was an abandoned farmhouse which had all of its windows and doors blocked up while small holes were drilled in the walls to drop the deadly Zyklon B pellets. It went into

* Rudolf Hoess, *Commandant of Auschwitz*, Orion Publishing Group, 2000, p 79.

operation in May 1942 supplanting those killings carried out in the crematorium.

Himmler decided that the relative isolation of Auschwitz, despite the fact that it was on an excellent railway line with links to the entire east, made it a perfect place to escalate the Final Solution. In July deportees from the rest of occupied Europe ended up in this camp. French, German, Polish, Belgian, Slovakian, Croatian, Italian and Greek Jews all began to appear in ever greater numbers and almost half a million arrived there in 1942–1943. Some prisoners were selected for work but most were sent straight to the death chambers. The Little Red House and the later Little Blue House could not keep up with the workload. Problems experienced at the other camps of mass graves full of rotting bodies engulfing the entire area in a sickening smell were viewed by Himmler as extremely distasteful when he visited in July 1942 and urgent upgrades were initiated.

Entirely new facilities were built. While not part of Operation *Reinhard* per se, these gas chambers were modelled on the three main death camps but had one major addition – huge crematoria. The scale was vast, eclipsing even Treblinka in its deadly potential. Massive new crematoria were built and, combined with the original one, allowed 120,000 individuals to be burnt every month. Basements were built below the crematoria which included rooms to undress as well as the gas chambers. Lifts were adjacent to the chambers allowing workers to load the corpses and deliver them straight to the ovens while powerful fans extracted the poisonous gases. These super killers could process 4,416 individuals every 24 hours, something that was proudly reported to superiors in Berlin.

The numbers are staggering and it they almost deaden the impact of such huge suffering. After the *Reinhard* camps closed Auschwitz became the main facility to kill Jews and achieve the final solution. But as transports rolled in from all over occupied Europe and peaked when the Hungarian

Jews were all but exterminated in a few months in 1944, each one of those millions of people experienced his or her personal hell as he or she was sent to die.

As transports arrived the camp staff were given fair warning by nearby stations and swung into action with well-practiced professionalism. Whistles were blown and all over the camp announcements were made on the camp loudspeakers. SS personal and *Kommandos* (inmate work parties) tumbled out of their barracks, leapt onto motorcycles and trucks and reported to their stations. Gas chambers were given a once-over, the crematoria were bought up to the desired heat while two camp doctors along with SS guards and their dogs headed for the *Judenrampe*. As the train pulled up to the lengthy wooden platform the troops formed a chain around the transport before the order was given to open the doors.

For many deportees this was the first time they had fresh air or light for many days. Any relief this may have given was cut short as they tumbled out onto the platform to be greeted with a torrent of abuse from SS men armed with whips and snarling dogs. Left behind were the corpses of those who had not been able to survive the long journey to the camp. Told to leave their luggage, the men and women barely had time to think before they were divided into two long columns, men on one side, women and children on the other. Frantic last hugs and tearful embraces took place as families who had suffered years of Nazi persecution were separated one last time.

The columns moved slowly forward towards a small group of SS men where the selection had begun. Those arriving at the *Reinhard* camps did not go through this process, they were all slated for immediate execution. In Auschwitz those being selected for either a quick death in the gas chamber or a slower death from months of hard labour were sometimes asked a question by the KL doctors. Age and profession were the most common queries but most just earned a quick glance before being told to go left or right.

Some of *Canada Kommando* (named after a land reputed to be filled with wealth and abundance), the Jews who received the transport and carried off the luggage, urgently whispered to children on the oncoming transport to lie about their age. Of the 210,000 youths destined to end up in Auschwitz only 2,500 survived the initial selection. Young women often survived. If they had children they did not. Those in charge of the selection soon learnt that it was much easier to send young women with their children to the chambers as trying to separate them disrupted proceedings as hysterical children clung desperately to their mothers. Canada Kommando personnel urged many women to hand their children over to older relatives.

On average 20 per cent of arrivals were selected for labour within the camp and sub camps. The rest would be killed within hours of the selection. The elderly and frail were loaded onto trucks. Some needed to be helped up onto the truck trays, aided by solicitous SS men intent on smoothing the process. The deception was extended to the rest of the condemned who had to walk to the chambers. The condemned arrivals were herded by SS men on either side of the snaking columns. These soldiers were under orders not to scare the arrivals. They asked polite questions about background and professions and explained that ahead of them lay delousing, and a warm shower before being reunited with the rest of their family in a comfortable barracks. Trailing behind the column was an ambulance with the Red Cross emblazoned on its sides, further proof of the Germans' good intentions.

Within the ambulance was the SS doctor tasked with carrying out the gassing as well as tins of Zyklon B. These were labeled with the manufacturer's marks and were specially printed to read, 'Only to be used for Jewish Resettlement.'

The column approached the gas chambers and individuals were funneled into the dank sealed gas chambers. The mask of helpfulness dropped from the SS as any who tried to resist entering the confined spaces were beaten or attacked by dogs. Some were shot on the spot. As the doors closed on the seething mass the SS yelled out coarse jokes and many lay bets with each other on which chamber would cease pounding and wailing first. The SS doctor ordered an orderly to throw in the gas pellets and the killing began.

Many transports did not go to plan. The belching smokestacks on top of the crematoria and the pervasive stench forewarned many. Hundreds of people would struggle to escape and as the doors slid closed they pounded on them to get out or smashed the glass peepholes desperately seeking to escape the gas. Sometimes the transports were too large for all to be accommodated. Prisoners were forced to wait under SS rifles for hours as they listened to the death throes of their friends and family before meeting their own end. The Special Squad of Jewish prisoners who helped move the transport to their deaths were ordered to maintain the lie that they were destined for a shower. Mostly they did this to minimise trauma. But survivors wrote after the war how they could not look the condemned in the eye. Too often they gave away the truth, with only a glance.

Roundups

The suffering of those earmarked to be dealt with by Operation *Reinhard* began well before they arrived at the extermination camps. Most Jewish populations had been confined in ghettos throughout the occupied territories. Given starvation rations and administered by the collaborating *Judenrat* (Jewish councils) the tortuous existence of the ghetto dwellers was merely a prelude to the nightmare to come. Although the Germans tried to keep some semblance of order and decent administration in these human holding pens, once a ghetto or community was to be cleared and its inhabitants shipped off for execution, all pretense of benign toleration evaporated.

The actions of Police Battalion 101 give a vivid example of the clearing operations conducted throughout 1942 and 1943. Not all Jewish populations were confined to ghettos but the areas where they were concentrated were well documented by the occupying authorities. Police battalions were assigned regions where they were to carry out *Aktions* to clear them of Jews.

Brutality was the norm and followed a set pattern. Police Battalion 101 was given the responsibility for clearing the Lublin district and by the end of 1943 were masters of their craft. In August 1942 they cleared several major towns and deported at least 16,000 Jews to Operation *Reinhard* camps. In October and November 1942 at least 26,000 Jews were rounded up in approximately eight major operations while large-scale massacres similar to those carried out in 1941 were also perpetrated.

A similar pattern was followed by at least 32 Police Battalions throughout the occupied territories. If it was decided to deport a population rather than liquidate them the required number of companies was given the task. If it was a large area auxiliaries might be bought in. One or two companies were usually nominated as the *Aktion* companies while other units would form a cordon to prevent escapes. The clearing of Jewish areas usually began at dawn. Germans armed with submachine guns, rifles, dogs, whistles and whips would systematically move house by house, block by block and street by street expelling all Jewish residents and herding them towards a central location. Those who were bedridden or too old to move were shot, as were any individuals who protested or resisted. Pets were bayoneted and infants shared the same fate or had their heads stove in. In larger ghettos whole hospitals or aged care facilities were exterminated along with their medical staff.

Once the initial sweep had cleared the bulk of the population special parties would move stealthily into the seemingly abandoned residences looking for dead space created by hidden partitions or using sniffer dogs to detect remaining people. Those found in these latter sweeps were almost invariably executed on the spot. These sweeps were repeated every two or three days to ensure that no survivors remained.

As the panicked population moved towards the staging area they would be surrounded by baying dogs and *Polizei* wielding whips screaming '*Raus, raus!*' ('Out, out!') Lining the gutter would be dead people shot during the action. These grisly tableaus served to terrorise the evicted civilians and cow them into obedience. Any illusions as to their fate would rapidly dissolve. The sudden extreme violence that seemed to emerge from a vacuum disarmed the Jews and ensured compliance in the harrowing scenes to come.

Once the survivors had been gathered at the collection point, usually adjacent to a railway station or within the town square, the terror was by no means over. Taking pleasure in brutalising and tormenting their charges the *Polizei* often gave any '*Hiwis*' (Eastern European auxiliaries) a free hand to do what they liked and both Germans and auxiliaries tortured the waiting Jews. Rather than being allowed to sit calmly they were often made to squat on their haunches. Painful after two to ten minutes such a pose became torture after several hours, often in the blazing summer sun. Any who toppled over or tried to sit risked a beating as several of their captors descended on them with flailing whips. The terrified captives would be praying or wailing to the annoyance of their captors who would wade into the crowd and silence them with rifle butts or even a bullet to the head.

Cruel games were enacted. Sometimes an empty bottle or even an apple would be tossed into the crowd. Whoever it hit would then be dragged out and shot. Sometimes they were not shot but set upon by a gang and beaten to death in front of their terrified relatives. Older Jewish men had to pose with their captors. Their beards were shaved off and they might be forced to play hopscotch or leapfrog in their long rabbinical robes. Anything that humiliated the former Jewish elites was considered to be tremendously amusing. Elders were forced to wear prayer shawls and the Nazis made them kneel as in prayer or chant while crawling to their destinations.

The thoroughly-cowed Jews were then herded onto prison transports. Usually crammed into cattle wagons they were forced in with standing room only and beaten until all were packed in tighter than sardines. The dead mangled bodies of earlier victims were thrown in with the living. As far as Police battalion 101 was concerned those corpses were someone else's business. They had been charged with dispatching the Jews to a *Reinhard* camp and that is what they would do, whether the cargo was dead or alive.

Conditions inside the wagons were intolerable. As far as the Germans were concerned it was a numbers game. If there was one train to take the Jews to a camp all of those rounded up had to be accommodated. In the press to get inside a wagon families often became separated. Since the mass deportations began in the summer of 1942 the German authorities decided to use closed windowless freight cars which quickly filled with the stench of excrement, urine and vomit. Those who were sent in cattle cars were perhaps slightly more fortunate. At least there were windows allowing in natural light and fresh air. Not so for winter transports. Freezing air whistling through the cars as they rocked on their way to a camp killed many, particularly the old and the young.

The passengers were packed so tightly that kneeling or siting was impossible. Often they could not reach any bags they had or were so constricted in their movements so as not to be able to pull out any supplies. Since their fate was predetermined the Nazi authorities did not schedule rest stops or provide food and water. Survivors from these transports talk of the thirst that became the dominant sensation. Babies stopped crying and children could not talk as a fatalistic lethargy overtook the victims. On occasion the train would stop and some relief could be given. One train stopping at a Polish station saw policemen appearing at the doors to ask for bribes. Those who had wedding rings or other valuables were given some water. On other occasions, as evil smelling transports pulled up in urban stations, outraged onlookers forced the guards to spray fire hoses onto the roof, through the doors and into windows to give some blessed relief. Children who were not separated from their parents only survived because for large parts of the journey they were hoisted onto their parent's shoulders.

The responsibility of the police battalions did not finish there. Once the company had herded its victims into the cattle trucks a detachment of one or two sections, approximately 30 men, accompanied the transport to its destination. Some of these journeys were quite short, lasting little over five hours. Others were longer and no food or water was provided to the captives. For the guards, German female auxiliaries provided comforts and refreshments at refueling stops when the death trains arrived. No such succour was given to the helpless women and children suffocating within the cattle trucks.

Once at the destination the train was handed over to camp personnel and the men of the Police Battalion rested in purpose-built barracks just beyond the gates of the killing centre. Fully aware of what was happening behind the wire fences they took their ease before returning with the empty transport for another load of human cargo.

An eyewitness account from a 'good German', one of the many who tried to stop the abuse of Jews is provided by Hermann Graebe. He gave evidence at the Nuremberg War Crimes Trial and described the events of 13th July 1942 when the ghetto in Volhynia was cleared. Graebe had been present to try and prevent the deportation of hundreds of workers employed in the engineering works of which he was a manager.

He proceeded to the ghetto where most of his Jewish

workers slept. He observed at ten O'clock that night a large detachment of what he thought were SS troops (probably a police battalion) with three times as many Ukrainian militia surrounded the ghetto with powerful electric arc lights.

Squads of militia and SS entered the Jews' houses either through the front door or by breaking through windows if the inhabitants had barricaded themselves within their residences. Some of the ghetto inhabitants had prepared so well that the Germans had to destroy doors with hand grenades to break through the barricades. The residents were then driven with rifle butts, kicks and whips into the street, many in their pyjamas and few had time to pack even the most meagre of possessions. Often children were separated from their parents, either because they had managed to hide or just due to the fact that in the confusion the little ones went missing. Many mothers cried out for their children as they were hustled away by the Nazi guards.

Once on the street the SS drove the people at a running pace to the waiting freight train and filled carriage after carriage with women, children and old men. Those who were too slow were whipped and in many cases shot. Graebe described how none were left behind;

> All through the night these beaten, hounded and wounded people moved along the lighted streets. Women carried their dead children in their arms children pulled and dragged their dead parents by their arms and legs down the road towards the train.
>
> Again and again the cries, 'Open the door, Open the door!' echoed through the ghetto.

Tadeusz Zaderecki described the August 1942 deportations from Lwów, to Bełżec.

* Bob Carruthers, The Gestapo on Trial: Evidence from Nuremberg, Pen and Sword, 2014.

They surrounded house after house, the sick were shot in their
beds. People jumped from the top storeys in order to hasten
their deaths and avoid being tortured. Jews were forced out
of rooftop hiding places with poles and fell to their deaths to
become a stain of blood on the sidewalk.*

Once the large population centres had been cleared
small patrols relied on local informers and visited minor
settlements where Jew hunting expeditions were mounted.

Endlösung – the Final Solution

These terrible atrocities did not happen by accident. They
were the result of a planned Nazi policy.

On July 31st 1941 Göring issued an order to Heydrich
to prepare, 'a general plan of the administrative material and
financial measures necessary for carrying out the desired
final solution of the Jewish question.'

These harmless phrases foreshadowed one of the most
tragic episodes in European history. After other options, such
as forced emigration of Jews to Madagascar or other regions
beyond the borders of the Reich proved unrealistic, it was
decided to eliminate the problem by eliminating the Jews.
The decision was already been made. It had to be decided
how to fulfill the goal.

On January 20th 1942, Heydrich convened the Wannsee
Conference in Berlin. He and 15 top Nazi bureaucrats
were to coordinate the Final Solution in which the Nazis
would attempt to exterminate the entire Jewish populations
of Europe and the Soviet Union, an estimated 11,000,000
persons. 'Europe would be combed of Jews from east to
west,' Heydrich bluntly stated.

* The Holocaust in the Soviet Union and Baltic States, Eyewitness Statements,
1941–1943 http://www.holocaustresearchproject.org/nazioccupation/Holocaust-
in-the-east.html

The minutes of that meeting, taken by Adolf Eichmann, one of the chief organisers of the Holocaust, have been preserved but were personally edited by Heydrich after the meeting. He used the coded language Nazis often employed when referring to lethal actions to be taken against Jews. 'Deportation' was double speak for elimination. The key goal was to eliminate the large remaining population of Jews kept in ghettos throughout the General Government (Occupied Poland). Heydrich was the chief planner of this operation and nominated many of the key personnel as well as authorising procurement of supplies and land.

The operation had four major goals; to 'resettle' the Polish Jews, to exploit the labour or skill of some Jews before their death, to secure their personal property, and to appropriate their major assets such as land, housing and manufacturing plants.

SS General Odilo Globocnik, SS and police leader in the Lublin District of the General Government, directed Operation *Reinhard* between autumn 1941 and late summer 1943. He established two departments on his staff for this purpose. The first was a Deportation Coordination team under SS Major Hermann Hoefle. This team was given the task of arranging personnel and transport for the planned deportations. The second department was the Inspectorate of SS Special Detachments under Criminal Police captain Christian Wirth. This crew was responsible for the construction and management of the three Operation *Reinhard* killing centres – Bełżec, Sobibór and Treblinka.

Construction of Bełżec, Sobibór, and Treblinka II began in autumn 1941. Wirth, who had played a significant role in the T4 program between 1939 and 1941, applied his experience of killing with carbon monoxide exhaust fumes to the construction of the Operation *Reinhard* killing centres. Killing operations at Bełżec began in March 1942. They continued until December 1942. Sobibór began operating in May 1942 and remained functional until October 1943. Treblinka opened in July 1942 and was closed in August 1943.

In all during Operation *Reinhard* it is estimated that around two million Polish Jews were executed with maybe three quarters of them killed in the designated death camps. Slovenian, Macedonian and Greek Jews were also liquidated, particularly in Treblinka.

The Reinhard camps

Operation *Reinhard* was carried out at four principle camps. They were Bełżec, Sobibór, Treblinka and Auschwitz. The first three camps were built solely for the purpose of eliminating Polish Jews and after the General Government was cleared they were decommissioned and shut down. Auschwitz began its existence as a normal KL before developing industrial plants as well as extermination facilities. In 1942 when *Reinhard* began Auschwitz was not capable of killing the huge numbers required. Two converted houses, 'The Little Red House' and the 'Little Blue House' were merely converted farm buildings and also lacking were crematoria facilities. Only late in 1943 were the huge gas chambers and crematorium complexes built that allowed its grounds to be used for mass killings and the Birkenau camp in Auschwitz was still in use and was the principal site where Hungarian Jews were killed in 1944 after the German occupation of that country.

By this stage the three extermination sites had fulfilled their role and been erased. The Nazis sought to eradicate them from history. Once they had performed their horrible task the *Reinhard* camps were destroyed and the land replanted with forest trees or returned to farmland.

The facilities built in Bełżec, Sobibór and Treblinka during 1942 are unique – specialised death factories with no other purpose than to kill civilians.

The SS staff at Bełżec wait for the next transport.

Bełżec

Bełżec was the first camp to be built. It began its life in November 1941 when construction began on a small installation 500 metres from the railway station of the small unimportant town of Bełżec. This was originally to be a small facility to kill Jews from the Lublin area. In December 1941 it was taken over by SS Captain Christian Wirth. This decorated war hero had fallen under the Nazi spell and after a short stint in the Gestapo he had pioneered the T4 program utilising carbon monoxide as his deadly substance of choice. Many of his subordinates were veterans of the T4 program and bought their expertise to this new industrial age facility.

Carbon monoxide was not the most efficient method of

killing people and that may be the very reason why Wirth decided to use it. He was known even in Nazi circles for his sadism and rabid anti-Semitism. He delighted in killing with his bare hands and enjoyed egging his subordinates on to commit despicable acts with a stream of profanities and by personal example. The petrol shortage of late war had not become a factor in 1942 and Wirth utilised normal combustion engines piped straight into the gas chambers rather than the cylinders of gas utilised in T4.

This choice of gas was ridiculed by Arthur Höss, the commandant of Auschwitz, and the Reinharders, as they were known, were viewed with contempt for their primitive methods. Wirth objected to using the bottles of carbon monoxide that had been used in euthanasia institutions of T4. The bottles, which were produced in private factories and which would have to be supplied to Bełżec in large quantities, could arouse suspicion. In addition, the factories were located at great distances from Bełżec and the steady supply of the bottles might cause a logistical problem. Wirth preferred to set up a self-contained extermination system, based on an ordinary car engine and easily available gasoline that was not dependent on supply by outside factors.

Wirth carried out experiments to determine the most efficient method of handling the transports of Jews from the time of their arrival at the camp until their murder and burial. He developed some basic concepts for the process of extermination and for the layout of the camp. The structure of the camp and the various orders the victims were given as soon as they left the train were intended to ensure that they would not grasp the fact that they had been brought for extermination. The aim was to give the victims the impression that they had arrived at a labour camp or a transit camp from where they would be sent to a labour facility. The deportees were to believe this until they were locked into the gas chambers camouflaged as baths.

The second principle of the extermination process was

that everything should be carried out with the utmost speed. The victims should be rushed, made to run, so that they had no time to look round, to reflect, or to understand what was going on. This also supported the basic principle of deceiving the victims. They should be shocked, and their reactions paralyzed in order to prevent escape or resistance. The speed of the extermination process served yet an additional purpose: it increased the killing capacity of the camp. More transports could be brought and their passengers annihilated in a day. The frenetic process led to an average life span of eight to ten minutes once the men arrived at the camp. Women were killed in approximately 15 minutes. It took longer because they had their hair shaved.

Wirth designed a killing factory divided into three chambers each resembling a shower block. Realising that since the majority of arrivals would be within minutes of their arrival Wirth dispensed with the large complex of barracks and buildings created for other KLs. The entire camp measured less than 300 metres by 300 metres and the most substantial buildings were wooden barracks for the camp personnel. A narrow platform leading from the station was all that was necessary. Unlike Auschwitz which needed a wider platform so that selections could be made, all who arrived at the *Reinhard* camps had already been selected, for death.

In political matters Adolf Hitler was possessed of an evil genius. But when it came to the mechanics of killing, Christian Wirth was without peer. An unpleasant looking bull-necked man he always seemed to be on the brink of a violent outburst and his round red face continually poured sweat as he denigrated and abused those around him. The Ukrainian guards nicknamed him 'the *Stuka*' due to his explosions of anger that seemed to come from nowhere. The mere sight of Jewish victims stirred an incandescent rage in him. Behind all the bluster was a keen mind, a mind that must have spent many hours thinking on how to turn small scale actions of T4 into huge factories of death.

Wirth achieved his aim. His three extermination camps were perfectly designed to kill civilians as smoothly as possible. Maybe 200,000 died in T4 installations over many years. 1,700,000 died in *Reinhard* in approximately one year.

As transports pulled into the station at Bełżec the new arrivals would have been struck by the orderly and peaceful nature of the camp. Surrounded by pine trees with an almost pastoral atmosphere it almost seemed to be a quiet refuge. The extensive wire perimeter had few guard towers and only one tower was armed with a machine gun. The wire was intertwined with boughs from pine trees, serving as both camouflage and ensuring that the internal workings of the camp remained a mystery to observers. In contrast to earlier experiences the guards at this new institution seemed almost kindly and understanding. Just as orderlies had gently chivvied patients into the shower rooms in T4, so the guards wanted the *Reinhard* victims to go quietly, if quickly, to their deaths. Marshalled into columns the Jews saw signs saying 'Delousing Centres' and such like harmless destinations.

Towards the middle of March 1942 Bełżec opened for business. The main track into the camp had two layovers. It was the station master's job to decouple the trains into relays of ten carriages. As each set of wagons was processed the others would be shunted up in turn. If there was a rapid influx of trains, some would have to wait on the sidings for one or two days.

Once the Jews were offloaded the entire camp organisation swung into action to ensure that the process of death went as smoothly as possible. Ukrainian guards stood by to remove from the deportees any who were showing defiance or in advanced states of distress. These were quietly manhandled directly to Camp 2, the killing and burial sector within Bełżec. Poised over the mass graves these unfortunates received a bullet in the back of the head before being tossed in with the victims of earlier transports.

Any who had died on the transport or were too ill to make their way to camp one were also taken on a direct route to Camp 2 and a burial pit.

The rest were lulled into a false sense of security with announcements over the camp loudspeakers. As a camp orchestra played jaunty tunes, Wirth or one of his subordinates repeated a basic message along the following lines:

> Welcome to Bełżec. You will not be here long. Soon you will be moved to a new camp where there is work for everyone, even housewives. All will be given work and women will be required to feed your families and keep your accommodation clean. Before we can move you to your new posting and before you can receive your rations you must be cleaned and your clothes disinfected. Women will have their hair cut to remove infestations. Proceed in an orderly manner.

This message repeated over and over, along with blaring music and orders from guards led to disorientation. The barriers corralling the Jewish victims meant the only response was to follow orders at the run.

Once off the train the columns of people moved into Camp 1, the processing sector. Narrow paths were surrounded on both sides by wire barriers covered with wooden slats preventing any view of the interior of the camp. The new arrivals could only look straight ahead or directly behind. The first destination was a large courtyard where all were told to stack their possessions and undress. The prisoners were assured that once they were showered and issued with clean clothes they would receive their luggage back.

Around the large undressing pen were secure warehouses. One each for storing clothing, food, silverware and one even for hair. Once the transport had moved onto the next stage of their 'processing' the Kommando of Jewish workers took all of the goods into two large sorting sheds where the valuables were inspected and packaged.

Men and women were separated and the men were 'showered' first. They were requested to remove their shoes and tie them together with string handed out by Jewish workers. The transported prisoners were then marshalled into long columns of 750 individuals marching five abreast. As they moved through various stations Jewish workers requested that they hand over clothing, possessions and money. Moving down the race to Camp 2 they were hurried along and SS men appeared with whips and dogs.

The next destination, Camp 2, was in fact the gas chamber. The bewildered column were sent along 'the race' a long curving walk way once again covered on the sides with timber. There was a small detour for the women. Females were guided into a long shed where workers waited with electric razors. Wirth allowed nothing to go to waste and the women emerged naked and shaved.

Emerging from the tight confines of the race, the inmates moved into a small holding yard before being packed into the gas chambers. Any who hesitated were ruthlessly beaten and the intensity of the Ukrainian guards went up several notches as many of the transported prisoners began to realise the Nazis' real intentions.

The initial gas chambers were in fact nothing more than a wooden barrack adapted and constructed to give the impression of a bathing facility. To enhance this deception false shower-heads were fitted and signs indicating a bathhouse were displayed. Despite all their efforts, the construction team were unable to make the building airtight. This led to several complications. At each gassing operation in the wooden barracks, sand had to be piled up against the outer doors to rectify this problem. After the gassing, the sand had to be removed to allow access to the corpses. It became apparent that major alterations were necessary, particularly since the gas chambers were proving inadequate in size.

Wirth travelled to Berlin and obtained permission to suspend the camp's activities temporarily while a new purpose built facility was created. The new chamber was located behind a copse of trees which shielded the structure from outside observers. The 'sluice' or race went directly into the doors of the new low concrete building. It was 24 metres long and 10 metres wide with a big vase of multi-coloured flowers in front of the entrance along with the sign, obviously written with grim humour, 'Bathing and inhalation space.' A bare and dark concrete corridor ran down the centre of the building and on each side were three chambers. Each was four metres by eight metres and had a thick wooden door a metre wide which slid open with wooden handles.

The chambers were dark, with no windows, and completely empty. A round opening the size of an electric socket could be seen in each chamber. These admitted the gas. The walls and the floor of the chambers were concrete. The corridor and chambers were lower than normal, not more than two metres high. On the far wall of each chamber there were exterior sliding doors, two metres wide. After asphyxiation the corpses were thrown out through these. This was done as soon as possible before rigor mortis set in. The chambers were a metre and a half above the ground, and at the same level as the chambers was a ramp at the doors, from which the bodies were thrown to the ground.

Wirth obviously considered that once his victims were inside the chambers there was no need for more deception. Shower heads were dispensed with. Once the victims were locked into the chambers a signal was given and the gassing engine was run for approximately 20 minutes. An inspection through the peephole in the chamber door confirmed that all inside were no longer living, and the engine could be turned off.

These facilities only took up a small proportion of Camp 2's space. Hidden from the rest of the camp was the real purpose of Bełżec. Lines of mass graves and funeral pyres were utilised to dispose of the dead as efficiently as possible. Kommandos pulled the dead from the chamber and began the disposal process.

Initially only mass graves were used and the disposal Kommando were tasked with disposing of the bodies. The doors were slid open and the corpses were thrown onto the ground. Each body was searched for valuables hidden in cavities and checked for gold teeth before being dragged to trolleys on which they were ferried to the mass graves. Other workers sluiced out the chambers and sprinkled fresh sand or sawdust on the floor.

If a mass grave was to be utilised the corpses were laid in top to toe with lime sprinkled between the rows to aid rapid decomposition. The burial pits had an average size of 20 metres wide, 30 metres long and 6 metres deep. These mass graves were located in the north-eastern, eastern and southerly sections of the Camp 2.

Other Kommandos sorted the goods left behind and sent them into the respective warehouses. After sorting the valuables were sent to the *Aktion Reinhard* warehouse in Lublin.

Wirth had thought of everything. A perfectly smooth functioning death camp where Jews did most of the work of death while Germans were mere bystanders. However, even he did not fully appreciate the scale of the Jewish Problem in the General Government. From July to October 1942 three to four transports arrived each day overwhelming the camp facilities. In August alone 130,000 were killed and in September approximately 90,000. The burial pits proved inadequate and in the particularly hot summer of 1942 masses of rotting vermin-ridden corpses were constantly joined with fresh bodies as the transports rolled in. It was due to this crisis that it was decided to exhume and burn the dead on huge pyres.

The final transports arrived at Bełżec in December 1942. By March 1943 the last corpses bodies had been exhumed and burnt by a special Jewish detachment *Sonderkommando 1005*.

Their task was surely one of the most revolting ever. The pyres were built by arranging railway line sections on top of large concrete blocks. Narrow gauge metal bars were then placed crossways on top to form a close-meshed solid grate. Four or five of these large constructions were built in Camp 2. The rotting corpses were then excavated from their mass graves before being soaked in oil and set alight. This went on for five months and the whole locality lay under a heavy pall of black oily smoke. Viscous material settled everywhere and the local inhabitants reported scraping human fat off their windows. The final remains were destroyed by using a bone crushing machine and the resulting coarse powder was spread over fields and used to de-ice roads. By spring 1943 the camp was demolished and landscaped with firs and pine trees. Approximately 434,000 died at Bełżec.

Sobibór

The problem of noxious fumes was evident even in the spring of 1942. Franz Stangl was another veteran of T4 and he was chosen to run death camp No. 2 – Sobibór. Wirth summoned him to Bełżec to fill him in on his duties. Stangl described the experience.

> I can't describe to you what it was like. The smell. Oh God the smell. It was everywhere. Wirth wasn't in his office. I remember they took me to him. He was standing on a hill next to the pits. The pits, they were full. I can't tell you, not hundreds, thousands, thousands of corpses. That's where Wirth told me – he said that was what Sobibór was for, and that he was putting me officially in charge.

> *The Bełżec Death Camp*
> http://www.holocaustresearchproject.org/ar/belzec.html

Sobibór was built in March 1942 and was designed with many of the lessons learnt in Bełżec in mind. Purpose-built accommodation for the SS and Ukrainian guards was included within the camp compound, far removed from Camps 1 and 2. Special barracks for the Jewish Kommandos were built within Camp 2, the execution area, to allow easier access to their work stations. Large holding pens were built so that women and men could be more easily separated and purpose-built storage and sorting areas were built within Camp 1. The chute leading into the gas chambers was wider and covered on top with wire and camouflage netting. Stangl took the deception of the camp's real purpose to new heights. Most walkways were lined with flower beds and all buildings were festooned with gaily coloured planting boxes.

Just as at Bełżec Ukrainians made up most of the camp guard. Sobibór accepted its first transport in May 1942. In a little over a year 250,000 people were murdered there.

Treblinka

Usually named Treblinka II, construction began in May 1942. Designed as a state-of-the-art facility its overall design allowed it to reach such a peak of efficiency that it far eclipsed the other two camps in the number of murders that were carried out there. It is impossible to reach an absolutely accurate figure due to the SS attempts to expunge the camps from the historical record but it is estimated that 900,000 died there.

However Treblinka got off to a less than desirable start as far as the coordinators of Operation *Reinhard* were concerned. Wirth, who was named inspector General of the three camps, visited the third camp and, shocked by what he saw, appointed Stangl to clear up the mess.

Treblinka II was built near a small KL called Treblinka I and its location was chosen due to its proximity to Warsaw.

The Warsaw ghetto represented one of the largest assemblages of Jews in the Nazi state and this facility was designed with the sole purpose of wiping them off the face of the earth.

All the camps had teething troubles as they started operations. Bełżec's gas chambers were shut down to allow new facilities to be built. Sobibór also had to rebuild its chambers at one stage as well as refining the rail links. These problems were nothing like the monumental problems encountered at Treblinka.

Treblinka was designed to kill 6000 people each day and when it opened it managed to carry out these heinous deeds relatively efficiently. By August numbers doubled and the system broke down. Dr Irmfried Eberl, another veteran of T4, managed to kill all those who arrived but it proved impossible to dispose of the mountains of corpses.

The smooth methods of killing weren't those planned by Wirth's evil genius. Eberl would not turn back a transport and since the gas chambers were being overwhelmed whole train loads of victims were shot while in a holding pen in the lower camp. This meant arriving transports immediately saw through any subterfuge leading to violent scenes as frantic captives sought to escape or at least plead for mercy. The entire aim of *Reinhard* was to carry out the final solution with the massed executions going under the radar. The turmoil at Treblinka led to many trains being stuck out in the countryside as thousands of people torn from the ghettos slowly died of thirst, hunger and exposure.

Oskar Berger, who arrived in August 1942, wrote how the camp had descended into complete chaos and as his transport pulled up they were witness to hundreds of bodies lying around intermixed with piles of clothes and luggage. As smoke issued form the crematorium pits forming a macabre backdrop the horrific scene SS soldiers and Ukrainian guards stood on the roof of the barracks firing indiscriminately into the arriving crowd. Women and children fell mortally wounded and the air was filled with screaming and weeping.

The mounds of unburied bodies led to a frightful stench that permeated everything for miles around. On still days the local Poles could not go outside their houses or open their windows.

By his own standards Eberl was tremendously successful, managing to kill approximately 10,000 a day in July and August 1942. His superiors viewed the matter entirely differently. One of their main concerns was the wastage of assets being stripped from the dead, further proof if needed that *Reinhard* was a massive criminal enterprise. Much wealth and loot was being destroyed whether it was rotting in the death pits, being spoiled on the railway sidings or being stolen by guards and workers. Eberl narrowly avoided arrest. He was sacked. Stangl was appointed as the new commander and the camp temporarily shut down to allow the premises to be cleaned up and certain structural changes to be made.

Stangl, an Austrian, turned Treblinka into the most efficient camp of all and used his sick sense of humour to ensure that actions would go off without a hitch. The new commandant bought some his most trusted men with him to reform the camp and ensure its smooth operation. Approximately 40 Germans were on staff but as with the other camps the majority of the guards were Ukrainians of which there were about 100. Between 700 and 1000 Jewish inmates performed most of the duties such as cutting pine branches to be used as camouflage on the wire and barbed wire fences, sorting bundles, escorting the transported prisoners into the holding pens, extracting teeth from the dead and getting rid of the corpses. To ensure the efficient employment of this labour force Stangl introduced coloured armbands for the different Kommandos. The blues were in charge of reception while those who seized goods were known as the reds due to their red armband.

One particularly horrible feature of the initiatives bought in by Stangl was the creation of a *lazaretto* just next to the reception ramps adjacent to the railway line. This was composed of a small wooden building and a small courtyard fenced off and hidden from the new arrivals. This *lazaretto* had two additional features, on top of the shack flew a Red Cross flag and in the yard was a deep pit which had a fire continuously burning. Those who were too weak or old, or unaccompanied children, were separated from the transport by outwardly solicitous guards, taken into the shed and made to undress. They were then shot in the back of the neck before being tumbled into the fire pit.

One peculiarly revolting individual to emerge from the Holocaust inhabited this little annex of the main operation. Samuel Rajzman described this German killer in his Nuremberg deposition.

> We had a Scharführer Menz, whose special job was to guard the so-called Lazarett. In this Lazarett all weak women and little children were exterminated who had not the strength to go themselves to the gas chambers … Menz who specialised in the murder of all persons brought to this *lazaretto*, would not let anybody else do this job. There might have been hundreds of persons who wanted to assist … but he insisted on carrying out this work himself.
>
> Here is just one example of what was the fate of the children there. A ten-year-old girl was bought to this building from the train with her two-year-old sister. When the older girl saw that Menz had taken out a revolver to shoot her two-year-old sister, she threw herself upon him, crying out, and asking why he wanted to kill her. He did not kill the little sister – he threw her alive into the oven and then killed the elder sister.
>
> Another example. They bought an aged women with her daughter to this building. The latter was in the last stage of pregnancy. She was bought to the *lazaretto*, was put on the grass plot, and several Germans came to watch the delivery. This spectacle lasted two hours. When the child was born, Menz asked the grandmother who she preferred to see killed

first. The grandmother begged to be killed. But, of course, they did the opposite – the new-born baby was killed first, then the child's mother, and finally the grandmother.

Nuremberg Trial Proceedings Vol. 8; Sixty-Ninth Day; Wednesday 27 February 1946; Morning Session

Stangl sought new and devious ways of fooling his charges. A fake railway station was built on the arrival platform. It had a wooden clock painted on the front. Signs reading 'ticket window', 'cashier', 'station master' with arrows pointing to future destinations were utilised, all seeking to reassure arrivals. There were even artificial timetables printed as well as large signs calling the station Obermajdan. The station was painted in gay colours and Stangl went even further and constructed a recreation area near the front gate with refreshments tables and sunshades as well as a Polish country-style gate bedecked with flowers. The guardhouse was made to look like a picturesque Tyrolian chalet, another folly designed to reassure the innocent victims.

As in the other camps arrivals were forced to undress and surrender their goods in several large assembly yards. Women were allowed to undress, for the sake of decency, in a large barracks which had at one end a group of Jewish prisoners who cut their hair.

The undressing square in the lower camp was connected to the extermination area by the *Sclauch* (The tube.) This was also known as *Himmelfahrtstrasse* (the road to heaven) by the guards. The naked Jews were driven along this long pathway, 80 to 90 metres long, by guards wielding whips. The last joke played upon the Hebrews as they entered the gas chamber was a ceremonial curtain taken from a synagogue suspended over the entrance's lintel. On the curtain which used to cover the Ark were written the words 'This is the gate way to God' were written. Righteous men will pass through.' The gable over the door had a large Star of David.

Once they entered the gas chamber the monumental scale

of this facility of death became obvious. The building was approximately twenty two metres long but only two metres high. Less gas was required to fill the low-slung chambers. Five chambers lined each side of the corridor. They were all eight metres deep and four metres wide and encompassed an area of 320 metres. Each chamber had a small glass panel set in the wall so that the SS men could observe the progress of the gassing. The gas chambers could exterminate 3,800 people simultaneously. On average 2,500 people were killed each time and while it originally took three to four hours to liquidate this many, practice led to the same number being

killed in only one and a half hours. Even as one transport was being asphyxiated a Kommando was cleaning up their wagons and shunting up another batch of deportees.

After death the industrial processes continued making Treblinka a true murder factory. The Jewish workers tossed the bodies out of the chambers before placing them on trolleys running on a narrow gauge railway to the burial pits. The ditches were massive, 50 metres long, 25 metres wide and 10 metres deep. Not dug by hand, an industrial excavator previously used in quarries shifted the enormous tonnage of soil and clay.

At this time, another team of approximately 50 prisoners collected the clothes and goods that had been kept in the undressing square and transferred them to the sorting square. Here a sorting Kommando searched the belongings for money or valuables and divided the clothes into neat piles. This Kommando was also responsible for removing the Jewish Stars from the clothing, and destroying identity cards and other documents the Germans considered to be of no value. Once sorted, the victim's possessions were stored, and at the appropriate time, were forwarded to the SS warehouses in Lublin. Made up of approximately 200–300 prisoners, the Kommando were employed in the extermination area on such tasks as the removal of the corpses from the gas chambers, cleaning the chambers, extraction of the victim's gold teeth and burial of the bodies. From the winter of 1942–43 corpses were cremated instead of being buried.

When the final gassing in August 1943 was completed, the camp area was ploughed over and trees were planted. The camp was turned into a farm, and a Ukrainian guard named Streibel was settled there with his family in order to protect the site from being plundered by the local population.

Many of the former SS guards were transferred to dangerous postings such as the Balkans and most died in combat. The camps and the personnel were deliberately eliminated and swept from the historical record.

6

BLITZKRIEG

Origins of *Blitzkrieg*

Cambrai. France. 1917. After three years of merciless and futile trench warfare, the two key ingredients that will determine the shape of the next hundred years of warfare are on show although none of the participants know this. The British throw a massed phalanx of armour at the German lines and achieve a limited breakthrough. German infantry counterattack using new assault tactics that throw the British back to their jump-off points and in some areas even take new territory.

In the 1930s Guderian combined the potential of armoured vehicles and the new assault tactics and gave Hitler a weapon that had the potential to give him domination of Europe, and possibly the world.

On 20th November 1917 at 6.20am hundreds of Allied guns opened up on the trench network that defended the town of Cambrai, a vital transport hub vital to the maintenance of the Hindenburg line. Following close behind the barrage were approximately 400 Mark IV tanks. Roughly half of the 30-tonne leviathans were armed with an array of Lewis machine guns while the remainder had 6 pounder cannon in side sponsons as their main weapons. They all moved at approximately six kilometres per hour in good going and were considerably slower over the shell-ploughed terrain of northern France.

Tough German resistance and frequent mechanical breakdowns meant that by the 21st of November less than half of these clumsy vehicles were available to continue the assault. Nevertheless the offensive penetrated the German defenses and the new salient was up to seven miles deep in some places. Church bells rang throughout England as it seemed the Allies finally had the means to bring the dreadful war or attrition to an end.

Not for long.

The problem was, as it was with all of these early tank offensives on the Western front, the years of intense artillery barrages had ploughed up the earth so much that a breakthrough inevitably had to be stopped to allow artillery support and supplies to catch up. Theoretically cavalry was intended to exploit any breakthrough but the built up nature of Belgium and northern France constricted mounted troops and they were unable to flank remaining machine gun positions or even take out skirmish lines.

The British attack petered out, new positions were dug, and the British settled down to wait for the inevitable counterattack.

Ten days later a German counterattack erupted from the lines defending Cambrai and threw the English back in a panicked retreat. The *Stosstruppen* (shock troops or Stormtroopers) assaulted the allied lines and reclaimed all of the lost territory as well as extra terrain behind the original British lines. This successful attack was a large-scale dress rehearsal for the Ludendorff offensives in 1918 that came within a whisker of winning the war for Germany. Had these later offensives succeeded Adolf Hitler would not even be a footnote in history.

Artillery specialist colonel Georg Bruchmuller was posted from the Eastern front to develop a fire plan designed to break British resistance and pave the way for the assaulting infantry in the Cambrai counteroffensive. Bruchmuller developed his tactics with the 5th Army on the Eastern Front. So successful was he that he gained the nickname *Durchbruchmuller* (Break-through-Muller). Rather than prolonged and wasteful preparation barrages that warned allied forces of an impending attack and allowed them to bring up reinforcements, he utilised sudden concentrations of fire immediately before the assault. These targeted the entire defense rather than the forward elements. Each battery received specific fire missions with designated targets and specified timetables. There were several stages in the delivery. The first targets consisted of headquarters, phone links, forward observation posts, enemy batteries and selected infantry positions.

Rather than relying on high explosives different shells were utilised for maximum disruption. Delayed action fuses kept the enemy off balance and mustard or chlorine gas shells were delivered along with explosives. Agents that rapidly nullified the defensive characteristics of gas masks forced the infantry out of the trenches where the poison gases settled, exposing them to the dangers of shrapnel and machine gun fire.

The German guns were on target from the first round. Thanks to ingenious artillerymen and painstaking mapmakers the Germans had figured out how to fire their big guns accurately without registration. Massed batteries could be moved into position and did not have to reveal their whereabouts with pre-offensive ranging shots.

Yellow-cross shells, containing mustard gas, were confined to the flanks of the selected target. Mustard gas tended to disperse slowly and could hinder attackers as well as defenders if it was delivered onto the German objective. By concentrating these deadly missiles on the flanks of the assault, they did not hinder the *Stosstruppen* and stopped reinforcements disrupting the German attack. Green-cross shells combined deadly odorless phosgene gas, which dispersed quickly. These were used on the forward trenches, the immediate target of attack. As well as killing front line troops they were also used on Allied artillery positions. The yellow cross and green cross shells were combined with one other ingenious ingredient. Contained within blue-cross shells was the non-lethal diphenyl chloramine. This fouled the British gas masks and caused men to expose themselves to the other lethal gaseous shells.

After the initial artillery phase, box barrages were employed on the flanks and rear of the target area to ensure that reinforcements could not get through. Heavy calibre long-range pieces penetrated far into the enemy rear destroying depots and marshalling grounds. A creeping barrage, or *Feuerwalze* (fire waltz) was employed to precede the assault waves. These exhaustive preparations were made in utmost secrecy ensuring defenders got the shock of their lives.

Those lives were likely to be short.

Following behind the diabolical array of shrapnel and gas and the German Stormtroopers were armed with an array of deadly weapons that broke Allied trench systems wide open.

As the Stormtroopers emerged from the trenches observers would have noticed their unconventional uniforms. Rather than having a clumsy backpack most had a blanket or greatcoat wrapped around a mess kit on their back. Gaiters and short boots replaced jackboots and knees and elbows had patches to reinforce their clothes. These troops were kitted out for speed. They were also the first to be issued with the modern coal scuttle helmet used for the latter part of the war and all of the WWII. This replaced the archaic *Pickelhaube* whose poor protection and spike on the top made it a liability in trench warfare.

German medical authorities had determined that 90 per cent of head wounds were made by small pieces of shrapnel, rarely the size of a pea. The *Pickelhaube* gave poor protection and the new helmet gave good neck cover, was set away from the head by an ingenious array of straps and pads but still allowed peripheral vision. The first production batch went straight to the Stormtroopers in 1916 followed by infantry on the Western front, then support services and finally to troops on the Eastern front.

Slung over each man's shoulder were one or two sandbags converted to carry stick grenades, the main offensive weapon. Stormtroopers often went into battle with their short carbines slung over their back. The Potato Masher or Stick Grenade had an official name *1915 Stielhandgranate* and was so efficient it remained the main German grenade right up until the end of WWII. The basic grenade was composed of a hollow metal cylinder packed with explosive attached to a hollow wooden throwing handle 225 mm long. This configuration allowed it to be thrown a long distance and as the users advanced they were able to lob it into remaining enemy outposts.

There were several grenades that the veteran soldiers could choose from. For long-distance throws the seven second fuse would be chosen, for close in work the three second fuse was appropriate while perhaps the most deadly variant exploded on impact as it was armed with a percussion fuse that was detonated by a spring-powered striker when it hit the ground. Maybe more convenient were the egg grenades introduced in 1916. A hail of these were thrown into British trenches at Thiepval in July, clearing out the British defenders in short order. Due to the close confines of the trenches most of these grenades relied on blast effect and caused shattered eardrums or ruptured internal organs, when thrown into crowded dugouts.

One advantage of the stick grenade was that it could be taped together into bundles to create an extraordinary close-in weapon that could take out the toughest defensive works.

An array of carbines, pistols and later submachine guns were available and Stormtroopers were allowed to choose what they were most comfortable with. The K-98 carbine was initially issued to cavalry and artillery units but its shorter barrel and lighter frame made it ideal for fast moving assault troops. The Luger and Mauser pistols were favoured weapons and the artillery model Luger often came equipped with a 32 round snail magazine making it almost as effective as a submachine gun. As Erwin Rommel explained, in single combat the winner is always the one who has the last round in his magazine.

In 1914 the principle infantry weapon was the magazine-fed rifle. Machine guns were used in support, usually in company or even battalion-sized formations. This was reversed in German formations by 1916. Section-based tactics where each platoon was divided into several groups led by NCOs became the norm. Each section was based around a light machine gun which could suppress enemy positions while troopers armed with grenades would close in to destroy the enemy defenses.

Light machine guns were required in this role and thousands of captured British Lewis guns were employed by the Germans and a factory in Brussels was tasked with maintaining them. The cut down Maxim-style MG/08 15 was also in use. This belt-fed weapon, though pretty cumbersome by modern standards, allowed a veritable hail of fire to be laid down on the opposition.

Stormtrooper battalions had other assets. The 7.62 mm Russian field piece was captured in such numbers that many were converted to make them perhaps the earliest version of assault artillery. The barrel was shortened from 2.28 metres to 1.25 metres. New close-in sights were added and a low-recoil carriage with small wheels was fitted. These light, low-profile guns could be manhandled right into the front line and pound enemy strong points with six kg shells of high explosive. In 1917 batteries of four German-made 7.7 mm field guns on purpose-built carriages were also introduced. The crews were trained in close support work as well as anti-tank duties.

For indirect fire mortars and grenade throwers were employed, including the massive *Minenwerfer* which lobbed such huge shells into enemy lines that the allied troops nicknamed them flying dustbins. They were guaranteed to obliterate anything that they hit but their short range made them vulnerable to counter-battery fire and capture.

Each battalion of Stormtroopers had an organic *Flammenwerfer* platoon armed with four to eight light flamethrowers. The psychological effect of these weapons often made whole enemy units break to the rear.

While this fearsome array of weapons made the German Stormtroopers the elite of their day it was the innovative tactics employed that made them into a potential war winner.

The German High command was not the monolithic organisation that it is often characterised as. Rather than prescribing tactics and drill that were to be followed by all units it actually encouraged independent thinking and initiative in its tactical formations. By 1916 infantry officers had been figuring out ways to break the trench deadlock and it was the distillation of all this experience that led to the game-changing Stormtrooper tactics.

These groups effectively invented modern-day infantry tactics. Small units would be given objectives and it was the responsibility of the NCO or officer in charge to work out how best to achieve the objective. Gun groups or rifle groups would utilise fire and movement to approach enemy positions. These positions would be suppressed with assault artillery, mortars and machine gun fire before being assaulted with close-in weapons such as grenades or pistols and, by 1918, the Bergmann MP 18 submachine gun. On a localised level riflemen would snipe at the enemy to support the machine gunners while the bombing parties worked their way forwards. Troopers were allowed to choose their own equipment.

Ernst Junger explained in his autobiographical account how he prepared himself for an assault. As an experienced fighter he knew what was appropriate for each mission. Firstly, he strung across his chest two converted sandbags each containing four stick grenades. Impact fuse bombs were on his left while delayed action grenades were in the right bag. In his tunic he placed a Luger on a long cord while stashing a small caliber Mauser in his trouser pocket. In another tunic pocket were five egg hand grenades for close-in work. Other equipment carried included a luminous compass, whistle, a bowie knife and wire cutters. Stormtroopers were under no illusion as to their life expectancy and Junger carried his wallet with his home address as well as his identification tags to aid identification of his body if necessary. His final bit of kit? A flask filled with cherry brandy.

Eyewitness accounts detail the appearance of these fierce attacks launched by the well-armed storm troopers. Rather than large linear assaults they noted how patrols preceded the heavily armed attack columns equipped with many light machine guns and flamethrowers. As the storm troopers closed with the British defenders German fighters bombed and strafed their positions causing casualties and distracting the Tommies as the Germans worked around their flanks and rear.

Flanks and weak points were sought. Troops were trained to bypass enemy strongpoints and take them from the rear or roll the remaining positions up from the flank. If these weak points could not be found a point of maximum impact would be chosen where all of the battalion assets would overwhelm the enemy with massed firepower allowing the assault troops to break through. Once a breakthrough had been achieved these elite soldiers were trained to penetrate the enemies' rear, disrupting communications, causing confusion and cutting off remaining enemy formations from supply.

The British Army and its allies were aware of combined arms attacks and the greatest proponent was Sir John Monash.

Sir John Monash was an Australian general who further developed the tactics used at Cambrai. His assault at Hamel on July 4th 1918 is considered to be the first modern combined arms battle. The troops of the Australian Corps attached to the British Fourth Army drilled with the tanks attached to the attack and experimented with tank-infantry cooperation, working out how best to attain set objectives.

Secrecy was paramount with few written orders and radio silence. Allied aircraft were deployed before the attack to ensure that troops were well camouflaged and to drown out the noise of tanks approaching.

The attack went according to plan. Ammunition was dropped to the forward troops as they advanced, waves of low-flying aircraft strafed enemy positions and smoke and dust concealed the troops as they stormed into the enemy trenches. A creeping barrage moved forward in front of the troops. The whole successful assault was carried out in 93 minutes. Monash had estimated it would take 90 minutes.

General Rawlinson who was the commander of the British Fourth army saw that the innovations were widely adopted by the rest of the British army and similar successful battles such as the battle of Amiens used the same tactic but on a wider scale. The other innovation pushed by Monash was to attack weak points and flanks rather than relying on frontal attacks. Amazingly even as late as 1918 this concept was novel to many in the Allied High command.

These tactics were formalised between the wars creating the brilliantly successful *Blitzkrieg* tactics.

Several other features of the *Blitzkrieg* that almost handed European domination to Hitler were already present by the end of the war. Combined arms where artillery, tanks, infantry and airpower combined to destroy the opposition were well understood. The infiltration tactics of the Stormtroopers were developed in the German army in particular. As well as almost handing victory to the Germans in the Ludendorff offensives of 1918 they were also used on the Italian front in the battle of Caporetta by quick-thinking light infantry officers such as Captain Erwin Rommel who won a Pour Le Mérite for his efforts.

Aerial bombardments and strafing combined with surprise attacks on weak points were common. Regimental or battalion battle groups combining artillery, machine guns, mortars and riflemen were common as was the idea of attacking the enemy's communications to disrupt defensive systems. Tanks were not the only tracked vehicles available to the allied forces. Armoured personnel carriers (APCs) and self-propelled artillery (SPs) were an established part of the Western arsenal.

Father of the *Blitzkrieg* – Heinz Guderian

Only one element was missing and that was provided by an outwardly nondescript German officer – Heinz Guderian. It was his idea to combine all of these elements with the most powerful weapon of all – the radio.

Guderian was not particularly tall and his round benign-looking face with its small moustache gives the impression of one who perhaps would have been more comfortable as a parish priest in a small town in Prussia. Born in 1888 he was destined to follow his father into the military. Indeed his father was disappointed with his eldest son when he agreed to a posting to a signals battalion before the outbreak of the Great War.

Below right: Heinz Guderian, father of the Blitzkrieg. Below left: Guderian leading Panzers in Operation Barbarossa before Hitler's stop order (second from left).

Nevertheless it proved to be an inspired posting. As the war progressed wireless and telegraph communications improved exponentially and their applications continued to increase. Guderian's next posting was as a staff officer at a divisional HQ followed by a position at corps HQ. After this he attended a Staff Officers course at Sedan. It is no doubt during this time that he was able to observe the shortcomings of the chain of command and begin to speculate how radio could make it more efficient.

Recognised as a bright up and comer he remained in the *Reichswehr* (post-war German army) after the war and was posted to another crucial position, the Inspectorate of Transport Troops. Despite its humdrum name it was in fact an innovative organisation ordered to develop strategies for the utilisation of motor transport in future warfare. During this posting Guderian read the works of British military theorists including JFC Fuller. These writings saw the role of the mechanised formations as hitting the command and communications centres of the enemy rather than combating front line positions.

Guderian combined all of the strands of modern technology with Prussian military traditions. He was able to understand and develop lessons learnt in the second half of WWI such as infiltration to avoid strong points, concentration of fire, combined arms teams and the use of concealment and misdirection in offensive actions. He joined to these ideas the potentialities of armoured formations, airpower, radio control and the novel ideas of theorists such as Fuller.

Guderian was above all practical. While some inter-war theorists believed massed armies purely made up of tanks could win wars or fleets of bombers could decimate an enemy and destroy their will to resist, Guderian's theories were realistic and achievable. His ideas were well received by his superiors and he became the commander of the first ever armoured corps in February 1938 just in time to spearhead the first operational use of the Panzer divisions – The *Anschluss*.

Panzer divisions – organisation and tactics

The new type of division that was envisaged by Guderian expanded on the ideas of the early Stormtrooper battalions. Whereas these battalion may have been made up of 1000 men at the maximum with separate platoons given different roles, the Panzer divisions had entire regiments taking on different tasks within the divisional organisation. In effect 17,000 men became a huge combined-arms team able to call on a range of assets to ensure the job was done. Its key task was mobile warfare. Guderian had much influence in tank and equipment design and he always saw mobility as the key to successful employment of the Panzers.

Blitzkrieg was stunning in its simplicity. Once an enemy's weak point had been identified the Panzer division was to direct all of its offensive weaponry at this point to achieve a breakthrough. Artillery and air assets would pound the opposition from above while armour and infantry would attack from the front once it had been sufficiently weakened. This was designated the *Schwerpunkt* or point of maximum effort. Once breached the Panzer divisions were to drive through the enemy lines. Panzer grenadiers (armoured infantry) would support the Panzers as they moved through built up terrain and would help widen the breach ensuring enemy anti-tank weapons or artillery could not harass the flanks of the advancing armour. Once the breach was wide enough, conventional infantry divisions would replace the Panzer grenadiers to hold or expand the shoulders of the breakthrough. Infantry would also march behind the Panzers to secure their flanks deep in hostile territory.

The Panzer division's aim was to get into open country. Once there they moved as an entire self-supporting battle group. Luftwaffe formations were ready to smash any communications, supplies, or strong points set up to impede the Panzers. It was here that Guderian's genius was apparent. The troops were to create maximum disruption in the enemy rear, destroying their ability and will to make a coherent stand. His maxim, 'Smash them don't tap them' sums up his thinking perfectly. His other maxim was, 'Order plus counter-order equals disorder.' This was a truly prophetic insight as would be seen in Russia. Once a strategic objective had been given it was to be followed no matter what.

The cutting edge of these new formations was of course the Panzer Brigade. Up until 1941 each Panzer division had approximately 300 tanks divided into four battalions which were further divided into two regiments. Each battalion contained both light and medium companies and some had heavy companies. Up until 1941 the bulk of Panzer production had been made up of light machine gun armed tanks such as the Panzer I and Panzer II. While fast-moving and reliable they were in real terms tankettes and could not stand up to other gun-armed tanks. Useful for exploitation and reconnaissance they needed the heavier Panzer IIIs and Panzer IVs to break resistance with their heavier cannon. Many Panzer divisions were equipped with Czech 35(t) and 38(t) tanks which were very well armed and armoured for the early *Blitzkrieg* battles.

The key role of the tanks was not always to fight in battles against enemy armour. Other assets had that role. Their key strength in *Blitzkrieg* doctrine was to burst through weak points in the enemy line and then using their superior fully-tracked mobility to range deep behind the enemy lines causing chaos and destruction on soft targets such as supply depots and HQs. The early generation of German tanks were in a sense over engineered. Carrying relatively light weapons their most dangerous kit was the radio. While other nations' tanks were controlled by flags or signal flares, each Panzer had a one-way radio at least, allowing the commander to spin his formation on a dime and cause the maximum damage.

Aiding the tanks in their break through and exploitation role were two rifle regiments. Each regiment was made up of two battalions and each battalion was in fact a combined arms command such as the Stormtroopers. Three rifle companies were supported by a heavy weapons company with anti-tank guns, mortars and infantry guns. Each battalion could therefore defend and attack and be able to draw on any required weapon for any tactical situation. The four battalions were called on by the commander for a multiplicity of roles. They were trained to apply the *Schwerpunkt* into the heart of the defenses, to roll up a defensive enemy line once the breakthrough had been made or to accompany the Panzers in their deep thrusts into the enemy rear.

Blitzkrieg doctrine called upon all of these infantry battalions to be carried in armoured personnel carriers (APCs) but few of the Sd Kfz 251 half-tracks had been built by 1940 so the grenadiers were carried in trucks. A fair proportion of these vehicles were four-wheel drive so they were still able to keep up with the tanks in unopposed advances deep into the enemy rear. The Panzer grenadiers as these infantry were called, would have to dismount if opposed by light arms.

The next-largest formation within the Panzer division was the artillery regiment. All German divisions at the time had a regiment built along similar lines. Two battalions had three batteries of four 105 mm medium howitzers while the third battalion had three batteries of four 150 mm heavy howitzers. However, while most infantry battalions employed horse-drawn artillery the Panzer artillery was towed by all terrain half-tracks. These 24 guns could rain a blizzard of high explosive onto any opposing formations and help batter a path through the defenses for the Panzers and their grenadiers to break through. The divisional HQ was equipped with a light observation plane the *Feiseler Storch* (Stork). These remarkable planes could take off and land on a small field and could act as a spotter for the divisional artillery, concentrating its fire onto a target until it was smashed.

Acting as defensive components to defend from enemy counterattacks were the *Panzerjäger* (tank hunter) battalion and the flak battalions. The former would be called up to fight off any armoured assault while the flak protected vital river crossings or other rear-area targets. Most of these weapons were towed although some of the flak was mounted on self-propelled half-tracks. The most deadly weapon in the entire German arsenal was the battery of 88 mm flak. These guns had proved themselves to be absolutely lethal against any air or ground targets. By 1939 they were all equipped with a range of shells including armour piercing (AP) allowing them to take on even the heaviest tanks.

The German genius at offensive organisation can be truly appreciated when the remaining two combat formations within a Panzer division are considered – the Panzer engineers and the reconnaissance battalion.

Just as the Stormtroopers had a small detachment of engineers armed with flamethrowers the Panzer engineers were fierce combat battalions trained to overcome the toughest array of opposition. Armed with flamethrowers and huge 210 mm short-range rockets, many mounted on half-tracks, they could pulverise the toughest blockhouse from close range. They also had as part of their arsenal hollow-charge bombs which could be fixed onto enemy bunkers with strong magnets and once ignited would burn any occupants to cinders. Engineers were armed with wire cutters and bangalore torpedoes to destroy wire entanglements and an array of mines which could be used offensively or defensively. Given the need to cross terrain quickly each engineer battalion was equipped with a pontoon bridge that could be thrown across wide waterways where the enemy had managed to destroy other crossing points.

The reconnaissance battalion was divided into four companies and could fight to obtain information. While the first companies were made up of fast-moving armoured cars the fourth company was a self-contained battlegroup and included artillery and anti-tank assets as well as infantry. While primarily trained to gather information these battalions could seize and hold vital terrain features until heavier forces could arrive.

At the heart of the Division was the command staff and the *Nachrichten* (radio-communication) battalion. The task of these units was to make independent decisions quickly and remain in radio contact with all subordinate, ancillary and superior formations.

While other nations still employed telegraph and dispatch riders as their main means of communication up to a thousand German soldiers were employed within these commands to ensure that radio communications were maintained with the entire division. As soon as orders were issued by the divisional commander they would be instantaneously relayed to all commands within the formation. This was two-way. Armoured cars of the reconnaissance battalion could range far ahead of the division and send communications back to their Company HQ who would send it to Battalion and up to Divisional HQ. Luftwaffe observers were implanted within the division allowing the division commander to call up air strikes where required or receive up-to-the-minute reports from recon flights.

Radios were not an afterthought but were integral to the organisation of even the Panzer battalions. At a platoon level individual tanks within a platoon were equipped with a radio receiver so that they could receive commands from their platoon leader. The larger Mark IIIs and IVs had a crewman whose primary function was as a radio operator. The platoon leader was equipped with a two-way set so he could communicate the tactical situation to his company commander. Each Panzer company commander had larger radios allowing him to communicate over greater distances with Battalion HQ. This was at the expense of ammunition storage and two such converted Panzers were issued to company HQ. One was operational and one was spare.

Panzer Regimental and Battalion HQs had three such command vehicles.

This organisation was replicated throughout the division ensuring every infantry platoon or artillery battery was in direct chain of command communication with Divisional HQ. Guderian had created an organisation that could turn on a dime.

The division was composed of approximately 15,000 men who through the use of the internal combustion engine and the radio could concentrate an unprecedented amount of violence onto a given objective.

There was one more trump card. The Luftwaffe. The German Army had always been the supreme decision maker in strategic matters and all other arms were subservient to its demands. The Luftwaffe was a tactical machine designed and built to support the *Blitzkrieg* ethos. The Luftwaffe never produced a successful strategic bomber – it was designed to lend tactical support to the army. Dive-bombers such as the fearsome Stuka were on call to bomb opposition while fighters ranged forward ensuring that opposition bombers couldn't interfere with the advancing motorised formations. Luftwaffe flak regiments were often attached to armoured groups guaranteeing the safety of rear communications and transport assets.

That was not all. Specialised formations such as heavy artillery regiments were often attached. These possessed massive artillery pieces of 170 mm to 210 mm which could lob shells 30 km into the enemy's rear.

Guderian and the German General Staff had revolutionised warfare and produced the perfect military machine. Nothing could stand in its way. Handled with purpose and daring the Panzer divisions were unstoppable.

Only one man stopped their ruthless conquest. Adolf Hitler.

This was not immediately obvious. The success of the early *Blitzkrieg* campaigns were a result of Hitler's political risk-taking combined with the military brilliance of the new Wehrmacht.

Early *Blitzkrieg*

Just as Hitler made no secret of his desire to destroy the Weimar Republic, so he made no secret of his desire to unite all Germans and obtain Lebensraum (living space).

His first success was the 1935 Plebiscite when the population of the coal-rich Saar Basin voted overwhelmingly to re-join the Reich. In 1936 he repudiated the treaties of Locarno and Versailles by marching into the Rhineland. This was a terrific gamble and Hitler was advised that the battalions marching to occupy the historical border between France and Germany had enough ammunition to fight for a matter of hours only. It was here that Hitler could have been stopped but the French and British did nothing.

Two years later the brand-new Panzer divisions were given their first dry run. On 12th March 1938 their armoured columns crossed the frontier to drive into Austria to perform the *Anschluss* (union) between the two Germanic countries. The German soldiers called this the *Blumenkrieg* (flower war) as the jubilant citizens of the Austrian heartland welcomed them enthusiastically. Nevertheless, significant problems were encountered with many trucks and tanks breaking down. A lack of petrol was particularly problematic and Guderian ensured that petrol lasting at least three days was with each tank unit thereafter. The *Anschluss* taught valuable lessons that would be used in later campaigns.

Once again the Western allies did nothing to intervene and Hitler used all of his hectoring bullying to overawe the British into handing over the Sudetenland. At this stage the Panzer divisions were largely paper tigers equipped with a majority of light tanks. The numbers of Panzer IIIs and IVs available to each brigade could be counted on one hand and there were still many problems with their organisation and equipment as demonstrated in the *Anschluss*. Hitler's use of propaganda overawed the Allies who thought themselves unready for war and allowed Hitler to gobble up those parts of Czechoslovakia that contained their state-of-the-art defenses and a state-of-the-art defense industry. In all likelihood the Czechs could have fought off the Wehrmacht but Hitler's sabre rattling unmanned any opposition.

HOW TO LOSE A WAR. LESSON ONE.
Attract a coalition against you

Then Hitler made his first blunder. At the Munich conference in September 1938 Hitler had been gifted the Sudetenland. In March 1939 he occupied the rest of Czechoslovakia. The sight of German troops marching down the cobbled streets of Prague was too much for the Western Democracies. Aware that public anger would not allow them to appease the dictator any longer, the British and French guaranteed the Poles that they would not allow Hitler to occupy their territory without a general war. Hitler had provoked a coalition to act against his interests. It was this coalition, in particular Great Britain, which would eventually be the agent of his downfall.

HOW TO LOSE A WAR. LESSON TWO.
Start a war

Hitler made what he thought were reasonable demands from the Poles. The treaty of Versailles had given the newly-formed state the Danzig corridor which separated East Prussia from the rest of Germany. The Free City of Danzig had been created although the bulk of the population was still German. Hitler sought control of railways and roads across the corridor and wanted Danzig to be returned to the Reich after a plebiscite. The Poles steadfastly refused to negotiate.

The German intelligence system unintentionally worked against their own interests. Telephone intercepts seemed to indicate that British and French delegates considered the Polish government was being intransigent. Hitler used this as his cue to set the invasion date for September the 1st 1939 believing that the Allies would not intervene. On August 31st the Polish ambassador contacted the German foreign Minister and indicated that they would be willing to meet the Germans and negotiate a peaceful outcome. The Polish ambassador was waiting to talk to Hitler but despite knowing this the dictator had given the final confirmation for the attack to begin.

Convinced of his psychological dominance over the British and French politicians and consumed by his hatred for the Poles, Hitler had misjudged the situation and provoked a general war. For two days the British hesitated but finally on the 3rd of September the British and French declared war. Von Ribbentrop, the German foreign minister, reported that on hearing the news Hitler was dumbfounded. The scale of his blunder sunk in and, seemingly unmanned, he turned to the minister and said, 'What now? What can we do?'

Hitler had unleashed unimaginable violence upon the heartland of Europe.

The Battle of Poland combined traditional Prussian strategic thinking with modern warfare techniques. Reservists had been called up in secret several weeks before the attack bringing all formations up to full strength. This rapid mobilisation allowed them to overwhelm undermanned Polish formations. From railheads in Germany concentric drives were launched designed to separate Polish armies from their neighbors, encircle them and then defeat them individually. The Germans had the luxury of striking from a range of points including East Prussia. Most Panzer divisions were supporting the largely infantry armies.

The first hint of the modern form of warfare released by the Germans occurred at 6.00am on the first morning of battle when bombers attacked Warsaw. This was followed by attacks on the Polish airfields that almost destroyed their air force. Communications and transport centres were next, paralysing already slow-moving Polish reinforcements. Up to a third of the Polish armed forces were in the Danzig corridor. Attacked from both sides they were shredded.

In the centre and south the Poles put up a tremendous resistance. Outgunned and outnumbered they fought on doggedly. Reports came through to OKH of whole German battalions refusing to advance or bolting to the rear. It was imperative that the last Polish formations be finished off and encircled.

Heinz Guderian was given this task and placed in command of the 19th Panzer corps. This was the first time an independent tank army operated on its own and plunged into an enemy's rear, daring them to counter-attack into the open flanks.

Made up of two armoured divisions the 19th corps could be considered the first tank army. The 3rd Panzer division had a staggering 391 tanks in its reinforced 5th Panzer brigade. This unit had two Panzer regiments plus the crack Panzer Lehr (tank demonstration) battalion. The Lehr had 20 Panzer II, 37 Panzer III and 14 Panzer IV on its strength. This was at a time when most regiments had only three or less Panzer IIIs and maybe eight Panzer IVs with most of the numbers being made up of machine gun-armed Is and IIs. The other division in the corps, the 10th Panzer only had one regiment but still mustered 150 armoured vehicles.

The greatest advantage this armoured corps had was its commander General Heinz Guderian. General von Bock, commander of Army Group North gave Guderian freedom of action and sent him south into the Polish army's rear. The Panzer corps raced southwards covering an unprecedented 200 miles in ten days. Encountering no serious resistance they shot up Polish reserve formations before they even knew they were in a war zone. One of the few existing

Polish armoured units was caught with its proverbial pants down and was destroyed while being unloaded at a railway siding. Guderian exceeded his objective of reaching Brest-Litovsk and south of this town joined forces with units of Army Group south.

This set the scene for the great *Blitzkrieg* attacks of 1940 and 1941. Deep thrusts into the enemy rear sowed such discord and disorganisation that rarely could a counterattack be organised by the defending army – they didn't know what to attack or where the enemy were. Only one thing could stop the Panzers – anxiety within the German High Command.

The Poles were surrounded, their army was destroyed. In four weeks the proud nation of Poland was dismantled and its intelligentsia was at the mercy of SS death squads.

The British and French had not even finished mobilising and except for a couple of limited attacks on several villages in the Rhineland, took no action to support their allies. Most of the French artillery was still in mothballs. The RAF and the French Air force dropped leaflets on the Germans.

It was these two countries who were next to feel the might of the reinvigorated Wehrmacht.

France 1940

The Ludendorff offensives of 1918 had succeeded in cracking twenty-mile wide holes in the Allied lines on the Western front. Whole divisions of storm troopers broke through French and British defenses almost routing the Allies and reaching Paris or the channel ports. Infiltration and storm tactics overwhelmed the defenses and the only thing that stopped German thrusts was the limitations created by the inability of foot or mounted troops to exploit the breaches hammered through the enemy lines. This last offensive gasp of the Germans saw hundreds of thousands of casualties and many of the storm divisions almost wiped out.

American and British reinforcements stabilised the line and overwhelming material superiority allowed allied offensives to break the German army by November 1918. The German military and civilian populations were exhausted after more than four years of attrition on the Western front. At least two million German soldiers were casualties of the industrial scale meat grinder of the trenches.

In 1940 the Germans military showed that it had learned from its mistakes. France fell in six weeks. The Germans lost approximately 160,000 casualties of whom slightly less than one third were killed. The French and British lost more than twice as many casualties and almost two million captured. The Allied armies were routed and humiliated and almost all of their equipment was added to German stockpiles.

Fall Gelb (Case Yellow) was the supreme vindication of *Blitzkrieg* tactics and only the escape of the British armed forces across the sands of Dunkirk prevented it from being a total victory which should have won the war. One man had ultimate responsibility for letting the British army escape – Adolf Hitler.

Fall Gelb originated in the minds of Adolf Hitler and Erich von Manstein seemingly simultaneously. Early plans envisaged a broad-front attack through the Low Countries (Belgium and Holland), Luxembourg and Northern France. This would fix the Allies in place and its only virtue would be to bring the German bomber fleet in range of the British Isles, a decidedly two-edged outcome.

The Manstein plan which was adopted as *Fall Gelb* was much more daring and took the concept of the *Schwerpunkt* to its ultimate conclusion. Army Group A, composed of seven fully-equipped Panzer divisions backed by three motorised infantry divisions and 35 infantry divisions were to unite in an unstoppable phalanx of armour, break through a weak point in the French defenses at the Ardennes and race through the French and British rear to the English Channel. Once there the following infantry divisions would seal the line behind the British and French divisions, cutting them off from supplies and command and forcing them to surrender.

At the same time Army Group B, composed of three Panzer divisions, one motorised infantry division and 24 infantry divisions, would advance through the Low Countries attracting the best of the allied formations and drawing them deeper into the German trap. The Allied major counterstroke played exactly into the Germans' hands. The Dyle plan would see their best formations advance into Belgium to take up station on the Dyle River.

However before the armoured onslaught of Army Group A could penetrate into the Allied rear they had to cross a series of imposing natural obstacles, the Ardennes forest and the Meuse River. It was the way in which the combined arms teams that made up the Panzer divisions breached these formidable obstacles that showed their true versatility and proved that they were worthy successors to their Stormtrooper forbears.

The Ardennes had been chosen for the site of the main German effort for several reasons. It was considered impassable by conventional military minds and was thus lightly held. The French 9th army under General Corap was given the task of holding the Meuse. Its seven divisions which included two in reserve was spread more thinly than any other formations and they were attempting to hold 75 miles of front. They were mainly made up of reserve formations and lacked heavy weapons. The natural obstacle was seen by the French planners to impose such a barrier to any German offensive moves that the Maginot line did not extend to the French frontier behind this line. Also it was correctly assumed that the dense foliage of the forest would conceal the huge columns associated with any Panzer division on the March. On the 10th of May the 7 Panzer divisions of Army Group A would see just how difficult it was.

Preceding the armoured cars of the reconnaissance battalions were specially trained units of the Brandenburger Battalion dressed in civilian clothes and trained to disconnect any demolition charges on bridges and road ways. There were occasional skirmishes with small units of Belgian cavalry but the advance was spectacularly successful. Each division took its own supplies of fuel and food while a pool of mechanics equipped with spare trucks and tanks ensured that any breakdowns didn't affect the operational elements.

The French High Command perceived that the advancing divisions were a threat and began to send reinforcements to the Meuse. However they were thinking along timelines appropriate to the previous war. It was presumed that it would take seven or eight days for the Germans to reach the Meuse and then another three or four days to prepare for an assault. They were wrong.

It took three days for the Germans to reach the Meuse and they began to attack immediately.

The first to reach the formidable river barrier was the 7th Panzer under General Erwin Rommel. Beefed up with captured Czech Panzers this was one of the strongest formations. Arriving on the 12th of May they found all of the bridges in the region of Dinant blown. Trained to seek gaps in the enemy defenses, light infantry from the division explored the river bank and found an ancient weir. They used this to cross and at night time stormed the opposing bank routing the enemy and setting up the first lightly-held bridgehead over the Meuse.

The next morning Rommel took personal command of the battle. He needed to expand his bridgehead. First he ordered that houses in the river valley be set on fire so that smoke would conceal offensive preparations. He then bought up 75 mm gun armed Panzer IVs to bombard opposing strongpoints. As well as calling in artillery stonks to pulverise the enemy he remained in contact with the rest of the division and corps command with two armoured cars in his personal retinue. The rest of the command staff was behind the front but such was the efficiency of the German communications that Rommel could command the entire division from the front line. The division commander then took personnel command of an assault battalion and led it across the river, just as he had in the Alps in WWI. His inspired leadership allowed the lightly-equipped infantry to fight off a French armoured counterattack with flare pistols!

By noon the combat engineer battalion had constructed a cable ferry that moved twenty anti-tank guns to the Western shore before beginning to move tanks and armoured cars over. By the next day he had a fully operational pontoon bridge over the river (appropriated along with some heavier tanks from the 5th Panzer Division) and was pouring troops over the Meuse and into the heartland of France. Unsure of what was happening the French High Command ordered counterattacks only to cancel them before the troops were even in place. A divisional-size Stormtrooper formation had cut up the enemy front and was heading for their rear.

South of the XV Panzer corps to which the 5th and 7th Panzer Divisions belonged was the XIX Panzer Corps led by 'Hurrying Heinz' Guderian. He had the toughest nut to crack, traversing the heart of the Ardennes and the conquest of Sedan.

Here the Meuse was defended by two fortress divisions manning a complex of bunkers on the shoreline and in the steep hills above. Although lacking heavy weapons they were well emplaced and supported by formidable artillery – a perfect defensive position. Guderian had drilled his corps with practice assaults on stretches of the Moselle that exactly reproduced the conditions here on the French border. His divisions swung into a well-rehearsed assault. On the 13th the Luftwaffe attacked the French positions with everything they had. Stuka dive-bombers dropped their half-ton bombs with unerring accuracy on bunkers and trenches. Even when they had exhausted their ordinance they continued to dive as their unholy ear shattering sirens were often enough to rout the shell-shocked French reservists. Guderian also bought up his 88 mm flak batteries. Shooting straight into the concrete bunkers' firing slits they reduced them to smoldering rubble one by one.

Crossing the Meuse in their flimsy inflatable the first infantry waves accompanied by the combat engineers took heavy casualties. But once across they found that the troops designed to protect the remaining bunkers had vanished. Veterans of WWI would have relished the following action. Using all the tactics of the Stormtroopers each bunker on the hills above Sedan were destroyed one by one. Stick grenades were thrown down ventilation shafts, flamethrowers incinerated the opposition, and mortars put smoke grenades in front of the firing positions blinding the defenders while explosive charges were thrust into the firing slits.

Reaching the heights above Sedan the soldiers of Guderian's corps, including the elite troops of the *Grossdeutschland* (Greater Germany) infantry regiment fanned out to expand the bridgehead and repulse anything the French could throw against them. Some counterattacks were launched and some of the Panzer grenadiers were mauled. At Bulson and Stonne the Germans received a rude awakening when the shells from their 37 mm anti-tank guns bounced off the thick French armour. But Panzers and artillery weapons were brought up and the bridgehead held. Guderian's HQ acting in support of the divisional staffs ensured that any threats were met with overwhelming force.

Not so the French. Their poor communications allowed rumours and hearsay to take hold, leading to a collapse in their line. The 55th Infantry division dissolved into a rabble as its commanders upped stakes and withdrew to the rear on unfounded reports of Panzers. Once the HQs were in motion they could not communicate to their troops resulting in whole regiments bolting to the rear, in some cases soldiers did not stop until they were 60 miles from the front.

Into this vacuum Guderian decided to lunge for the French rear with his three Panzer divisions. Leaving behind some infantry formations he drove into the French heartland. Following him were five other Panzer divisions driving for the coast.

There was no Allied force with the ability to stop the expanding torrent of armour. However, setting a deadly precedent was a communication from German High Command on the 15th of May. The point divisions were given an order to halt. Guderian's superior Kleist determined that it was important to secure the Meuse bridgeheads. Guderian was at the front and saw the dissolution of the French at first hand and wisely ignored the order. Kleist visited Guderian and reiterated the order. The Panzer commander stuck to his guns and insisted that some formations would continue a reconnaissance in force. That these formations were entire Panzer divisions was not discussed. Honour satisfied Kleist butted out and left the advance to continue. In the following days there were reports that Hitler had a nervous collapse and raged and screamed at his commanders to stop the advance to the channel. They managed to circumvent these orders and the drive continued.

However, Hitler had shown that while he was a lion politically, he could panic and see imaginary dangers in a military setting. Not a good characteristic in a supreme commander. The advance continued against Hitler's wishes.

Belatedly French and British bomber formations tried to blow up the vital crossing points over the Meuse. The Germans had three or four days to encircle these bridges with their flak formations and the slow moving bombers were shot out of the sky. 80 per cent to 100 per cent losses were not uncommon.

Whole French formations were captured as they marched to the front. Just as in Poland, many tank units were cut to pieces as they detrained from railheads but many were left stranded when they ran out of fuel. Unsure of where the *Blitzkrieg* had placed the German units the Allies only managed one serious counterattack on the spearhead of the 7th Panzer at Arras.

While this was meant to be a corps-sized attack using a British armoured division along with a French armoured division and several infantry formations, poor communications meant that only a couple of brigade-sized groups were able to attack the Germans. The superiority of the Allied armour caused a dent on the German formations and momentary panic but once again Rommel's ability to lead from the front averted a catastrophe.

The British artillery was delayed and the infantry didn't reach its jumping off points in time but on 21st May heavily armoured Matilda I and II infantry tanks crashed into the German formation.

Suddenly coming under fire from several directions at once Rommel immediately grasped the fact that his division was under heavy attack. While it had taken several days for the French and British to coordinate their forces for a combined arms attack, Rommel acted instantaneously to bring all of his divisional assets to the fight. Dismounting from his command vehicle Rommel and his aide de camp first approached a battery of the 78th Artillery Regiment.

The General was a seasoned campaigner and immediately recognized the signs of panic as his units were in danger of being overrun by the Allied tanks. The artillery crews had fled with some retreating infantry and his first task was to get them back to their guns. Once the men were back in position Rommel gave each gun its target-rapid fire at the nearest tank. Rommel and his adjutant then organized some light anti-aircraft batteries to fire over open sights at the enemy until most of the divisional assets were pouring fire at the allied armour. Even though the thick armour of the British Matildas could not be penetrated by the German rounds the volume of fire was enough to convince them to back off.

When another assault was launched from a different direction the dose was repeated and the British counter attacks were finally beaten off. In the final moments of the battle as firing died down Rommel's adjutant, Lieutenant Most sunk to the ground with blood gushing from his mouth. A stray bullet had hit him in the throat inflicting a mortal wound.

Rommel saw this attack for what it was, a minor setback. As the fighting was raging around Arras the leading elements of Guderian's Panzer corps reached the channel.

Facing little opposition he decided to turn his three Panzer divisions, still at full strength, onto the channel ports and ensure that the entire Allied force trapped in the gigantic pocket would have to surrender. Boulogne, Calais and Dunkirk were all but defenceless.

Then came an order from Hitler. The Panzers would halt and Göring's Luftwaffe would finish the job.

HOW TO LOSE A WAR. LESSON THREE.
Don't finish off a beaten enemy

Hitler had decided to halt the Panzers. Various reasons have been given but none explain why the Panzer were not permitted to engage with the rear of the BEF (British Expeditionary Force) – a demoralised and defeated enemy retreating in panic to the channel. Hitler made a political decision. All of the glory could not go to the traditional Prussian military of the Wehrmacht High Command. The Luftwaffe and Hitler's political creature Göring had so far played second fiddle to the army in the dazzling Western triumph. The Führer succumbed to the Reichsführer's bombastic claims that he could finish off the Allies by bombing them into submission at Dunkirk. Hitler stopped the army and let the British get away. Three hundred and fifty thousand trained British troops were rescued along with approximately 50,000 French. The British love the adversity of a fighting retreat as shown by Agincourt in the 15th century and Corunna in the 19th. Hitler gave the British the propaganda victory of the Dunkirk evacuation. Had Guderian not been stopped a defenceless Britain would in all probability have sued for peace.

Hitler had the political will to attack France and Britain, but not the military will to finish them off.

Sixty divisions were left to fight off the German Army as it turned westwards to finish the job. After an initially robust defense the French cracked and the now veteran Panzer divisions drove hundreds of kilometres into France, only stopping at the Swiss border. Four years of humiliating occupation followed.

The French campaign did not only set the precedent for lighting war, rapid advances and huge encirclements. It also saw the first large-scale massacres of captured troops by members of the Waffen SS (fighting SS).

The first, the Paradis massacre, occurred near the Pas de Calais on May 26th. A company of the Royal Norfolk Regiment, trapped in a cowshed, surrendered to the 2nd Infantry Regiment, SS Totenkopf (Death's Head) Division under the command of 28-year-old SS-Obersturmführer Fritz Knöchlein. Marched to a group of farm buildings along the Rue du Paradis (thereby giving this massacre its name) they were lined up in the meadow alongside the barn wall. When the 99 prisoners were in position, two machine guns opened fire killing 97 of them. Knoechlein then ordered a group of his men to fix bayonets and stab or shoot to death any who showed signs of life. The bodies were then buried in a shallow pit in front of the barn. Two men managed to escape. Privates Albert Pooley and William O'Callaghan of the Royal Norfolk Regiment emerged from the slaughter wounded but alive. When the SS troops moved on, the two wounded soldiers were discovered, after having hidden in a pigsty for three days and nights, by Madame Duquenne-Creton and her son Victor who had left their farm when the fighting started. She cared for them until they were captured again by another, more civilised Wehrmacht unit to spend the rest of the war as POWs. Members of the Wehrmacht were shocked by what they saw. Major Friedkerr von Riedner, who was at the scene of the massacre on that day, reported that most of the dead prisoners had suffered from head shots that had been fired at point blank range. The others had their whole skull smashed in, an injury that von Reidner instantly recognized as being caused by a rifle butt.

One day after the Paradis massacre a similar atrocity took place. Around 100 men of the 2nd Royal Warwickshire Regiment, the Cheshire Regiment and the Royal Artillery, were taken prisoner by the No 7 Company, 2nd Battalion of the SS Leibstandarte Adolf Hitler. These captives posed no threat as most were wounded and lacked small arms. At Esquelbecq, near the town of Wormhoudt, about twelve miles from Dunkirk, the prisoners were marched across fields to a nearby farm and there confined in a barn with not enough room for the wounded to lie down. There the massacre began. About five stick grenades were lobbed in amongst the defenceless prisoners who died in agony as shrapnel tore into their flesh. When the last grenade had been thrown, those still standing were then ordered outside, five at a time, there to be mowed down under a hail of bullets from the rifles of the executioners. Fifteen men survived the atrocity in the barn only to give themselves up later to other German units to serve out the war as POWs.

7

THE EASTERN FRONT

A new direction

Just as the encirclement battles of the German *Blitzkrieg* in Russia dwarfed those seen in France, so did the massacres that took place as all rules of civilised warfare were torn up and ground into the Russian mud.

August 1941. Army Group Centre has paused to regroup. Panzer Group 3 under Hoth and Panzer Group 2 under Guderian have smashed the Russian forces before Moscow. The top army commanders want the drive to Moscow to continue. Once Moscow has fallen the war will be won. Hitler disagrees. He considers the Russian army to be already beaten.

Arguments raged back and forth between OKW (German High Command of all Armed forces) and OKH (Army High Command). Russian troops launched offensives against stalled Army Group Centre allowing Stalin to convince himself that his genius had stopped the Germans. The Army High Command began to realise what their oath to Hitler meant. As commander of OKW he was able to make operational decisions which they could not disagree with. He was determined to interfere with Barbarossa. He was determined to stop the drive on Moscow.

Hitler's ascendancy over the army had begun in 1933. Just as they had sworn an unconditional oath of allegiance to Kaiser Wilhelm I and II the armed forces swore personal allegiance to Adolf Hitler, a man who was given unconstrained powers by his manipulation of the constitution and had been a homeless vagrant less than twenty years earlier. The oath recited was as follows.

> I swear by God this sacred oath, that I will render unconditional obedience to Adolf Hitler, the Führer of the German Reich and people, Supreme Commander of the Armed Forces, and will be ready as a brave soldier to risk my life at any time for this oath.

The military machine that had 20 years earlier almost taken supreme power in the heartland of Europe was now at the beck and call of an outsider, an Austrian by birth. It was this oath of unconditional obedience that allowed Hitler to destroy his army on the Eastern front and kept the armed forces fighting to the last until his suicide, even though most of his top commanders knew he was stark raving mad.

The German military forces had come under the domination of Hitler when he became The Supreme Commander of the OKW – the High Command of the Armed Forces. The Armed forces were divided into three subsidiary organisations – the Luftwaffe, the Kriegsmarine (German Navy) and the OKH, the Army High command. It was in his role as commander of the OKW that Hitler was able to wreck the plans of the OKH.

Hitler made the correct political and strategic decision to attack France using the Manstein plan but then blew his chance for outright victory by unnecessarily interfering with operational matters. Only the scope of the victory concealed the faults of his leadership.

Not so with Russia. Once again Hitler made the correct political and strategic decision to launch operation Barbarossa and in real terms the military had the Russians on the ropes within five or six weeks. Just as the spaces of Russia extended any operational matters far beyond what was in France, so did changes in plan take a lot longer to implement. When Hitler interfered with the military operation in Russia almost two months of campaign time was wasted. This window of opportunity was used by Stalin to rally his shattered forces and mount a desperate last-ditch defense of Moscow. Even this defense was crumbling and it was only the arctic conditions of the Russian winter that stopped the exhausted Germans.

Hitler's decision to invade the Soviet Union

In early 1940 Hitler would have been mad to engage in a war on two fronts by invading the Soviet Union. However by 1941 the strategic situation had been turned on its head. France had been humiliated in a six-week campaign and was now either occupied by the German military or else ruled by the sympathetic puppet Vichy government. Britain's ground forces had been decimated, first in France and later in the Balkans where whole divisions had been captured. Small forces remained in North Africa and in colonial possessions but these in no way threatened Hitler's European Empire. True, the Luftwaffe had been defeated in the Battle of Britain but the RAF was at this stage largely a defensive force with short-range fighters and an antiquated bombing arm. America had not entered the war and it would be years before Britain could think of challenging the Nazis on the continent.

If Hitler could knock out the Soviet Union with another Blitz campaign his Thousand Year Reich would be all but assured.

1941 was in many ways the perfect time to attack the Soviet Union.

Hitler had always seen the quest for Lebensraum as the prime motivation of his Reich. It can be argued that France and Britain were only a threat to him because they sought to limit his advances in the East. Now that they were no longer a threat he could pursue his goals. As a student of history Hitler knew America would likely become involved on the side of the Allies and it was critical for him to act before that happened. Also Hitler was convinced that he was not to live for much longer. Whether his heart problems were real or imagined he was sure that he had five to ten years to live at the maximum and within this narrow space of time Hitler wanted to see his Reich on a firm footing.

The purges of the Russian military in 1937 and 1938 had removed the most talented military commanders, including many innovative generals who might have been able to mould the Red Army into a flexible modern army that could use armour and air power effectively. The Red Army was in many ways a headless behemoth. Their poor performance in the Winter War against Finland had shown that a mighty power with an army of millions of soldiers could be humiliated by the professional dedicated Finnish army.

Nevertheless the Red Army was rearming. Intelligence reports spoke of modern weapons and arms pouring from Soviet production lines. If allowed to continue some German estimates said that by late 1942 the Red Army would be superior to the Wehrmacht. Additionally the Soviets had not been able to fortify their new frontier gained in the non-aggression pact with Hitler when the two powers had divvied up Poland between them. One or two more years might see the frontier becoming a much tougher nut to crack.

Accepted wisdom was that the late start to the campaign due to the Balkans invasion was the reason Hitler lost the war. However the winter of 1940–1941 was so severe a late thaw combined with heavy spring rains would have pushed back the invasion date by three weeks from 15th May regardless of the Balkans sideshow.

What's more, German planning forecast a rapid-fire defeat of Russia. Intelligence put the number of Russian armoured vehicles at 10,000 and it air force at 14,000 combat planes. These figures proved to be remarkably accurate and planning took into the account the destruction of these machines. The

OKH plan put together by General Halder which delivered a *Schwerpunkt* into the heart of Russia to take out Moscow would have seen Russia defeated in six to ten weeks with a further 17 weeks required for consolidation. By taking Russia out of the war, a friendless Britain could do nothing but arrange a generous peace. Wargames calculating possible casualty figures and approximate drive times proved to the High Command that a drive on Moscow and several hundred kilometres beyond was realistic. Once Moscow was seized the German troops would have been able to spend the hostile Autumn and Winter months in the most densely populated areas of Russia, sheltered from the elements with good transport infrastructure.

Precise timetables were laid down for the coming offensive. Railhead supply bases near the border of the Soviet Union had been upgraded to double or quadruple line networks and all had been converted to German gauge. Fleets of trucks able to take tonnes of equipment and supplies were assembled and were able to take the stockpiled material deep into the Russian interior. Battalions of armed railway engineers had been assembled at the six major railheads and it was their task to convert Russian gauge lines to German gauge. Armed and organised as light infantry detachments these battalions were staggeringly successful and could convert 20 kms of railway lines a day. In many instances during the initial advances these battalions were so close behind the advancing military that they were engaged in firefights with retreating Russian forces.

The Wehrmacht was at the peak of its powers. Huge stores of transport and weaponry had been stripped from conquered foes. All of her formations had been blooded and most were veteran divisions, unlike the untried military that had attacked Poland. Negligible losses had been sustained in these earlier campaigns and all formations were at full strength. Raw materials such as steel from Sweden and fuel from Rumania were guaranteed. Half a million tonnes of gasoline were stockpiled as were 91,000 tonnes of ammunition. Additional signal troops were organised and they were specially equipped to be able to communicate over long distances. Fifteen thousand Polish pattern horse-drawn carts were acquired. They were chosen for their suitability for crossing poor roads and utilised the local *panje* ponies.

Ten Panzer divisions had been expanded to twenty of which 17 took part in the initial drive into Russia. The Germans had been able to double the Panzer divisions so rapidly by halving the number of tank regiments within the division. Although the number of tanks deployed was reduced they were of a much better quality. Most Panzer Is had been stripped from the tank regiments and replaced with large numbers of Panzer IIIs and IVs. Many of the Panzer IIIs had been vastly improved with a more powerful 50 mm tank gun and thicker armour.

Adolf Hitler had specifically ordered that the new 50 mm gun should be the long version but in defiance of his wishes the short version was installed. At his birthday demonstration of New Panzers in April 1941 Hitler saw that his wishes had not been carried out. Furious, he ordered the more efficient L60 to be installed at once. Events proved him to be correct and the L42 could not take out the T34 whereas the longer version could. The first Panzer III Lang (long) did not reach the troops until the beginning of 1942.

Despite the fact that the number of tanks per division was reduced they still had their full complement of supports. Due to improved production of half-tracks many of the artillery regiments were fully cross-country capable. Additionally some motorised infantry regiments were able to mount a battalion of infantry in armoured half-tracks, giving them off road capabilities and tremendous fire power.

Most important was the tremendous increase in the number of motorised infantry divisions. Fifteen were available for Operation *Barbarossa* and these proved to be tremendously important for the large encirclement battles to come. Fully motorised these units had all of the support battalions of the Panzer divisions including artillery and anti-tank assets but in place of the armoured regiment had an extra infantry regiment. This allowed a much wider defensive front to be established, crucial in the wide spaces of Russia. One hundred and four German infantry divisions were present on the Eastern Front. These were not the slow marching formations of WWI. Built for speed they included a motorised anti-tank detachment and reconnaissance battalion that could be brigaded together to take on fast-moving missions.

In all the German army deployed approximately three million men, 3,350 tanks, 7,200 artillery pieces, 2,770 aircraft, 600,000 motor vehicles and approximately 700,000 horses. Added to this impressive total were 14 crack Finnish divisions as well as numerous other allied detachments including 13 Romanian divisions. Approximately 3.8 million men were ready to 'Kick down the door' of the rotten edifice that was the USSR.

It seems that Hitler had another good reason for attacking the Soviet Union, even without knowing it. Almost three million communist solders were arrayed on their western frontier. With a preponderance of material in the south and centre, it is possible that Stalin was considering some offensive actions of his own while Hitler was tied down in the West.

Nevertheless the Axis forces had numerical superiority in men at the beginning of Operation *Barbarossa*. Experienced and well trained, the German soldiers were optimistic about the outcome of the war.

Operation *Barbarossa*

The attack came before dawn on 22nd June 1941, commencing at 3:15am with the largest artillery bombardment in history. Thousands of artillery pieces and rocket launchers rained thousands of tonnes of shells on Red Army positions. Simultaneously 3,277 Axis combat aircraft launched a record-breaking aerial onslaught targeting the Soviet air force on the ground. In the first 24 hours 2000 Soviet planes were destroyed in the air or on the ground. In the same period only 17 German aircraft were lost to enemy action. Columns of tanks punched holes in Red Army defenses, followed by motorised and regular infantry, all supported by a continuing air assault, now targeting Soviet ground forces.

The invasion had three main objectives. Army Group Centre, consisting of 1.3 million troops mounted a massive drive on Moscow. Meanwhile, Army Group North, consisting of 700,000 troops drove north from East Prussia through the Baltic States towards Leningrad, with the assistance of Finnish and German troops from Finland. Finally, Army Group South consisting of one million troops invaded the Ukraine with Romanian troops targeting the Black Sea port of Odessa.

The German *Schwerpunkt* drove into the heart of the Russian defenses. Packed into the frontier many Russians had been ordered not to shoot at any Axis forces lest they provoke them. The distances covered were huge. Motorised divisions routinely travelled 60 km a day. Once the initial crust of Russian border fortifications were broken they found little to delay them. The Wehrmacht soon developed procedures that made the victory in 1940 look insignificant.

Panzer divisions were teamed up with motorised infantry divisions into armoured corps. Their role was to drive through the stunned Russian defenses and drive for the rear with all speed. Once they had reached their objective, often hundreds of kilometres behind the Russian formations, the motorised infantry was to shake out into defensive positions and face backwards towards the encircled Russian formations. Meanwhile infantry corps marched at blistering pace to come up with the motorised elements and close the trap around the enemy formations trapped within the *Kessel* (kettle). The speed of these manoeuvres was unprecedented. After four days of campaigning the 7th Panzer Division (nicknamed the Ghost Division) had penetrated 275 km into the Soviet Union, seized the main Moscow highway and only two days later was joined by infantry divisions to erect the first major pocket around Białystok. In the same day, one week after jumping off, the second major pocket 400 km east of the frontier was founded around Minsk.

Luftwaffe units were as mobile as the advancing army. Flying into occupied territory they were experts at setting up forward air bases which enabled them to support the deep thrusts of the Panzers. In close touch with advance elements, many Soviet tank attacks were broken up by Stukas before they even got close to German formations.

Within two weeks the bulk of Western Soviet formations had been destroyed. Unlike the Russian army in 1812 which withdrew before Napoleon's army, the formations defending against the Germans were told to stand and fight to the last cartridge. Conflicting orders were given and many formations were told to attack the advancing columns while others were told to dig in.

Soviet High Command (STAVKA) lost all communication with its forward units and whole corps went missing, neither able to report their positions nor receive orders.

Despite this confusion millions of Russian soldiers and their command realised one thing, they had to break out to the East, they had to escape from the *Kessel* and regain their lines. German reports from this period are all similar. They speak of thousands of Russian soldiers employing human wave tactics to try and break through the German encirclement. Often the Russians were drunk. Goaded on by their Commissars (Communist Party enforcers attached to each formation) they literally ran onto the German guns. Infantry often came onto German lines with arms linked and lacking weapons. As one soldier fell another would pick up his weapon and keep advancing. Artillery support was often misdirected due to poor communications and massed tank attacks disintegrated into confused assaults. The veteran German divisions were ideally equipped to stop these onslaughts.

The heart of the Wehrmacht was the infantry squad. Gone were the green novices of the Polish campaign. Forty five thousand highly trained and professional ten man squads were deployed in Barbarossa. These were the ultimate fire and movement units distilled from the early crude beginnings of the *Sturmtruppen*. Each squad was equipped with the state of the art MG 34. This lightweight machine gun could spit out 750 rounds per minute (rpm) decimating any targets to its front. Supporting the MG's firer and loader were seven riflemen and one non-commissioned officer armed with a submachine gun. All members of the squad carried extra ammo for the MG 34 allowing uninterrupted firing of the deadly weapon.

Each battalion had at least 36 of these squads. They also had a heavy weapons company that deployed the MG 34 on a heavy tripod mounting as well as several 81 mm mortars. This company could deliver an unprecedented weight of ordinance onto a given target. The 12 MG 34s of this heavy company could stop any infantry attack in its tracks and many reports tell of mounds of dead Russian soldiers stacking up in front of the German positions while more soldiers tried to clamber over the top.

Even more deadly were HMG Battalions. As corps troops they were thrown into where the fighting was at its hottest.

Each Infantry unit had similar radio communications to the Panzer divisions. While they lacked the speed of the motorised units they could still act as flexibly as their more modern counterparts.

German divisions thrown in front of the massed outbreak attempts report similar things. Once the Russian soldier knew he could not break out of the encirclement, he surrendered. Luftwaffe planes dropped thousands of leaflets over the encircled troops. These were 'safe conduct passes' and encouraged whole formations to shoot their officers and commissars and surrender. The Soviet soldier was an excellent defensive fighter but the sophistication of German military technology unnerved them. They were particularly demoralised by combined air and artillery attacks and if they heard firing to their rear it was often the final straw. Thrown off balance by rapid and confusing German assaults the soldiers readily surrendered.

The Russian soldiers weren't helped by their clumsy tactics and poor communications. Human wave assaults were launched at the defending Germans holding the base of the *Kessel*. As the first wave was destroyed by massed machine gun and artillery fire the second would be launched over the same ground, in some cases eight waves of infantry marched to their deaths. Egged on by political commissars any who sought to retreat would be shot out of hand. No weak points were aimed at and little tactical finesse was displayed. Troops would arrive at the German lines in march formation and launch themselves directly at the defenses without shaking out into attack formations or waiting for heavy weapon support. Many Russians made deadly pacts with their comrades and committed mutual suicide to avoid being captured. Artillery stonks often landed where there were no German formations and armoured attacks usually went in piecemeal allowing the German anti-tank weapons to decimate the thinly armoured Soviet tanks.

Few German formations reported Soviets breaking into their defensive lines. Remarkably few German casualties were inflicted and a ratio of 29 Russians killed to one German may have been typical. This does not include the number of Russians captured. The numbers are staggering. One motorised infantry regiment took 36,000 Russian prisoners in a week. One machine gun battalion took 8000 prisoners on the 4th of July in the Minsk pocket.

Confusion in Russian command centres didn't help.

From the opening hours of the campaign communications infrastructure was seized and destroyed by the advancing Germans. Operational maps became meaningless as the speed of Axis armoured and foot assets meant that Russian commanders had no idea where they really were. Total domination by the Luftwaffe meant any reconnaissance flights had little chance of gathering or reporting accurate information. Any phone or telegraph communications were placed along roads and as the German pincers met on these main thoroughfares hundreds of kilometres behind the front lines the first thing they did was cut these vital links to the rear. Russian formations blundered around without any direction. On the 25th June the 7th Panzer division found itself on the main highway between Moscow and Minsk and cut the railway line and the telephone trunk line between these cities essentially rendering the troops in the first great *Kessel* incommunicado. HQs were usually situated in towns and villages, making them easy targets for bombers and artillery. Rendered unable to direct the movements of their formations in any meaningful way, stock orders such as 'hold to the last cartridge' and 'attack the enemy wherever you find him' only made matters worse, leading to the disintegration of whole armies.

Such was the rapidity of the German advances that the Soviet Army Headquarters facing the German Army Group Centre was 40 km behind the advancing Panzers four days into the campaign. Two weeks after the offensive began the fast-moving infantry formations formed a pocket 300 km to the rear of the Soviet line. Most German infantry divisions had one or two fully-motorised components. These included motorised pioneers, an anti-tank battalion, an armoured car company and some motorcycle formations. These were combined into fast moving battle groups that could clear opposition for the marching infantry and artillery regiments and provide a link between the fast-moving armoured columns.

After two weeks fighting the Soviet armies on the central front had been all but annihilated. The Western Special Military District troops were encircled in two massive pockets centred on the towns of Białystok and Minsk. Army Group Centre had numerical superiority on this front and 750,000 German soldiers well trained in *Blitzkrieg* techniques were more than a match for the approximately 675.000 Soviets. By the 3rd of July the Russian forces were decimated. At least 280,000 surrendered and approximately 130,000 were killed or wounded. A vast amount of booty fell into German hands. More than 2,500 tanks were destroyed or captured along with 9,000 artillery pieces and almost 2000 aircraft.

Well before the larger Minsk pocket was finally cleared on the 3rd of July the next stage of Operation *Barbarossa* had been set in motion. Guderian had pulled his Panzers from the pocket perimeter and launched them towards the next major objective on the road to Moscow – Smolensk.

It appeared to German High command that the Russians were all but finished. Earlier, on 2nd July, Colonel Kinzel of the general staff Intelligence Department reported to Halder on the supposed strength of the Red Army. Halder wrote in his diary:

> In general, one can say that our mission to destroy the mass of the Russian Army west of the Dvina and Dnepr has now been fulfilled ... it would not even be too much to say that the campaign in Russia has been won within 14 days.

Halder's impressions were further confirmed when on 8th July Colonel Kinzel reported that of the 164 Soviet rifle divisions that had been identified since the beginning of the war, 89 had been fully or partly destroyed and only 46 remained on the battle-fronts. Another 14 divisions were tied down facing Finland and four more were in the Caucasus. The Russian rearward reserve was reckoned at

11 divisions. Of the 29 Russian tank divisions that had been created, only nine were still considered to be battle-worthy.

For the German troops on the ground there was no illusion that the Russians were finished. STAVKA were throwing everything they could at the Central front and Marshall Timoshenko was given several armies to counterattack the German forces and hold Smolensk. However, the Russian attacks were piecemeal and poorly coordinated. Most of the troops were recently-raised and poorly-trained levies – only eight divisions were pre-war formations. As Guderian approached Smolensk from the south and his fellow Panzer commander Hoth approached from the north, the Russians threw hundreds of thousands of soldiers westward, deeper into the German noose.

The fast marching Wehrmacht infantry divisions rapidly followed up the advancing Panzers and by the 27th July the Panzer spearheads linked up 40 km East of Smolensk. In this advance they had forded several rivers and broken through any natural defensive positions shielding Moscow. Six infantry divisions pounded the pocket and by the 5th of August it was annihilated.

Three Russian armies had been destroyed. Three hundred and nine thousand were taken prisoner and thousands of tanks and guns were destroyed. STAVKA's strategic reserves were no more. The road to Moscow was open.

The German commander of Army Group Centre, Von Bock, was able to state:

> Only in one place on the eastern front – in front of Army Group Centre – is the enemy really smashed … Now is the time to attack with all mobile troops towards Moscow.*

* R.H.S. Stolfi, *Hitler's Panzers East – World War II Reinterpreted*, University of Oklahoma Press, 1991

The two encirclements, Minsk and Smolensk had shattered the Soviet armies in the central theatre. By the 19th of July STAVKA had committed 56 divisions to the North, 103 to the south and 160 to the central fronts.

Thus more than half of the Soviet divisions had been shattered in the giant central pockets. While many soldiers had managed to escape the German noose those that did were without heavy weapons and demoralised. The German achievement had been stupendous, dwarfing anything achieved in Poland or France. Six hundred and thirty four thousand prisoners had been captured along with 5,537 tanks and 11,000 guns destroyed or captured. Whole armies and their commanders had been destroyed and the Germans had driven 700 km towards Moscow which was only 300 km away.

Moscow – the end of the war in reach

The German forces were still in incredibly good shape. As the infantry divisions cleared out the last great pocket at Smolensk by 4th August most of the armoured and motorised divisions were pulled out for rest and refitting. Losses among personnel had been surprisingly light. By 3rd July they had approximately 55,000 casualties, by 16th July this had increased to 100,000 and by the last great battles around Smolensk they had lost 180,000 men. But these figures were for the entire front, not just Army Group Centre. Army Group North had managed to bounce through most of its opposing enemies and was approaching Leningrad. Army Group South had fought an equal number of Soviet troops at the beginning of the campaign and had much stiff fighting before they managed to get into the Russian rear and cause tremendous casualties. But Army Group Centre had outnumbered their foes at the

* Stolfi, ibid, p 77.

beginning of the campaign, despite facing half of the Soviet operational units and by August its numerical dominance was complete. Shadow armies faced the Germans and although they launched attacks at the regrouping Panzers of Hoth and Guderian these costly failures were shrugged off by the Germans.

The Germans had suffered approximately 180,000 casualties on the entire front. This was killed and wounded. Of the latter many would be expected to return to the colors. The OKW estimates for this period before the invasion were that the Germans would lose 275,000 and this many soldiers were available in the Field Replacement Army to replace the losses.

Many units were bought up to full strength and the cutting edge formations such as Guderian's Panzer divisions were at least 80 per cent combat effective. The Germans had begun Barbarossa with 3,100 Panzers and after two months fighting had only lost 15 per cent as totally destroyed. Army Group Centre began the campaign with 1,780 tanks and in early August had 1,157 operational and 356 being repaired. By this time the German workshop companies were past masters at recovering Panzers from the battlefield, cannibalising write-offs and getting the damaged vehicles back into action in short time frames. In real terms they still had 85 per cent operational or near operational.

What's more the efficient railway pioneer battalions were able to bring the railheads right up to the main German formations replenishing ammunition, gasoline and foodstuffs. By 5th of July Minsk was being converted into a massive rail transit point using German gauge rails. By the end of July these lines reached Smolensk. By Mid-August Army Group Centre had enough supplies accumulated to report that they had total operational freedom and could advance on Moscow.

Moscow was the target of Barbarossa. The Halder Plan had called for an uninterrupted drive for the capital of

Soviet Russia and all of the OKH planning had been aimed at this one outcome.

Moscow was the heart of the Communist state and if it fell the entire edifice of the Soviet Union would come crashing down around it. The leader of the Red Army Leon Trotsky had recognised this and he made it his first point of business in the October Revolution in 1917 to secure it from counter revolutionary forces. Moscow was not just the ideological heart of the Red regime. From its headquarters at the Lubyanka the Russian secret police spread its terror network throughout the Soviet Union. From here the vast network of slave labour in the forced labour prisons, the Gulags, were administered. In the Kremlin Stalin and his *apparatchiks* organised purges and programs of mass starvation to keep the population in terrified thralldom.

The terror state needed Moscow to survive and if it fell to the Germans it was unlikely that the Bolsheviks would be able to maintain their reign of terror. Already millions of people behind the German lines were welcoming the invaders with open arms and actively helping to throw off the Red tyranny.

The region around Moscow was also necessary for the continued military survival of the Red Army. It stood at the heart of the only real transport infrastructure in Russia, the railway lines carrying raw materials and manufactured goods emanated from Moscow like a great spider's web. By seizing Moscow the heart of the system was removed, materials would not be able to be transported around the empire and isolated centres such as Leningrad and Kharkov would wither on the vine. Army reserves would not be able to be shifted between theatres and the Germans would be operating on interior lines.

Approximately 40 per cent of Russian industrial manufacturing was in the Moscow region. Tula was one of the key weapons-manufacturing centres in Russia and

Kutuzov, the Russian commander fighting the French invasion in 1812, had been particularly keen to keep it out of Napoleon's clutches. The T-34 medium tank was manufactured in Moscow and this lethal weapon would not have been able to cause so much trouble in the future if its factories were seized while only a comparatively small number had been manufactured.

If Moscow fell, the Soviet Union would fall.

The spectacular victories of Army Group Centre, led in many respects by the creator of the *Blitzkrieg*, Heinz Guderian, had placed the domination of Europe in Hitler's grasp is he chose to seize it.

OKH's brilliant assaults had all but broken the Russians. A new danger had emerged into the German rear, one that would lose the battle.

Adolf Hitler.

HOW TO LOSE A WAR. LESSON FOUR.
Allow economic and political concerns to override military goals

Just as the last great *Kessel* around Smolensk was about to slammed shut Adolf Hitler issued Führer Directive No 33 on 19th July 1941. The unstoppable central Panzer Groups were to be divided. Basic military precepts such as not dividing your forces in the presence of the enemy and concentration of resources to fulfil one key goal were abandoned, demonstrating the naivety of Hitler as a Supreme Commander.

This was the reckoning for the Wehrmacht. They had allowed Hitler to eliminate all political opposition in the 'Blood Purge' and let him pervert the Constitution before voluntarily pleading allegiance to the dictator. Hitler chose this moment to assert himself against the army commanders. He would brook no opposition.

Führer Directive No 33 stated that Moscow was no

longer the primary military objective. Once the Smolensk pocket had been destroyed Guderian's Panzer Group was to drive south and join up with Army Group South to encircle forces in the Ukraine centred on Kiev. At the same time two Panzer Corps were to be detached to drive north and assist with the capture of Leningrad.

The enormity of the stupidity here is amazing. While Moscow was only 300 km away over paved roads and with abundant transport due to the denser population, Guderian's Panzers would have to travel at least 600 km to the south moving laterally across roads and rail. Hoth would have to do the same except moving while moving north.

A storm of protest erupted from both OKW and OKH. Halder, the OKH Chief of Staff, Jodl the OKW Chief of Staff, Von Bock the commander of Army Group Centre as well as Hoth and Guderian protested vehemently. Alternative plans that tried to pull the wool over Hitler's eyes such as the 'reconnaissance in force' of May 17th 1940 were provided but Hitler had learnt his lesson and would have none of it. For two weeks the Panzers of Army Group Centre sat on their haunches and did nothing. On the 17th of August Hitler's key military advisors submitted a formal memorandum explaining the military imperative of seizing Moscow. This strategic survey made the case for the drive to Moscow, arguing once again that Army Groups North and South were strong enough to accomplish their objectives without any assistance from Army Group Centre.

Most importantly it pointed out that there was only enough time left before winter to conduct a single decisive operation against Moscow.

Hitler had his line in the sand. He denigrated his military saying that they had no understanding of the economic aspects of the war. Leningrad had to be secured to safeguard Swedish iron ore. The Ukraine had to be seized so that its agricultural bounty would be available for the Germans for the long war he envisaged.

Hitler here showed that he did not have a true appreciation of the capabilities of the *Blitzkrieg* formations under his control. He was thinking in terms of WWI where the idea was to seize territory and seek to destroy an enemy through attrition and economic warfare.

Hitler was also thinking as a politician. Determined that the Germans would not suffer the privations they experienced under the Allied Blockade in The Great War he was seeking to guarantee his popularity with the voters by ensuring bountiful produce.

He was also suffering a bout of nerves. Unmanned by inaccurate reports of Soviets breaking out of the pockets and believing German tank losses were more severe than they were he allowed his fears to dictate his actions. As well as this he seemed to have an overwhelming self-confidence and he oscillated between the two states, nervous anxiety and bombastic self-congratulation.

Most importantly as a supreme commander, he had two character flaws – a distrust of his military advisors and an inability to finish off a beaten foe.

The seeds of this seemingly arbitrary decision had been laid many months before. On Hitler's orders OKH was moved out of Berlin, 20 km away from OKW which remained in the Chancellery grounds. No formalised lines of communications were maintained between the two bodies and the Army planners often had no idea what was being planned in Supreme command. This was exacerbated by Hitler's inability to give clear instructions or hold a calculated line of thought.

The first recorded aim of Hitler for Barbarossa was in Halder's diary on 22nd July 1940 when the dictator outlined three aims.

To defeat the Russian Army or at least to occupy as much Russian soil as is necessary to protect Berlin from air attack. It is desired to establish our own positions so far to the east

Hitler's decision to halt the Panzers led to the Wehrmacht being exposed to four Russian winters.

that our own air force can destroy the most important areas of Russia.

These are conservative aims and show no appreciation of the ability of *Blitzkrieg* to knock out an enemy. OKH prepared the Halder Plan which placed the strategic imperative of the war on knocking out Moscow. But true to form Hitler requested a plan from OKW. Known as the *Von Lossberg Plan* this dictated that the speed of the central thrust should be determined by what happened on the flanks and placed the most emphasis on Hitler's hobby horses – the Ukraine and Leningrad.

These operational chickens came home to roost as Army Group Centre stayed stalled before Moscow.

After several weeks of bickering which wasted more precious time the Kiev encirclement began late in August 1941. Guderian's Panzer Group 2 drove south, away from Moscow, to meet up with Panzer Group 1. By September

12th the pincers met up 120 km east of Kiev. Six hundred and sixty five thousand prisoners went taken and the Russian south west front ceased to exist.

Few Russian tanks were captured in this major victory. Some in OKW had argued that the south had to be secured to avoid a Soviet counterattack into the flank of Army Group Centre. The lack of Soviet mechanised weapons captured shows that such a Russian counterattack was not a real threat.

Two months too late Hitler ordered Operation *Typhoon*, the conquest of Moscow, to begin. The Panzer divisions which had driven north and south to fulfil the Führer's capricious objectives had spent at least a month away from major transport infrastructure. For the first time the tough conditions of the Russian front had led to massive breakdowns. Regiments which were at 80 per cent strength in July were down to 10 tanks. 25 per cent efficiency was common. Motorised rifle companies were at 25 per cent strength. Sickness was increasing as the weather turned sour and by 26th September losses had risen to 534,000 men. Hitler continued to make crazy decisions. Replacement Panzers were shipped to new Panzer Divisions forming in the West. He stopped his victorious troops on the outskirts of Leningrad deciding that a slow siege would be a greater propaganda victory than a rapid assault.

Had Hoth's and Guderian's Panzers been able to attack Moscow in August they would have been 200 km behind it with transport infrastructure and shelter at their disposal. The war would have been won.

Instead they kicked off Operation *Typhoon* on 30th September. Even though the Russians had had two months to reinforce their front before Moscow the defenses were cracked wide open by the Panzers. Two huge pockets were formed around Vyazma and Bryansk. When these were eliminated two weeks after the start of the offensive at least 900,000 Russians and a further 1,277 tanks were destroyed while more than 4,000 artillery pieces were accounted for.

Moscow was only 100 km away but by this time the weather had turned. Roads became quagmires, trucks which had covered thousands of kilometres on Russia's primitive roads finally gave up the ghost. Whole columns of horse-drawn wagons disappeared in a sea of mud. Spare parts could not reach the front and rations and ammo were in short supply. The shorter days and foul weather meant the Luftwaffe could not maintain operational efficiency. By 24th October the front came to a dead halt. No more assaults would be launched until 24th November.

Too late. Early in October the brilliant General Zhukov who had recently destroyed the Japanese Manchurian army was bought from the East to take command of the western front. Through desperate innovations he was able to solidify the defences. The Germans launched one last-gasp offensive and came within 6 km of Moscow's outskirts. By now the frozen conditions were playing havoc with German supplies and weapons.

On the 4th December Operation *Typhoon* was called off. The Soviets launched counter offensives over the coming months that forced Army Group Centre back from Moscow for several hundred kilometres.

A potentially bloodless advance on Moscow had been turned into a catastrophic defeat for Army Group Centre. Exceeding any previous losses they had suffered 110,000 casualties, 496 tanks, 938 artillery pieces and 800 anti-tank guns in Operation *Typhoon* alone.

HOW TO LOSE A WAR. LESSON FIVE.
Pick a fight with the US

As his troops were freezing, starving and dying on the outskirts of Moscow Hitler made another blunder of heroic dimensions. Perhaps trying to block out the bad news from the Russian front he declared war on America.

On December 7th 1941 Japan attacked Pearl Harbor. The Germans had a defensive alliance with Japan and were only obliged to come to their assistance if attacked by a third country. Despite advice from his Foreign Minister, Hitler decided to declare war against America. Without consultation he announced his decision to the Reichstag. Exhibiting dangerously delusional thinking he declared:

> I can only be grateful to Providence that it entrusted me with the leadership in this historic struggle which, for the next five hundred or a thousand years, will be described as decisive, not only for the history of Germany, but for the whole of Europe and indeed the whole world.

American aid under the Lend Lease agreement began to pour into Russian arsenals. This included 13,000 armoured vehicles, thousands of planes, almost half a million trucks and

Hitler lost the strategic initiative when he declared war on the USA, 11 December 1941.

motorcycles, four and half billion tonnes of food, two and a half million tonnes of petroleum, 66 locomotives, 10,000 railway wagons and millions of dollars of other war material.

While the Russians were allowed to mobilise using their almost unlimited resources the Wehrmacht was never at full strength again and could not replace the losses suffered due to Hitler's bungling. As the campaigning season for 1942 came around the German armed forces on the Eastern front were short 625,000 men, 2,000 artillery pieces and 7,000 anti-tank guns. 2,300 armoured vehicles had been lost and some tank battalions had 20 or fewer runners. One quarter of a million horses, half of those that had set out with the army, had perished and needed to be replaced.*

In the space of five months decisions made by Hitler had reversed the strategic balance of the war.

Had Hitler followed the advice of his military, Russia would have been knocked out of the war by early November at the latest. The tremendous resources of Europe would have been his to use as he saw fit. Only one major power, a weak and diminished England, would still be facing him on a one front war.

Thanks to Hitler's catastrophic blunders three major powers were arrayed against him, Great Britain, America and the USSR. Combined they would be able to marshal their military might and bring down the thousand-year Reich in less than four years.

* Albert Seaton, *The German Army: 1933–45*, Weidenfeld and Nicholson Ltd, London 1982, p 188.

8

DRESDEN

A new kind of war

Monday 26th April 1937 began in Guernica began like any other market day. Spanish peasants crowded into the narrow streets of the old market town and the market square. By 4.30am the town was still busy and a church bell rang an alarm. Nationalist troops had sent small air raids against the Republican held town but little damage had been inflicted and the population expected that this day would be the same.

Nevertheless Catholic priests exhorted the population to flee to their shelters and most people moved to what they thought would be places of safety.

Five minutes after the church bells rang a single German bomber appeared and circled at low altitude over the town before dropping a paltry six bombs aimed at the railway station. Several houses were set alight but people began to emerge from their dugouts thinking the raid was finished.

Not so. Those five bombs were merely the opening salvo of the Western world's introduction to terror bombing aimed at civilians. The Chinese were well aware of the devastating impact of raids against soft targets but European nations had not experienced the full fury of air war.

Soon after another solo bomber appeared and dropped its load in the centre of the ancient town. No military objective was hit but some cellars collapsed and fires broke out. Fifteen minutes later a wave of Junkers bombers appeared followed by an entire squadron of modern Heinkel 111s. The bombing continued for more than two hours. Not only high explosive was dropped but incendiaries were mixed in, ensuring that ancient medieval structures burst into flame. After the centre was a smoking rubble-strewn ruin the bombers continued to range around the countryside shooting up hamlets and even isolated farmhouses.

While it was reported that leftist Republican soldiers were in the town, destroying them was not the real objective of the raid. It was a terror raid meant to impress upon the civilian population the strength of the Nationalist forces and the consequences of fighting against them.

Many civilians died in the bomb shelters. In one street 50 people, mostly women and children were trapped in a shelter and perished when burning buildings collapsed on top of them. Most of the shelters were insufficient to protect against half-tonne bombs which gouged out 25 foot deep craters.

Hitler's support of Franco against the Republicans comprised, in part, the Condor Legion – an adjunct of the Luftwaffe. The Condor Legion provided the Luftwaffe with the opportunity to develop aerial warfare tactics that were to be perfected in the *Blitzkrieg* campaigns.

Both Hitler and Göring were pleased with the dire results produced. Göring testified at his Nuremburg War Crimes trial after World War II that the Spanish Civil War had allowed him to blood his Luftwaffe giving invaluable experience to his aircrews while testing tactics and equipment.

Some of these experimental tactics were tested on that bright spring day with devastating results – the town of Guernica was entirely destroyed with a loss of life estimated at 1,650. The world was shocked and the tragedy demonstrated the destructive powers of modern weaponry.

While the Nazis were gloating over the devastation caused, eyewitnesses were shocked by what they saw. Noel Monks was a correspondent with The *London Daily Express* covering the war who witnessed the entire event and its horrific aftermath.

There were flames and smoke and grit, and the smell of

burning human flesh was nauseating. Houses were collapsing into the inferno...

A sight that haunted me for weeks was the charred bodies of several women and children huddled together in what had been the cellar of a house. It had been a *refugio*.*

A new horror had been launched upon the European battlefield. Hitler had initiated the procedure with a relatively small raid. It was his subjects who would feel its full fury as the industrial might of England and USA was bought to bear on Germany's civilians.

The RAF – night bombing begins

After routing the Allied armies and forcing the capitulation of France in six weeks, the German military switched their attention to the British Isles. It was decided to destroy the RAF Fighter Command to allow the Luftwaffe and Kriegsmarine to dominate the channel. This was the prerequisite of the army before they could launch Operation *Sea Lion*, an amphibious attack on England.

During the ensuing Battle of Britain Göring promised his Führer that he would smash British air defenses in four days and destroy the RAF in four weeks. Initially he was quite successful and the RAF was on its knees. Göring was not aware of this and unbeknownst to Hitler, and in direct contravention of his orders, he widened his bombing to include docks and shipping. On 24th August 1940 German bombers were ordered to attack at night as well as day in order to increase pressure on the British.

The fortunes of war took a dramatic turn when a small flight of Heinkel HE 111 lost its way and, rather than attacking factories located in Rochester and Kingston,

* *The Bombing of Guernica, 1937*, EyeWitness to History, www.eyewitnesstohistory.com (2005).

dropped its bombs over the city of London. Churchill seized upon the opportunity to widen the war and ordered an immediate attack on Berlin. This early attack of 81 bombers was small compared to later attacks but it was followed up with four more attacks in the next 10 days.

HOW TO LOSE A WAR. LESSON SIX.
Take the enemy's bait

Churchill had succeeded in goading Hitler into his second catastrophic error of the war. Furious at the first terror raid on German civilian targets Hitler launched the first of his revenge attacks against British civilian targets.

For the second time he let the British off the hook. Just as the Panzers had been stopped outside the Channel ports and allowed the British army to escape and fight another day, Hitler took the pressure off the RAF at a crucial time and ordered the annihilation of British cities, swearing to raze them to the ground. On 7th September an armada of 318 Luftwaffe bombers swarmed over London and began to pound the city. Nearly 2000 civilians were killed or wounded and thousands of homes were destroyed along with many commercial premises and churches. The RAF Fighter Command was at the end of its operational rope at this time and had only two fully-functioning fighter bases in the south east of England. As the Luftwaffe switched their attacks the air defenses were able to rebuild. It was this switch in strategy on the orders of Hitler that led to the Germans losing the Battle of Britain.

The tit-for-tat battle of civilian bombing increased and many raids were sent into the German heartland. As a result of efficient German fighter and flak defenses the British began to bomb by night. Most RAF bomber pilots were only trained for daylight operations and when flying by night had to rely on primitive guidance equipment. While much was made of these attacks in the British press a Cabinet paper revealed that most British bombers were missing their targets. Only one aircraft in three was dropping its payload within five miles of its aiming point and when encountering heavy flak only one in ten got near its target.

Night fighters and flak batteries were putting up a stout defense against British bombers and so heavy were the casualties among the British aircrew that more were being killed than German civilians.

The thousand bomber raid

Bomber Harris could in many ways be likened to Guderian. A firm believer in the motto 'Smash them don't tap them' he was determined to ruthlessly propagate a campaign of terror bombing against German targets. He still clung to many outdated concepts from military theorists of the twenties and thirties who believed war could be won by air power alone. Nevertheless while derided by some of his contemporaries he did his utmost to prove his theories and began an unremitting slaughter of German civilians that culminated in the horrific slaughter at Dresden.

Upon being given command over Bomber Command in February 1942 Air Marshall Arthur 'Bomber' Harris sought to secure his position and the importance of his bomber fleets by staging the 'Thousand Bomber Raid' over Germany. Believing that the strategic importance of long-range air raids was not fully appreciated he hatched the diabolical plan of using massed bomber formations, of at least 1000 planes, to obliterate three German cities. Not aimed at military or industrial centres the raid's aims were frighten the people of Germany to such an extent that they would rise up and force their leaders to sue for peace. Considering that this plan was hatched in May 1942 when Hitler's empire was still at its peak with an almost uninterrupted string of victories it is obvious that, like many crusaders, Harris was delusional.

Nevertheless his tremendous organisational energy

allowed the Air Marshall to gather together 1000 bombers for his first raid. To do this he used his permanent air fleet of 400 bombers combined with the 250 or so bombers from Coastal Command. In addition he rushed through the training of green aircrews and put them into obsolescent bombers that were scrambled out of repair or storage. By scraping the barrel and putting every resource available into the sky he managed to scrape together the desired number for his spectacular raids.

On May 30th clear skies were reported over Cologne. The once-free imperial city with its mighty cathedral, the tallest building in Europe before the building of the Eiffel Tower, had little military value except that it was a transport hub with several important rail and road crossings over the Rhine. The bombers took off beginning at 22.30 hours from 53 bases across Britain. As the stream of bombers crossed over the channel to Axis territories fighter command launched raids against German night-fighter bases while Coastal Command streamed out of the channel ports ready to rescue any crews ditched in the channel.

Bomber crews were instructed to pick out the Rhine River and use it to lead them into Cologne. Some of the more modern types were equipped with the GEE navigational equipment which gave an accurate fix on their location and they were the first to arrive. Ordered to attack the *Neumarkt* in the city's old town the first wave dropped incendiary bombs to set the medieval structures alight and act as a beacon for the stream of following bombers. These later waves were ordered to bomb one mile north and one mile south of the old town, the heart of residential Cologne. This fine old city had established a reputation throughout Europe as an independent and proud city, the centre of learning and culture as well as fine arts. The cathedral – construction commenced in 1248 – was seen as the most impressive example of Gothic architecture in Europe. The old town was largely composed of 15th and 16th century buildings laid out in narrow, winding cobblestone streets. This priceless heritage was sacrificed as a propaganda victory for Harris and his Bomber Command.

The intensity of the attack allowed the final run of bombers to see their target from 100 miles away. Smoke from the fire rose to 15,000 feet and the ruined town threw up so much smoke that the RAF could not get any reconnaissance photos for a week after the raid. 600 acres of the city was destroyed, 13,000 homes were destroyed, 6,000 homes were damaged, 45,000 people lost their homes and 500 lost their lives. Thirty nine bombers were lost to night fighters and flak. Industrial enterprises were dislocated for about a week. This contrasted with the Blitz on London where there was less than 120 acres of devastated housing. Thirty five German churches were destroyed.

Although the death toll was comparatively light, a Swiss eyewitness wrote of the human cost of this raid.

> Except for the cathedral and a few isolated houses, the old and inner city of Cologne has ceased to exist. ......I seemed to be on another planet. In front of houses lay goods and chattels, and also people in a state of utter exhaustion. In the Glockengasse I came on a woman searching among a score of corpses for a relative. Further on in the city, in a big square, I saw bodies laid out in hundreds.
>
> Vera Brittain, *One Voice: Pacifist Writings from the Second World War*, A&C Black, 2005, p 130.

Harris had proved his point, Churchill and the Joint Chiefs began to see the strategic potential of Bomber Command. Churchill wrote:

> This proof of the growing power of the British bomber force is also the herald of what Germany will receive, city by city, from now on.
>
> Winston Churchill, communication to Harris.

Harris followed through with a second raid two nights later, fielding 956 bombers against the industrial town of Essen. Due to the target-acquisition problems endemic to the foggy Ruhr Valley, relatively little damage was done. A third raid, in which 960 bombers targeted the coastal town of Bremen, took place on 25th June. Damage was more extensive than in Essen, although it fell far below the levels of the Cologne raid. While some military installations and several shipyards were hit, most of the damage was to residential areas.

Pathfinders

Although known as 'Butch' by his crews, short for 'Butcher', Harris knew his 1000 bomber raids had been a propaganda victory but new navigational aids were needed. He demanded new equipment and more equipment. His wish was immediately granted and in March 1942 the new Lancaster was introduced. This incredibly tough bomber flew a total of 156,000 missions and was armed with the new Mark XIV bombsight as well as the Gee navigational aid, a radio intended to allow bombardiers to hit the mark even if it was occluded by cloud.

These measures were only partially successful. German defenses did not only rely on flak. They also jammed 'Gee' and lit fire decoys miles from the targets to distract bombers coming in on latter waves. Human error also played its part and bombers coming in latter waves tended to drop their load as soon as they saw fires leading to creep back where bombs became further from the target with each subsequent bomber. The need to use inexperienced crew with faulty or older equipment also played its part in making bombing less than effective.

To counter these problems Pathfinder Group was established in August 1942. This elite group of crack bomber pilots bought a new deadly professionalism to the art of killing German civilians.

Many deadly devices were used. The pathfinders were trained on all kinds of planes so that each squadron or bomber group could be led by a like plane. The elite of the elite were the crews of the fast moving Mosquitoes. They would appear above the target area hours before the main bomber stream, scouting out opposition, checking the weather and laying flares to light up the sky for the main pathfinders.

Target marking was effected by dropping a marker bomb stuffed with flares called a 'pink pansy.' This was followed by incendiary bombs to attract the following bomber stream. Often these were dropped ahead of the target so the bomber stream would 'creep back' to the intended target. No concern was paid to suburbs in the way. Pathfinder Force found improved navigational success with Oboe in late 1942. This system employed a steady radar pulse sent to bombers from a site in Kent. Another pulse was sent from a station in Norfolk and when the signals intersected the pathfinders knew when to drop their bombs.

In January 1942 pink pansy was replaced by Target Indicator Bombs. These were devilishly sophisticated pieces of equipment. Different flare colors indicated different parts of the bombing target and delineated the approaches guiding the bombers to the correct location. Different colors were used for each raid meaning the Germans couldn't utilise dummy flares to confuse the incoming planes. Some were sky markers hung above cloud or smoke on the ground to delineate the target. There were even 'correction' TIBs which cancelled out improperly laid markers.

Oboe was replaced by the H2S – an on-board radar transmitter and receiver that created a map like picture of the landscape beneath. Pathfinder force also carried 'Window'. This was a cloud of metallic strips that reflected radar signal creating so much interference that German radars were overwhelmed.

These two deadly new innovations would be first used over Hamburg as the night-time air war escalated over Germany.

Hamburg

As Hitler sowed so his people reaped. Henni Klank and his family were lucky to survive. They decided to flee and emerged from their shelter to see and inferno where everything was ablaze, trees, houses and roofs. Some burning horses thundered past them throwing off flecks of melted tarmac that had been torn up by their hooves. Many died stuck in the sticky tarmac or collapsed overwhelmed by the fierce heat. Klank's wife's hair began to burn but fortunately he had a bucket of water with which he put out her hair and cooled his hands.

Two aspects of the carnage struck Klank in particular – many families that sought to flee together became fused masses of ash and flesh no larger than a child and all who were still alive were silent, their throats were too dry to scream.

The bombing raid on Lübeck on 28 March 1942 had created a firestorm, this had occurred almost by accident. Local factors had created an almost self-sustaining fire that virtually destroyed the wooded historic centre. Non-industrial areas were fair game after Churchill issued an Area Bombing Directive in February 1942 which authorised the specific targeting of civilian targets.

By 1943 RAF technology sought to immolate as many civilians as possible. Hamburg was a spectacularly successful example of Bomber Harris' art. The attack on Hamburg was called Operation *Gomorrah*. It was a joint British-American venture. Many of the attacks on Germany before *Gomorrah* had been separate British (at night) and American (at day) attacks. The combination of both bomber forces gave Harris a substantial number of planes and therefore a substantial number of bombs that could be dropped.

Hamburg was well defended. The Nazis were aware of its historic significance as the major port in the old Hanseatic League. The city was ringed with anti-aircraft defences and there were 1,700 shelters for 230,000 citizens. Radar around the city could pick up enemy bombers when they were 100 miles away.

Operation *Gomorrah* was scheduled to last for three nights, starting on July 24th. In eight heavy raids a total of about 10,000 tonnes of high explosives and incendiaries was dropped on this city of 1,800,000 inhabitants, completely destroying nine square miles, or 77 per cent of the built-up area.

The first attack came in the early hours of Sunday 24th. In one hour, between 1am and 2am, 2,300 tonnes of bombs were dropped which included 350,000 incendiary bombs. Fifteen thousand people were killed and many more wounded. In previous bombing raids, the RAF had sent in pathfinder planes to illuminate the target by dropping incendiary bombs. The main bulk of the attack followed on to what was now a burning target. For the attack on Hamburg, the RAF combined the use of high explosive bombs and incendiary bombs, which were dropped together. The result made any form of firefighting hazardous and largely useless. May of the high explosive bombs were on delayed action fuses, perfect for killing civil defence workers as they tried to save civilians or put out fires.

The Americans attacked on Monday 26 July and sustained heavy losses as a result of Luftwaffe attacks. The raids were resumed on the Wednesday. Seven hundred and twenty two bombers were loaded with an extra 240 tonnes of incendiary bombs and dropped a total of 2,313 tonnes of bombs in just 50 minutes. The impact of this attack led to a firestorm with temperatures estimated to have reached 1000°C. There had been no rain for some time and everything, including the wooden buildings of the old town, was exceptionally dry. The clear visibility allowed the bomber crews to concentrate their payloads on the nominated targets. This led to a vortex and whirling updraft of super-heated air which created a tornado of fire almost half a kilometre high. Bomber crews reported smoke reaching 20,000 feet. Winds on the ground reached 195 kph. While not exclusively a wooden city, Hamburg did have many old wooden houses and after a dry summer they burned easily. An estimated 30,000 died in this raid. On the Thursday the smoke blotted out the sunlight associated with July.

The firestorm created scenes that had never been seen in warfare. Whole streets and districts were obliterated. The heat caused even dense trees and grass to ignite. The large eight-story shelters were scenes of panic as their 6000 inhabitants became terrified of the tremendous explosions. Many tore out their fingernails – they had gone mad with fear and threw themselves biting and clawing against the doors locked by the fire wardens.

Those in smaller shelters didn't survive, not because of the blast effect but because of the firestorm. The most densely populated part of town, the old worker's district which for so long had been a bastion of Communist resistance to the Nazis, was wiped out. The combination of mines, high-explosives, phosphorus bombs and hundreds of thousands of incendiaries was deadly. Fires sucked in oxygen causing air chimneys, up which raced ever faster and faster pyres of flame. The fires covered several square kilometres engulfing rows of apartments until a blanket of flame covered the entire old town and rushed upwards to almost six km according to Allied pilots. It seemed as if a huge bellows were pumping oxygen into the flames and the streets served as channels feeding flame, ash and oxygen into the conflagration.

German civilians and the inferno competed for oxygen and of course the fire got the best of it. Breathable air was sucked from rooms, cellars and subterranean shelters as well as devouring all the oxygen in the streets. Thousands of civilians, women, children and the elderly began to experience breathing difficulties even if their shelters weren't hit by high explosives. The heat within the shelters began to rise unbearably but to leave the shelters for respite was almost impossible as the deadly cocktail of lethal ordinance rained down on Hamburg. Men with their larger lung capacity and bigger bulk could make a break for it and survive but women and children emerging from shelters would often be overcome by smoke and fine particles of dust and rubber. Men were more likely to be dressed in heavy military or firefighting clothes which would shield them from referred heat. Women and children in light summer clothing who emerged from the shelters were quickly converted into living torches. Many were found along the outer walls of houses where they sought shelter completely charred.

Those who stayed within the shelters fared no better. German authorities were never able to ascertain an accurate number of those who died. Air raid shelters were stripped of their oxygen before becoming ovens hotter than a crematorium. Doctors found human remains where the bones were of a finer dust than those found after cremation. Hundreds of people, impressed foreign workers, children, POWs, Nazi officials – all were reduced to ash. Belongings and ID papers were destroyed eliminating any record of those who had died. Records of Block leaders along with parish birth and death certificates were destroyed. Where once a thriving community had existed, all was now reduced to dust. Salvage parties searching for survivors could not access buried shelters two weeks after the raids. These last refuges were still so hot that any introduction of oxygen made the fires flare up again. To escape the conflagration many women threw their children into the canals found throughout Hamburg. Few survived. Windows and metal frames did not melt. They were reduced to ash.

Charred corpses were everywhere. Littering the streets or thrown into treetops by explosive blasts. Adults were shrunk to the size of children although many who had suffocated had no visible injuries at all. Some unburned bodies were found naked. The force of the wind had stripped them of their clothes as they gasped out their last.

Dazed survivors wandered around unable to deal with the enormity of what they had experienced. The wounded were left unattended. Swedish sailors who bought cargoes of iron ore to the devastated town reported that Hamburg had ceased to exist and not more than fifty houses survived.

Bomber Harris' deadly art had been all but perfected. Targets were acquired and destroyed throughout Germany and on 18th November Harris launched the first of 16 major air assaults on the German capital of Berlin. By 1944 so skilled were the pathfinders that marking incendiaries could be dropped from a height of 60 feet! Only the furthest reaches of Germany were safe from Bomber command and the dreadful reality of war was being bought home to the German people and the Nazi leadership. Fifty five thousand men of RAF bomber command lost their lives but due to an error by Hitler in the summer of 1940 their sacrifice had been instrumental in helping to bring down the thousand-year Reich.

Day bombing USAAF

Bomber Command's night strikes weren't the only weapon in the Allied armoury. The Americans entered the war and bought a new dimension to terror bombing – daylight bombing. The USAAF (United States of America Air Force) took on the Germans in broad daylight and smashed the German fighter defences.

This victory did not come immediately. From 1942 through to early 1944 the Germans were able to fight off the Americans and almost held the upper hand.

The USAAF began daytime heavy-bomber operations from England in August 1942. Throughout 1942 these attacks were mere pinpricks against the Reich territories and the Eighth Air Force rarely exceeded 100 operational aircraft with only one fighter group assigned for escort duties. Most American forces were committed in North Africa at the time and the Eighth focussed most of its activity on fairly soft targets on the French coast.

By April 1943 the bomber fleet had expanded to 264 bombers and 172 escort fighters. The first large operation against Germany was aimed at the Focke-Wulf Fw 190 plant in Bremen. The Focke-Wulf was the best German fighter at the time and it was crucial to try and reduce its production. The Losses were high during 1943 with many raids experiencing eight per cent losses. Crews were required to fly 25 missions on their rotation. They therefore had a 200 per cent chance of being shot down over the Reich, exploding in mid-air or plummeting to earth as their bomber became a fireball. Although given lots of fighter protection, the range of these single-seat interceptors was severely limited. They could escort the bombers part of the way to the target area and part of the way back. But for most of the time the bombers were left to their own devices as German twin-engine and single-engine fighters attacked them.

The American bombers, chiefly the B-17 Flying Fortress and the B-24 Liberator, were literally dripping with heavy machine guns. Seemingly covered with 50 calibre belt fed turrets and hatches they flew in 'boxes.' These were designed so that a bomber squadron comprising six to 12 planes flew in close box formation so that any incoming fighter would be met with a hail of heavy calibre bullets vividly illuminated by tracer. Squadrons were arranged into larger boxes so that the entire bomber mass of a group, four or more squadrons, could throw tonnes of lead at any oncoming German interceptors. The aim was not necessarily to shoot down German fighters but to keep them at a distance. Nevertheless optimistic reports from gunners wildly inflated the number of kills, leading the USAAF to overestimate the impact they were having on the German day fighter force.

The Germans used novel means to break up the boxes. One of the most unusual was firing 210 mm *Nebelwerfer* rockets from tubes slung under the wings of their fighters. Heavy twin-engine fighters had two slung under each win while single engine planes had one under each wing. These devastating rockets were fired into the middle of the box formations, throwing shrapnel in all directions and causing the box to break up allowing the fighters to engage their foe one by one.

The German fighters had been equipped with better guns and once a bomber came into their sights they could pour high explosive shells into their victim. The ME 110 was armed with two 20 mm cannon in a nacelle in its belly and two 30 mm quick firing machine guns in its nose. Any bomber unlucky enough to stray in front of this armoury was sure to come unstuck. It was estimated that 20 hits from a 20 mm and three from a 30 mm high explosive shell were enough to bring down a four-engine bomber. Single-engine fighters such as the Focke-Wulf 190 had their original 7.92 mm machine guns stripped out and replaced with 20 mm MG 151s as well as two powerful 30 mm rapid-fire self-loading cannon. The ultimate bomber killer was the Me 410 armed with a 50 mm pneumatically powered auto-loading PAK 38 Anti-tank gun with a magazine capacity of 22 rounds. Any bomber hit with one of these shells disintegrated immediately. Special squadrons of FW 190s were formed with heavily-armoured fighters that could penetrate the hail of defensive fire and take the attack right up to the bombers. These special *Sturmstaffel* groups were attached to each fighter group. Sophisticated radar systems alerted the Germans to oncoming attacks and fighter squadrons were vectored on to the approach runs to attack from above while massive flak installations attacked from below.

During 1943 it seemed the Eight Air Force was destined to lose the battle. By this time the RAF were ranging deep into the German heartland with area attacks on built-up zones. The USAAF preferred pinpoint attacks on specific industries and it was decided late in 1943 to try and knock out the ball bearing works at Schweinfurt deep inside Germany's heart. In August 367 B-17s attacked the ball-bearing plants and 60 were shot down. In October the Americans received an even greater mauling attacking the same target. Of the 291 that attacked 67 were destroyed, 17 suffered such heavy damage that they had to be scrapped and 121 suffered damage that could be repaired.

Known as Black Thursday by the traumatised crews the 14th October began badly. As they crossed the channel most of their fighter escorts could not take off due to fog or missed the rendezvous point. Many of the bombers got lost due to the poor weather and couldn't proceed. German fighters massed towards the oncoming Americans and one bomber group separated from the main formation over Aachen. Here 1st *Jagddivision* pounced on the outnumbered Americans and in the space of a few minutes 13 of the 16 planes were shot up and crashed. As the rest of the bombers flew on 275 heavy rocket-armed fighters descended on the boxes shooting them up and launching their rockets into the densely packed bombers. As the American bombers tumbled from the sky the only thing that caused the German fighters to sheer away from their targets was the massed concentration of flak around the target. The exceptionally heavy flak around Schweinfurt reportedly shot down more than 40 bombers and once their payloads were dropped they returned through the waiting fighters who continued the turkey shoot.

However these tactical victories won by the Luftwaffe glossed over the strategic defeat that the American daylight bombers inflicted on the Reich. In December 1943 the Luftwaffe had 1,222 day fighters defending the Reich. Added to this were the 430 on the Western Front, stationed in France and also used against Allied bombers. Compared to this the eastern front had less than a third of the planes arrayed against the Americans. As the German army reeled back from the Soviet offensives after July the entire Eastern front could only call upon 428 fighters. Without the American offensive at least 1000 fighters could have faced the Red air force, seized air superiority again and perhaps stopped the Russians in their tracks.

HOW TO LOSE A WAR. LESSON SEVEN.
Give up a technological edge

Hitler too was partly to blame. Refusing advice from aces such as fighter supremo Adolf Galland he continued to order manufacturing to concentrate on producing bombers rather than fighters. Encouraged by Göring, Hitler was thinking in terms of punishing the Allies rather than protecting Germany. Wrapped in the fantasies that were rapidly coming to characterise his thinking, Hitler envisaged building fleets of the Heinkel 177 to launch devastating attacks on Britain. The 177 was perhaps the most troublesome bomber in aviation history. Four engines were coupled to two propellers and this complicated arrangement had the unfortunate side effect of causing the engines to catch fire and the airframe to collapse. Hitler dreamed of these bombers terrorising Britain in tandem with the new wonder V1 and V2 weapons. While he fantasised the fighter arm had to compete for manufacturing resources, trained pilots and fuel.

Hitler also delayed for more than twelve months a weapon that could have ravaged the Allied Bomber offensive and caused catastrophic losses. In May 1943 Galland flew a Messerschmitt 262 prototype. This revolutionary jet fighter was armed with an array of 30 mm cannon in its nose and could outfly any Allied fighter. Despite enthusiastic reports Hitler refused to countenance large-scale production. In December 1943 he saw the prototype but, once again, rather than ordering large-scale production, decided that it should be produced as a bomber. This so delayed training and manufacturing that by the end of the war only limited numbers had been produced. Even in 1945 they achieved spectacular successes. Had they been available mid to late 1944 in large numbers they could, possibly, have decimated the Allied daylight bombers. Overall, about 1400 Me-262 aircraft were produced, but the number of operational aircraft was usually below 100, mostly due to lack of fuel. The top scorer with the Me-262 was Heinz Baer of the crack fighter unit Jagdverband 44, who scored 16 victories with it.

By the time the Me-262 became operational Allied fighters were ranging over the heartland of Germany. Rather than trying to defeat the jets in air-to-air combat the American pilots followed their targets back to the German airfields and shot them up as they landed. If Hitler had allowed the revolutionary fighters to operate earlier they would have in all probability been able to keep the Allied interceptors beyond the Reich's borders.

This meddling occurred before 1940. In a colossal misjudgment he ordered the suspension of all research work into anti-aircraft missiles or radar defences if they were not expected to become operational in 18 months. This gave the Allies a technological edge which they exploited in their bomber campaigns. Teams of innovative scientists and engineers were broken up and when they were reassembled two years later it was too late to get many projects operational.

Without interference from Hitler the Germans may have been able to maintain their technological edge over the Allies. However the Americans in particular were learning rapidly from their mistakes and these costly raids late in 1943 proved to the Americans that they could no longer send bombers in daylight over the Reich without protection unless they were willing to accept unsustainable losses. They learnt their lesson well. By January 1944 the Eight Air Force was ready to take on the German Day Fighter Command. Named Operation *Pointblank* a sustained attack on German fighter capabilities was launched.

Winter 1943–1944 was particularly bleak and most

days saw heavy cloud over most targets in Germany. While something of a respite for the German population the USAAF in England used the time to rearm and reequip.

By February 1944 the Eight Air Force could deploy 1,129 four-engine bombers. Allied advances in the Italian theatre meant the 200 bombers of the Fifteenth Air force could contribute raids into southern Germany. More importantly by February P-51 Mustangs began to be equipped with pressurised drop tanks that allowed them to escort bombers as far as Vienna. Non-pressurised tanks could not be used at high altitudes and the new equipment allowed escort fighters to range ahead of the bombers and shoot up German airfields or fly above the formations ready to hunt down Axis fighters.

Along with the new equipment came a new aggressive attitude. The USAAF had debated whether preservation of the bomber force or destruction of German fighters was the priority of escorting fighters. A New Year message to the Eighth and Fifteenth removed any ambiguity.

> This is a MUST – Destroy the Enemy Air Force wherever you find them, in the air, on the ground, and in the factories.

When General Doolittle visited VIII Fighter Command he noticed a sign that proclaimed:

> The first duty of the Eighth Air Force is to bring the bombers back alive.

He had this sign torn down and replaced with:

> The first duty of the Eighth Air Force is to destroy German fighters.*

* Steven J Zaloga, *Operation Pointblank 1944: Defeating the Luftwaffe*, Osprey Publishing England, 2011, p 55.

The weapon that won the air war ... the Mustang with disposable fuel tanks.

The Americans set about this with a will. The aptly named Operation *Argument*, part of the larger operation named *Pointblank* set about bombing the Nazi fighter factories, oil generation plants and airfields. The escorts were tasked with hunting down Nazi fighters. The new policies paid dividends immediately. Previously American escorts were prohibited form descending below 5000 metres. Now they began to hunt the German fighters and on January 25th whole squadrons were pursued and decimated by Mustangs.

The German fighters were categorically ordered to avoid the fighters and attack the bombers by none other than Herman Göring. This was the death knell of the fighter arm. American interceptors knew they could position themselves perfectly as the Germans were ordered not to interfere. While the American fighters terrorised the German planes they also had free reign to attack airfields, strafing hundreds of German planes as they sat and waited for fuel. Continuous raids into Germany used up fighter resources but while many raids suffered 6 per cent losses to the bomber fleets the Germans were suffering on average

10 per cent. Particularly vulnerable were the twin-engine heavy fighters. So catastrophic were their losses to the more nimble single-seaters that they had to be withdrawn. It was during this time that the cream of the German fighter pilots, unable to cope with the numerical superiority of the Americans, were shot down. Years of priceless experience and talent were forever removed from the Luftwaffe. Most German pilots by June 1944 had between eight and 30 days combat time. Babes in the wood or lambs for the slaughter.

Simultaneously the raids hammered German fighter production and plants across Germany were reduced to so much twisted metal. However most of the machine tools were saved (75 per cent) and these enabled the Germans to maintain production. They dispersed manufacturing into small plants scattered around the countryside but this caused wastage and problems with manufacturing.

In April and May 1944 the bomber streams shifted to attacking synthetic fuel production and refineries. The effect was felt throughout the German armed forces immediately. Heavy flak was withdrawn from the Eastern Front to protect fuel assets. The Kriegsmarine had to cut back consumption and entire fronts were deprived of vital fuel. The Wehrmacht alone required one million tonnes per month but it was estimated that by June 1944 German production had been halved from 1.2 million to 600,000 tonnes.

A vicious cycle was set in train. Lack of fuel led to lack of training. Poorly-trained fighter pilots were sent up to combat the bomber fleets. They were shot down and even more poorly-trained pilots were then sacrificed. The attrition rate by May 1944 was reaching 11 per cent per mission. I Jagdkorps lost 70 per cent of their force in this month alone. In the first three months of 1944 the Luftwaffe lost 2,180 planes. In the next three months they lost 3,057 and from July to September the staggering total of 4,043 fighters were destroyed. Three out of every five pilots were killed or wounded every month.

Flying Fortresses over Germany. By 1945 camouflage was no longer necessary.

By 1945 the Americans had asserted total superiority over the skies above Germany. The German sorties per month were in the hundreds while the Allies were in the thousands.

Flak defence

The need to defend the Reich from the escalating bombing campaign imposed an enormous cost on the economy and detracted from the Luftwaffe's ability to support the army in the field, its original purpose. Flak weapons defending instillations and cities were largely manned by Luftwaffe personnel. The best-known artillery piece of the war was undoubtedly the deadly 88. In August 1944 the Luftwaffe was manning no less than 10,704 while the army had approximately 6000 in its arsenal. This weapon had an effective ceiling of almost 15 km and had a vast array of deadly shell types to shoot allied bombers out of the sky.

Berlin flak tower in 1943 before the devastating raids of 1944–1945.

The next large purpose-built flak piece was the 10.5 cm Flak 38. Its ceiling was slightly less than that of the 88 but the weight of its explosive load ensured that any bomber near an exploding shell from this fearsome weapon would be destroyed. Almost 2000 of these were deployed to protect German industry and population centres. Many of these guns were in fixed installations but others were mounted on railway cars and trundled around the Reich to protect vital war industries and give the allied bomber crews a nasty surprise.

The deadliest heavy flak in the German arsenal was without question the 12.8 cm Flak 40. This precision built instrument cost 105,500 Reichsmarks but was a supreme bomber killer. Able to reach 15,000 metres it could crack out 15 rounds a minute. Powered loading was provided but even so two ammunition handlers were required to place each round in the holding tray, where a fuse setting machine set the nose fuse the instant before the power loader took over. After the firing the spent cartridge was automatically ejected allowing for the devastating rate of fire.

Even more deadly was the *Flakzwilling*. This mounted two Flak 40s on a dual mount. Able to throw almost one quarter of a ton of high explosive into the air in one minute, bomber crews quickly learnt to avoid them. Each gun required an enormous crew of 20 men. Fit adults were required for this task due to the weight of the shells. The smaller guns could be manned by adolescents at a pinch.

Also present in the Luftwaffe armoury were the light flak. Designed to combat low-flying aircraft the mainstays were the 2 cm Flak 38 and the 2 cm *Flakvierling*. Dubbed the meat chopper this combination of four heavy calibre machine guns with a cyclic rate of 1800 rounds per minute took a fearful toll on Allied fighters. In May 1944 the Luftwaffe had almost 20,000 of the single barrel guns in action and 3,000 of the *Flakveirlings.*

Even this stupendous arsenal of at least 35,000 purpose built anti-aircraft guns could not protect Hitler's Reich. In 1943 flak consisted of a staggering 29 per cent of the German weapons budget and 20 per cent of the munitions budget. Half of the Luftwaffe was manning fixed defences which rarely saw battle. From 1943 the Reich batteries doubled from 629 in January 1943 to 1,300 in January 1944. Hitler had opened up a war on two fronts – now he had a war on three fronts on his hands. Without these distractions Hitler could have taken on the Soviets or the British easily.

Dresden

The attack on Dresden displayed the absolute dominance of Bomber Command and the USAAF over the skies of Germany by 1945. So precise were Bomber Command's pathfinding techniques that almost the entire bombloads of thousands of planes were dropped exactly where desired.

So effective were the British deception methods that less than half a per cent of the attacking planes were shot down, an unheralded amount for a long-range penetration assault. So brazen were the Americans that they took their bomber fleets in a straight line to the attack without seeking to hide their destination. By this stage of the war they no longer painted their bombers in camouflage colors. The silver bombers were supported by long-range fighters and they actually sought to tempt the German fighters into retaliation so they could be shot down.

There were many reasons that the Allies decided to bomb Dresden. It was a vital transport link to the Eastern Front and only two weeks before the attack large elements of the several crack Panzer armies had passed through the town on their way to relieve Budapest. There were many key industrial concerns in the city, including oil storages, shell manufacturers and most importantly the camera and lens manufacturer Zeiss-Ikon. This factory was the city's largest employer and made bomber sights, artillery range finders and time-delay fuses for U-boat torpedoes. Dresden was only one of several cities slated by the Allies to be appropriate for saturation bombing but due to several factors, including the weather, Dresden found itself as the main target for a massed bomber assault on the 13th and 14th of February 1945.

With the benefit of hindsight it is now easy to see that Hitler's empire was finished by early 1945. To the Allied planners things were not so cut and dried. The Nazi armies had just launched two large offensives in the west 'Watch on the Rhine' and 'Northwind.' The Rhine River was still a large, defended obstacle stopping any British or American drive into the Reich and V1 and V2 weapons were still raining down on Allied territory. If Goebbels' propaganda machine was correct there were still many new 'revenge weapons' about to appear on the European battlefield.

Once the decision to bomb Dresden had been made the Allies executed their plan with clinical efficiency, destroying a once great city with a dreadful ease. The earlier Luftwaffe attacks on London and even the 1000 plane raids were now primitive relics of the past. The Allied air fleets had become the most fearsome killing machines on the earth.

Bomber Command loaded up each of its Lancasters with 2000 gallons of petrol for the return journey. Each carried one large blast bomb of one or two tonnes and a full load of incendiaries. The first wave of 246 Lancasters were preceded by a task force called 'Blind Illuminators'. Their task was to drop strings of flares above the city to illuminate if for the following 'Visual Markers'. These planes were high speed Mosquitoes which dropped bright red indicator bombs from as little as 500 feet using individual landmarks to orientate themselves to the targets. These were dropped a couple of kilometres before the actual targets and as the approaching bomber fleet passed over the markers they released their bombs. As the bombs were moving forward as they plummeted to the defenceless city below they then hit the targets dead on. A Lancaster called the Master Bomber circled the target city and ordered different bombers onto different axes and controlled the placement of visual markers ensuring the bombs were dropped into different sectors.

Just as the second wave of 550 bombers hit, the firefighting units of Dresden emerged to try and combat the flames breaking out throughout the city. The first wave was equipped only with high explosives to disorientate the defenders while another team of visual markers and blind illuminators dropped mixed red and green indicators to guide in the following five waves. Each of these waves consisted of approximately 100 bombers and came in at three-minute intervals. In the space of 15 minutes a concentrated rain of high explosive and incendiaries overwhelmed the defenses and caused the maximum amount of destruction.

As the massive bomber stream proceeded on its way to Dresden a range of measures were utilised by Bomber command to ensure the Germans could not throw the full

Victims of the Dresden firestorm incinerated in a bomb shelter.

weight of their defenses at the attacking planes. Up until late 1944 the bombers had to fly over massed flak batteries in the Netherlands and France. As the ground forces came up to the borders of the Reich much of the hostile territory was now friendly reducing the time the bombers were exposed to German attack. It was easier to confuse the Germans and preceding the advancing bomber streams were a screen of ten Halifax bombers flying north and south for hundreds of kilometres employing the radar jamming device known as Mandrel. This acted as a huge electronic curtain stopping the Germans from detecting the axis of assault. Several screens were in operation baffling the German *Freya* radars. Another artificial means of confusing the Germans was a force of aircraft dropping clouds of chaff far to the south of the bombers. This massed chaff gave the impression of a huge fleet of aircraft several hundred kilometres from the real attack. Simultaneously to the north feint attacks composed of up to 70 fast moving Mosquitoes bombed Magdeburg and Dortmund while the same happened south towards Nuremburg. Night fighter Mosquitoes were present to hunt down any German night fighters drawn out by this activity.

The sophistication of the Allied offensive capacities was in stark contrast to the ramshackle nature of the German defensive measures around Dresden. The Luftwaffe had always presumed that Dresden was out of range of Western bombers and by the time the Americans and British began to penetrate the airspace around the Saxon capital it was too late.

The day fighter arm had been severely weakened during Operation *Pointblank* in 1944 and its back was finally broken when Göring sent them out en-masse in support of the Ardennes Offensive. Hundreds of fighters were shot down in futile attacks on Allied airfields. The Allies conducted 35,000 day fighter sorties over the Reich in January 1945 while the Germans were able to mount a paltry 591. One hundred and seventy two German fighters were shot down. During the attack on Dresden only one of the 316 American day bombers was bought down. The American fighter escorts had been able to scatter the German fighters south-east of Leipzig before they had been able to attack the bombers.

In contrast the night-fighter arm had a multitude of effective weapons and a month before Dresden had about 1020 operational planes, many of them technically superior to Allied planes. The potential could not be exploited. Lacking fuel, only ten managed to get airborne to attack the British bombers. Of the 796 attacking bombers, six were destroyed in the two waves but three of these were destroyed by 'friendly bombs' dropped by other planes. No night fighters rose to meet the second wave and the pathfinders were able to roam at will with little or no interference from the German defenses. Those night fighters that did manage to get airborne were effectively without radar as the British managed to jam their signals.

In contrast to most other major cities the flak situated around Dresden was woefully inadequate. At a maximum they had four batteries of 88 mm flak and maybe three or four batteries of 85 mm Russian flak, captured in the heyday of the early advances into the east. While these guns were effective early in the war the Germans had rebored many of them to be able to take German ammunition and many of the barrels were worn out reducing their accuracy. To make matters worse late in 1944 and into 1945 456 heavy flak batteries had been removed from air defense throughout the Reich and shipped east to try and stem the avalanche of Russian armour. Most of those in the Dresden region had been moved by January and a minor raid by 127 Liberators on the 16th of January encountered no flak whatsoever. The only real impediment to attacking Dresden was the weather.

In the city things were just as bad. Few permanent, large air raid shelters had been built leading to most of the citizens hunkering down in their cellars. One thing the civil authorities had done was to connect underground shelters with a maze of connecting tunnels. These were meant to help people escape if their shelter exits were covered but merely served to funnel heat and smoke through the makeshift protection adding to the carnage.

The raid followed the precedent set in many other unfortunate German cities. So used to saturation bombing techniques were the Lancaster crews that their performance was flawless. So light was the German resistance that it enabled the Master Bombers to circle the city at an unusually low ceiling, guiding the waves of planes onto their targets with pinpoint accuracy. The initial marking flares were dropped three minutes early and bathed the city in an eerie red glow. The pinpoint target flares followed soon after, using as their chief aiming point the Dresden football stadium. These new improved flares exploded a set distance above the ground spreading red pyrotechnic candles over a wide area. Spread over hundreds of metres it made it impossible for the civil defense workers to suppress their fierce light and acted as an unmissable beacon to the following bombers. The first 244 Lancasters converged on the city. Each squadron was on a slightly different course ensuring that their bombs covered the entire sector. The bombers came in on steady runs – no evasive action was necessary to avoid flak or night fighters. It was turning into a milk run.

Not so for those on the ground. The high explosive

bombs reduced many wooden houses in the old town to a pile of shattered beams and splinters making them that much more combustible. Those houses that weren't demolished had their doors and windows blown in turning each house or apartment into an individual chimney through which the fires caused by the thousands of incendiaries roared skywards. A steady westerly wind was present and this combined with the combustible raw materials allowed the fires to coalesce into a firestorm. Within the *Altstadt* (Old Town) the heat from thousands of fires superheated the air above causing violent up draughts which sucked ever more oxygen into the centre of the inferno. Individuals were swept off their feet as they tried to flee along the roads – the tar on the roads was melting and turning into a molten river. Even if they were not in the fire, those houses or people on its periphery would combust while those on its outskirts found it increasingly difficult to breathe. Many of the old or young simply gave up and lay down to die. Tremendous amounts of carbon monoxide were produced and this seeped into many underground cellars, asphyxiating all below.

The fire brigade could do little to contain the fires. Only 1000-strong, their vehicles were antiquated and in many cases lacking petrol. Most of the population immediately fled to the shelters rather than staying above ground to help fight the small incendiary fires. This resulted in many small fires coalescing into a large fire that only became apparent when it suddenly burst through ceilings, collapsing the fourth and fifth stories and raging through the roof. As the inferno took hold firefighters and civilians leapt into the water tanks constructed for the city's firefighters but most of these luckless souls were boiled to death.

This was just the first taste. Just as the initial target flares were being dropped the second wave of 550 bombers was taking off from myriad bases around England. Once again this bomber stream was untroubled on its approach to Dresden. Once there the Master Bomber ordered

Hitler's reckoning ... victims of the Dresden bombings.

skymarkers, parachute flares that were able to pinpoint the target even though it was shrouded in smoke. Even then the fires were so huge that it was almost impossible to find landmarks so the order was given to bomb the centre of the fires. As the bombers pulled away they could see the blazing city of Dresden up to 100 miles away.

In two concentrated attacks the two waves had dropped one and half thousand tonnes of HE and over a ton of incendiaries. They had also dropped 404,400 individual 2 kg magnesium incendiary bombs and 2,099 incendiary clusters, each holding 150 individual 2 kg incendiaries.

The second wave was particularly deadly as the city defense force was out vainly trying to put out fires and they were caught in the subsequent rain of HE shells and shrapnel. Many civilians emerged from their shelters during the gap between raids and these too died in the even larger raid. They had sought to flee the city but were caught unprotected in the open.

As the stunned survivors emerged from their refuges they were greeted by a horrific moonscape interspersed with fires still blazing out of control. At midday the next day the third and final act arrived in the form of 316 Flying Fortresses from the USAAF Eighth Air Force. These bombers had proceeded in pretty much a straight line from the channel coast to their destination. There was no attempt to hide their path and the screen of escort fighters would have welcomed a fight from the Germans. None was forthcoming. The German day fighter arm was all but impotent. The initial squadrons bombed the suburbs to the north of the *Altstadt* and the marshalling yards but soon cloud and smoke obscured these targets so most dropped their bombs once more into the centre of town. The next day another 211 bombers dropped their load. In all the Americans dropped a further 1,235 tonnes on the stricken city, 40 per cent of which were incendiaries.

The peculiar nature of the Dresden air raid shelters, or

lack thereof, led to a uniquely unpleasant problem for the civil authorities. Thousands had asphyxiated in the streets and were half submerged into the now dried and hardened bitumen which they had sunk into in their desperate efforts to escape. Some were half-burned or smoldering match stick people shrunk to half size by the flames. All had to be counted, registered or identified if possible and then disposed of. In the *Altmarkt* (central market) huge funeral pyres were set up upon which countless thousands of corpses, men, women and children, were tossed. Thousands had perished in their bomb shelters, either as the building collapsed upon them or else as the carbon monoxide insinuated itself into the shelters making the civilians unconscious. Many died from heat exposure even though they were below ground. These shelters had to be located, often through piles of rubble, and the lifeless victims pulled to the surface where they too joined the pyres. Many individuals were nothing but a greasy smear on burnt cobblestones or against a wall in the heart of Dresden where the firestorm had raged at its fiercest.

Many refugees from the East were passing through Dresden and the savage nature of the attack meant that it was impossible to accurately determine how many died. 40,000 to 50,000 could be a realistic number. The USAAF and the RAAF lost 6 bombers. This amounted to less than half a per cent casualty rate. Well before the final collapse in May 1945, Germany was supine beneath her conquerors' boots.

9

SUICIDE

Götterdämmerung

When Hitler moved back to Berlin for the final time he entered his own personal *Götterdämmerung* (twilight of the Gods). On January 16th he returned to a small bunker complex deep in the government district after witnessing the collapse of his last two Western offensives – Watch on the Rhine (*Wacht am Rhein* – the Battle of the Bulge) and Northwind (*Nordwind*). While he returned voluntarily the inhabitants of Berlin had had no choice in the matter. Berlin had been subject to saturation bombing raids for several years now. The Americans came during the day with their Flying Fortresses and Liberators. These tough machines were arranged in box formations enabling each bomber to protect its neighbours with a deadly array of 50 calibre machine guns. The English came at night, guided onto their targets by pathfinder Mosquito fighter-bombers. Often the pathfinder squadrons weren't required as smoke and flame from previous raids acted like a beacon, visible up to a hundred kilometres away.

One bombardment had lasted for 21 days and nights. The sprawling city had lost 62 per cent of its housing but in the heart of the city it was more like 85 per cent. Given that Berlin, the heart of the Prussian state, covered 240 square miles this was a catastrophe. At least 52,000 people were killed in the bombings in early 1945. Twenty two thousand had heart attacks in April alone, half of them fatal. Six thousand four hundred people committed suicide during the same time.

Berlin was like a burning ghost town. While most Berliners spent their time in shelters the business of the once-great metropolis had choked on the incessant fumes and dust of the Allied bomber campaign. Many ministries had been evacuated and no longer ran government. The great department stores had closed down. Shops that had not been bombed were looted. No restaurants, theatres, cinemas or cafes were open. Buses, trams and trains had ceased to function and nobody had petrol to drive cars over non-existent roads. Some trams and buses had been tipped over and filled with rubble to form makeshift anti-tank obstacles.

Only major thoroughfares were kept open by slave workers and conscripted civilians. A number of small, narrow-gauge locomotives had been brought from the Ruhr mines and they were used to carry rubble out of the city centre. Bombs and shells were essentially pulverising old rubble. By mid-April it was estimated there were 100 million square metres of debris – rock, paving, bricks, glass, sandstone, destroyed furniture and the detritus of a once great city, all piled in huge mounds. The national railway estimated there was enough rubble to fill four million freight cars or else to create an artificial mountain higher than the tallest peak in the Harz Mountains.

Ever present in the streets of Berlin were the columns of traumatized civilians fleeing their own personal *Götterdämmerung* as the Soviet juggernaut forced millions of German civilians to flee the eastern territories that had taken hundreds of years to settle. Many had been forcibly relocated after the Nazi–Soviet pact signed in 1939. From January 1st to April the 15th 1945 700,000 refugees had passed through the city. The cavalcade rode on anything they could find – cars, horses, cows or bikes. Some farmers in traditional dress drove what livestock they could in front of them while others brought their dead relatives in homemade coffins. This caused an obvious health scare and the dead and their coffins were confiscated. The corpses were burnt and the coffins resold on the black market for huge profits. Eight million civilians fled to the west and East Prussia, Pomerania, Posen and Silesia were depopulated as the heartlands of old Prussia were stripped of their German heritage. Hitler's glorious vision of Lebensraum for the Germans was looking horrifically ironic

But although Berlin was engulfed in a sea of fire, smoke and gas, resembling a vision of hell that might be painted by a medieval artist, gigantic flak towers projected like holy mountains above the chaos and destruction that was Berlin in 1945. Night and day these giant towers poured fire at the armadas of Allied bombers as they pulverised Berlin. Built in 1942 these defensive constructions were placed in three locations around the heart of Berlin.

Mounted on their top platforms were heavy 12.8 cm anti-aircraft cannons. These state-of-the-art guns were upgraded versions of the famous Flak 88 and could hurl their massive shells almost fifteen thousand metres into the air. At lower levels each tower had a plethora of lighter flak guns, mainly the quadruple 20 mm flak cannon which was aptly nicknamed 'the meat chopper.' Any low-level fighter that came within range of these heavy calibre machine guns was soon shot out of the air. This ensured the towers were the last bastions to fall as the Red Army battled for the Nazi capital.

The towers were built in pairs. The main tower was the gun tower *Gefechtsturm* while the smaller tower was known as the *Leitturm*. These latter structures had large retractable radar dishes that could detect incoming bombers more than 50 miles away. Each of the gun towers had eight 128 mm guns, some on dual mounts. With a maximum rate of fire of 12 rounds per minute per gun, almost 300 26 kg shells were pumped into the oncoming bomber formations every minute, a deadly arc of steel protecting the heart of Berlin.

Packed into these flak towers were up to 30,000 desperately frightened civilians. Built in 1942 they were repositories of food and water as well as innumerable state treasures. With autonomous power and water sources their fifteen feet thick concrete exteriors made them invulnerable to shell and bomb fire. They were designated a priority building project by Adolf Hitler and were erected in only six months. The priority of the project was such that the national railway timetables were rearranged to provide the huge amounts of steel and concrete required for their construction. Vienna and Hamburg were similarly protected by other sets of towers all designed by the architect Freidrich Tamms, although Hitler made some contribution to their design.

As Hitler returned to Berlin the flak towers were one of the few safe havens in fire swept Berlin. Equipped with hospitals and supplies each could reportedly hold 10,000 civilians. Also packed into the towers were priceless artefacts from Berlin museums. These included the Pergamum marbles as well as a multitude of paintings and artworks. But while Hitler retired to his comparatively spacious underground bunker, food and water was running out in the towers and the overloaded sewerage systems were failing to cope with the demands placed upon them by the mass of humanity sheltered behind the concrete walls. Conditions deteriorated and the women, children and elderly began to contract illnesses and disease.

On January 26th Hitler descended into the bunker complex known as the *Führerbunker*. He was never to spend more than one hour above ground and never saw another dusk or dawn. Hitler's health was so poor that he was well suited to the troglodyte existence he and his retinue now experienced. He would occasionally venture to the surface to give his dog Blondi a walk but in real terms he had reached the end of his physical endurance. He could barely lift his legs and shambled along, occasionally having to grab hold of some object when he had a sudden giddy spell. The Führer had been complaining of lack of balance for months and often his entourage saw Hitler take a sudden lurch to the right. He and Blondi took these short strolls at night, usually when the British had departed and before the American bombers arrived. During the few times he was outside in daylight Hitler complained that the light was hurting his fast failing eyesight. Basic services were hard to come by and while Hitler had a Faustian vision of dying heroically in his capital among his still adoring people, many witnesses mentioned his dingy field blouse covered in mustard spots and other food stains. These were caused when his shaking hands caused the founder of the thousand-year Reich' to spill his dinner down his front.

Hitler had been on a diet of uppers and downers for years and it seemed to be leading to a system collapse during his time in the bunker. Although he doped himself with a range of sedatives he often had sleepless nights and could only occasionally snatch an hour or two of sleep. He was not disconcerted by the ongoing bombardment and reckoned it was like distant barrages in WWI.

The fatigue affected his appearance. Many visitors to the bunker who saw him for the first time or after a prolonged interval of time were shocked by what they saw. His once bright blue eyes were glazed, bloodshot and sunken into his puffy sallow cheeks. His brown hair was almost entirely grey and as he shuffled along his left leg dragged behind. There was often spittle on Hitler's lips and occasionally he whistled through his teeth when exhaling. The left hand shook violently needing to be held steady with the right.

By mid-April much of Berlin was encircled. On April 18th the first shells from Russian field artillery began to be lobbed into the government district. At first the bunker inhabitants thought these may be a result of delayed action bombs detonating but soon so many shells were crashing into the heart of Berlin that it was realised that they were from heavy 15.2 cm field artillery. Hitler was at first convinced that they were from long-range artillery guns but reports confirmed that they were in fact from the Havel River, fifteen miles north of their target.

On April the 22nd Hitler lost all control and for the first time blurted out, 'The war is lost.' Hearing that soviet tanks were reported to the west of Berlin and that a final counterattack by SS General Steiner's Panzer corps could not relieve Berlin, Hitler became convinced that not only the Army had let him down but the SS as well.

By the 27th April Russian artillery was only two miles from the Reich Chancellery and the inviting target that stood out above the shattered remains of the Berlin skyline was under almost continuous fire. Hitler knew that his time was come and he made two decisions, marry Eva Braun on the 28th and commit suicide on the 29th.

Even this occasion proved unlucky for the poor fellow who administered the happy couple's vows. As *Gauleiter* of Berlin it was Goebbels who had to track down an official with notary and registrar credentials. He found one Walter Wagner and the poor fellow was pulled out of his *Volkssturm* (Home Guard) unit and hustled down into the bunker. Wagner was a bit of a stickler for protocol and before the ceremony he made sure that he asked the couple to prove that they were third-generation Aryan. Once the two had proven their ancestry he raced through the formalities and declared them man and wife. Wagner noted on his watch that the clock had ticked past the midnight hour and with an angry scribble changed the date on the marriage certificate from the 28th to the 29th April 1945.

Walter was then treated to a liverwurst sandwich, a glass or two of champagne and a chat with the bride before being hustled out of the bunker. Thirty minutes later he lay dead in the street with a Soviet sniper's bullet through his head.

After the brief ceremony the newlyweds both prepared to die. Hitler by writing his last will and testament and Eva by disposing of her worldly possessions.

As he pondered his fate on the 30th April it was obvious

Adolf Hitler and Eva Braun, 1942. By this time he had already made the decisions which would bring ruination to Germany.

that Adolf Hitler had not learnt from his mistakes and remained a boiling chancre of hatred. His last will and testament read in part:

> It is false that I as Führer wanted war in 1939. The war was provoked exclusively by the international Jewish politicians belonging to the Jewish race or working for the Jews.

Having attained psychological fulfilment by dragging all of Germany, Austria and Europe into his own private hell his work was done and the exit beckoned.

Displaying remarkable bravery and sang-froid, the often-despised Frau Hitler went to her death with composure and grace.

The newly-married Eva Hitler took herself to her small bedroom in the bunker to sort out personal possessions and small gifts that she would give to other members of their retinue. Trudl Junge, Hitler's secretary, found her sitting at her dresser preparing a bundle of valuables for her faithful maid while Trudl received a silver fox wrap from the strangely exuberant newlywed.

While Eva was somehow fulfilled by her marriage and impending death, a visitor to the bunker met Hitler and saw that he was a man at the limits of his physical and mental strength. Professor Schenk came directly from the aid station under the Reich Chancellery. At first stunned to be standing in front of the Führer he soon began to look at the small shrunken man in front of him with a doctor's eyes. As one of the last eyewitnesses to see Hitler alive on April 29th, just before the double suicide of Hitler and Eva, Schenk's trained medical eye saw a man on his last legs. The first thing he noticed was that while Hitler was wearing his once immaculate uniform of grey tunic, green shirt and black trousers that he had chosen to wear on the first day of the war, they were spattered with dried food and soup stains, showing obvious signs of neglect. Although Hitler still wore the Iron Cross First Class that he had earned as a runner in World War One and his golden party badge, Schenk saw how he had completely lost his military bearing and had a hunched spine and curved shoulders, seeming to disappear into his coat almost like a turtle.

Hitler's shoulders and arms were jerking and shaking and out of his hooded brows his eyes peered out, lacking focus, bloodshot and rheumy. They were not the piercing blue he knew from the past but rather pale grey and filmy, almost like a soft poached egg. Hitler had deep dark sacks under his eyes and the months spent underground had given him a lifeless grey and yellow sheen that was reflected in the lack of expression in his voice and facial features. Deep fold lines ran across his brow and on either side of his fleshy nose. As Hitler shook the doctor's hand there was no strength in his grip and for an instant Schenk saw that this was not the Führer standing before him but rather a tired palsied old man who was way beyond any medical help and would soon die. Whether of natural or unnatural causes he was not sure, although he was convinced the man was senile.

Schenk passed by Hitler's study soon afterwards and saw him discussing a topic with Professor Hasse, the SS bunker doctor who was in charge of distributing cyanide capsules. So intense was the discussion, probably about Hitler's method of committing suicide that Schenk was able to observe him for a period of time without being overawed at being in the presence of the Führer. He was able to use his experience as a doctor to diagnose Hitler's ills. He noticed that unless Hitler held on to something solid such as a tabletop his left hand would tremble and shudder uncontrollably. Even while grasping the table his arm kept tapping it rhythmically, despite the fact that he had braced himself by wrapping his left leg around the table leg. His leg too, was throbbing and shaking and it was only with the greatest will that Hitler could control himself. Just as he had lost control of the military situation, the dictator was descending into classic Parkinson's disease, *paralysis agitans,* and Schenk predicted that within a short time he would be a hopeless invalid with no control of his body or mind.

Schenk also witnessed the end of Hitler's faithful Alsatian Blondi. Hitler intended to commit suicide using pills supplied to him by Himmler and he mistrusted their efficacy. Hitler's veterinarian Sergeant Tornow held open Blondi's mouth and held the capsule in the dog's mouth between a pair of pliers. Closing his mouth over the pliers he broke the capsule and saw the dog expire. On being told that the cyanide had worked Hitler shuffled into the toilet where Blondi had been killed, checked that she was dead and returned to his rooms without a word. Blondi had four puppies that she whelped just before accompanying her master into the bunker. They got a bullet in the brain fired by the sergeant. Tornow had to kill Eva's dogs and his own dachshund. These acts sent the poor man over the edge and he ran into the canteen screaming that Hitler was dead and it was every man for himself! He was hauled out of the bunker raving and gibbering after being forcibly restrained in a straitjacket.

Hitler and his wife then came together and made their final goodbyes at 3.00am on the 30th of April. The remaining members of the Reich Chancellery group, including Martin Bormann and Joseph Goebbels, were present for this final leave-taking which only lasted a few minutes. No stirring last immortal sentiments were expressed and, stepping in to end an awkward silence, the senior valet Heinz Linge opened the door leading to Hitler's private apartment. Hitler motioned for Eva to precede him into their rooms and, after asking Linge to check the apartment after 10 minutes if he heard no sound, the heavy door swung shut. Linge lost his composure and bolted up the stairs of the bunker into the Reich Chancellery garden where he was greeted by a fusillade of Russian artillery fire. He bolted back down the stairs to his post outside Hitler's chamber, watched by the bemused entourage.

Major Otto Guensche was the next to make a move. He rounded up members of the Führer's guard to carry the corpses upstairs and stationed himself directly in front of Hitler's door, feet splayed and with a pistol clasped to his breast. Obviously if he heard someone thrashing around in their death throes it was his role to go in and finish the job.

The Hitlers were not seen alive again. However, what happened in the room can be reconstructed. Hitler had followed the advice of Professor Hasse on the most efficient form of committing suicide. Hasse had recommended that Hitler bite down on a cyanide capsule before shooting himself in the temple with a pistol.

Hitler had in his possession two pistols. The larger gun was a standard Walther 7.65 calibre, which he had been carrying in his tunic pocket since at least April the 22nd. The smaller pistol was a Walther 6.35 which he had been carrying as far back as his days in the Wolf's Lair hidden in a leather holster sewn inside his trousers near the right pocket. This is the weapon that was chosen and Hitler withdrew it from his trousers and placed it on the table in front of the sofa upon which the two were sitting.

Eva was sitting on the corner of the couch with her legs drawn up under her after kicking off her shoes and she too placed a Walther 7.65 on a side table. Both had two cyanide capsules. Their last wish as a couple was that they should die simultaneously. Both ground the capsule between their teeth but only Hitler shot himself. The thick door to the private quarters ensured that none waiting in the corridor heard the discharge. Eva Hitler was the only person to hear the single shot that countless millions would have been delighted to hear.

Presuming that Hitler had followed his doctor's advice he would have put the muzzle of the 6.35 Walther directly next to his temple right angled at eye level. He then would have squeezed the trigger while biting into his capsule. The pistol would have slipped from his grasp and clattered to the floor while Hitler slumped forward dripping blood down the side of the lounge and onto the carpet. Most people who commit suicide with a pistol are found still gripping the gun but the double action of the cyanide and pistol shot must have led to muscle spasms that allowed it to slip from his grasp.

After 10 minutes Linge was the first to enter the Hitler's 'quarters. The acrid smell of cordite with the poisonous almond smelling fumes from the cyanide caused him to choke and withdraw. After the fumes had dissipated he entered again to find Hitler's body slumped over with blood steadily dripping from his right temple. Eva was still sitting snugly in her corner.

With Linge were Bormann, Guensche, Goebbels and Artur Axmann, the head of the Hitler Youth. The men stood and stared at the tableau for two minutes before Guensche broke the trance and ordered Linge to make room so that two blankets could be laid out, ready to receive the corpses. Before they were moved Colonel Stumpfegger the surgeon entered. It didn't take all of his medical training to reach the obvious conclusion and he promptly declared the couple deceased.

Three guards then came in and rolled the two bodies into blankets and started manhandling Hitler along the narrow, dank corridors where he had spent his last months as the Reich crumbled around him. Spared no indignity the Führer's legs protruded from the blanket which was drawn up high to conceal his shattered temple. He was still quite heavy and it was difficult getting him up the winding stairs out of the bunker. The body was taken headfirst with one guard under each shoulder and the third pushing from below with a firm grip on the ankles. The smaller lighter body of Eva brown was initially carried by Bormann but Eric Kempka, Hitler's chauffer of many years, suddenly appeared and grabbed her warm corpse from his grasp and carried her up the remaining stairs with the aid of another officer.

Most SS personal had been ordered away from the Reich Chancellery grounds but one or two witnesses were present to view the attempted cremation of the leader of the 1000-year Reich. One saw the three officers lower the corpses into a makeshift and shallow ditch only a short distance from the bunker exit. Those who had scraped out the pit had needed the bunker entrance nearby so they could scramble back into its shelter whenever incoming Russian shells were heard. They then poured two jerry cans full of petrol onto the corpses before running back into the bunker entrance and tried to set the lot alight by tossing matches towards the trench. Smacking into the grounds were Russian Katyusha rockets. These comparatively short ranged rockets show how close the Soviets were to capturing the final Berlin bastion. They were nicknamed by the Germans 'Stalin Organs.' An ironic accompaniment to Hitler's Wagnerian end.

Linge finally came up with one last way to serve his master. He twisted some paper into a makeshift flare, lit it and passed it to Bormann. Bormann threw it as if it was a paper plane and on the second attempt landed it straight into the ditch. A second later with a fierce whoosh both corpses ignited. The participants gave one last Hitler salute before scuttling back into the bunker.

The cream of the Nazi crop made no real attempt to make sure that the remains were destroyed. It wasn't until 10.00am that it occurred to someone to send a guard to ensure that they had been thoroughly burnt.

The guard did not do a particularly fine job of fulfilling his duty. He returned to report that Eva Braun had been reduced to a fine ash and Hitler was no longer recognisable with the face and head entirely burnt away. Another soldier sent up soon afterwards reported the same thing.

Obviously inspecting charred corpses in the dead of night while under intense Soviet artillery fire was not a job that the young soldiers, a private and a corporal, wanted to linger over. Their appraisals were wildly over-optimistic.

None of the criteria for a successful immolation of the Hitler's' corpses had been met. For a human body to be successful temperatures of up to 1800 degrees Fahrenheit are required. This allows the body fats to combust and reduces the corpse to ash. For these conditions to be met an appropriate heat source is required and air must be able to circulate around the body. The makeshift grave used in the attempt to cremate the Hitlers did not meet any of the required criteria. It's likely that most of the petrol soaked into the ground and only the surface skin and fats were charred. Hitler's skeletal system remained intact and the teeth were hardly burnt at all. This allowed rapid pathological identification of his corpse when the Russians took it.

Eva's body had undergone an even more frightening metamorphosis. The heat from the superficial burning combined with rigor mortis to cause her body to sit up in a jack-knife position. Otherwise known as the equestrian posture by morticians, she sat upright as if riding on a saddle and her arms were outstretched as if holding a set of reins.

As the Soviets approached it was decided to bury the corpses. The three soldiers who had been detailed to drag the Hitlers from their shallow trench would have had the unpleasant task of stomping on Eva's body to flatten her out before burying the couple in a new grave approximately eight feet deep. This grave was a shell hole and it too was close to the entrance to the bunker. The bodies were thrown in. No flag could be found to wrap them. They were covered with rubble and dirt that was pounded flat with a wooden pestle.

An inglorious end to one of the most evil men ever to walk the earth.

Stalin heard soon afterwards of Hitler's suicide. He had often dreamed of bringing Hitler to Moscow in an iron cage and lodging the ex-dictator in the bowels of the Kremlin where he could torment him at his leisure. He expressed his disappointment that Hitler had evaded capture: 'So, the beast has escaped us.'

His corpse had not escaped the Soviet authorities. On Wednesday the 2nd of April the first Russian combat troops entered the bunker and they were soon followed by Colonel Ivan Klimenko, a detective with the NKVD who soon located the body of the Goebbels. His next startling discovery was the body of a Hitler double who had been hauled out of a water tank that was filled with other corpses. It was originally supposed that this was the corpse of Hitler and it was displayed in the Reich Chancellery main hall. Who this body double was and who killed him is a mystery.

Thinking that they already had Hitler's body the discovery of two individuals and two dogs buried in another makeshift grave was not considered important and they were reburied. Only when senior German personnel proved that the intact body was not that of the Nazi dictator did the

Colonel exhume the correct corpses and send them off for identification.

On May 8th both bodies were dissected and Hitler was identified by a crown bridge on two of his molars. Two dental technicians who had worked on Hitler's teeth in the thirties were asked to sketch the teeth before pulling them out of an old cigar box where they had been placed with a range of other similar teeth. Case closed. The pathologists couldn't use Hitler's fingerprints as his fingers and hands were charred and crisped.

Hitler's body was then correctly cremated and his ashes were scattered at an unknown location. It is possible that they were sent to Moscow. It is also possible that a piece of Hitler's skull along with some of his dress uniforms and the settee on which he shot himself were also sent to Moscow where they now reside in the Kremlin.

Death of Goebbels

Several days before Hitler committed suicide in his bunker his secretarial staff noticed a change. For months the RAF had been pounding Berlin with night-time bombing raids while the USAF dropped their loads during devastating daytime attacks. Long-range shellfire had been noticed on the 18th of April. But now they recognised something different – shellfire from standard divisional field artillery. Long-range fire was replaced by 122 mm and 152 mm howitzer shells and even short-range rockets began to pound the government district including the Reich Chancellery and Hitler's bunker below.

By the May 1st the artillery fire formed an almost continuous drumfire. Hitler had committed suicide on the 30th of April and Joseph Goebbels and his wife put into effect their plan to kill their five children.

Joseph Goebbels was a notorious ladies' man and had enjoyed many affairs with a cavalcade of beautiful women.

Magda Goebbels was infatuated with Adolf Hitler and whenever she was in his presence 'She was like a bitch in heat.' according to a Nazi aid. Hitler had arranged the union of his two powerful friends and the marriage of convenience had produced six children who appeared to be the perfect Aryan offspring.

Helga, the oldest daughter, had bright blue eyes and an affectionate temperament. She was 12 years old in 1945. Hildegard was two years younger and was followed by her brother Helmut. It is possible he heard Hitler's suicidal pistol shot and exclaimed, 'It's a direct hit' thinking it was a mortar round. Holdine was a shy young girl who was eight at the time of her death. Hedda was four days shy of her seventh birthday. Heidrun, an energetic four-year-old girl was seen as a little ray of sunshine by the denizens of the bunker.

Up until Hitler's suicide there had been a sliver of hope for the children. The Berlin commander had offered the family the use of a Tiger II to extract them from the encircling Russian pincers and others had offered to include the children in their breakout attempts through the Berlin subway system. All to no avail. Previously Goebbels had suggested alternative options to whisk the children to the Bavarian redoubt but Magda had been firmly against such options. She did not want her precious jewels to have to live in a world without Hitler. Upon learning that the Goebbels were preparing to murder their own children, Hitler had taken off his Gold Party badge and fastened it to Frau Goebbels' frock.

Life in the bunker was a new experience for the Goebbels children. Removed from the sprawling family estate on the river Havel where the children had their own ponies and were able to ride in the family carriage or cruise in their family motor yacht *Baldur*, they were now confined to a dank and dark existence in the Führer bunker as the Third Reich sputtered towards its inevitable extinction.

The family had arrived in the bunker on Sunday April

22nd. They brought some happy relief to the doleful existence of the subterranean inhabitants. Young Hedda wanted to marry a SS subaltern who had lost his eye in battle and could now pop out his glass eye to the delight of the siblings. The children were excited with the change of scenery and the excitement around them and managed to enchant even the most hard-bitten front line soldiers. They also relished the chance to talk with Uncle Dolf who always doled out chocolate and let them use his bathroom, a real treat as it had the only bath in the bunker complex. The children played with Hitler's dog Blondi and put on small theatrical numbers or sang stirring Nazi songs in unison.

And they always had the loving attention of Magda, the perfect German mother.

In the early evening of the 1st April she put her plan into action. She intended to sedate the children before manually crushing a cyanide tablet between their teeth as they slept. Goebbels disappeared somewhere during this time and none of the bunker personnel were able to explain his whereabouts.

The children began the evening sitting around a workstation while their mother brushed their hair and sang a little song. The eldest daughter Helga seemed to sense something was wrong and was observed to be weeping as bed time approached. Magda gathered her brood and ushered them to their quarters as bed time approached. Helga seemed to be reluctant and needed to be chivvied along by her mother.

There seem to be conflicting stories about the sedative that was given to the children and the story that was dreamed up to ensure that they went to sleep peacefully. One version has them taking chocolates laced with an oral sedative which their mother explained would allow the children to sleep well because they had a long journey the next day with Uncle Adolf up to the Bertchesgarten the following morning. The other story has an attendant

The Goebbels family in happier times (above) and the children, killed at the hands of their parents (below).

physician or dentist injecting them with some knock-out drops to render them unconscious although the children were told that they were being inoculated to ensure they didn't pick up any bugs that might be floating around in the subterranean environment.

What is not in doubt is that the children were killed with cyanide. Dr Stumpfegger, Frau Goebbels' attending physician, had also been distributing cyanide capsules all week. Many inhabitants of the bunker saw that Magda had six of these blue plastic phials with a brass ring neck in her possession. Magda herself had written in a letter to her son from a previous marriage that she thought god would forgive her murderous acts as she had the courage to carry out the deed herself, rather than asking others to commit the act. In her perverted worldview she explained that her mother's love that would ensure they received a soft, painless and peaceful death with sleeping potion followed by poison.

She led the children into the family quarters within the bunker and once the sedative had been administered she placed them into their bunk beds and waited for them to drift off. While this was happening Dr Stumpfegger and SS Major Ludwig Kunz, the bunker dentist, were standing in an adjoining room. It seems that it took Frau Goebbels about an hour to kill her children.

Once they were asleep she placed the cyanide capsule between their teeth and clamped their little jaws down to break the vial, releasing the poisonous gas into their lungs. After each one or two murders she left the room and went into one of the upper bunker corridors for a cigarette. She was seen by at least three individuals several times between five and six, pale and drawn, leaning against a wall as if marshalling her resources.

One fact that is not in doubt is that the eldest child Helga fought off her mother and had to be subdued before she was killed. Kunz or Stumpfegger would have had to assist the murderous mother in this killing. Two sets of defensive wounds were revealed on Helga by the Soviet autopsy once the bodies were recovered. The oldest sibling may have refused to eat the candy or else the sedative was not strong enough. Whatever the case she resisted her mother fiercely and her wrists were severely bruised as one adult pinned her to the bunk bed, or maybe the floor. She also had black and blue bruising around her lips and cheek indicating that another adult had to use brute force to open the girl's mouth and force the deadly vial between her teeth. It is possible that her jaw was broken in the struggle.

The children were left sprawled in their bedroom wrapped in winding sheets. As a final indignity there was no attempt to bury them.

Magda was next observed choking down a piccolo of champagne and chain smoking. Her husband reappeared and the two began to prepare for their own suicides. Goebbels was encountered walking in the Reich Chancellery gardens scouting for a spot for their cremation while several aids managed to locate some jerry cans of gasoline which were moved out of harm's way into the emergency entrance to the bunker. He went downstairs, dressed as if for a chilly evening and offering Magda his arm they ascended out of the bunker. The last words from the maestro of propaganda were strangely considerate. He explained to his attendants that they would not have to lug him and his dead wife up the winding stairs of the bunker as they had walked up themselves.

Standing in front of a shallow ditch they killed themselves using the Führer-approved method – cyanide and a bullet. Magda went first. She bit into her capsule before sinking slowly to the shell-torn earth. She was still wearing the golden party badge given to her by Hitler. Josef stepped forward and put a bullet from a Walther P-38 into the back of her head. He then bit into his own capsule before firing a bullet from the same gun into his right temple. The SS captain who was standing by in case a *coup de grâce* was needed didn't have to intervene. The bodies were bundled into the ditch and kerosene was hurriedly poured over them before they were set alight. United in infamy and united in death.

Death of Himmler

Heinrich Himmler entertained notions that he could cooperate with the Allies and become a member of a new government allied with the Western powers to fight off the Bolshevik menace. His manipulations came to nothing and when the BBC broadcast a news report that detailed his negotiations on the 28th of April, Hitler flew into a rage. Betrayed by *'der treue Heinrich'* (faithful Heinrich) he considered that it was the worst betrayal he had experienced in his long career in politics. Himmler was stripped of all his military and security powers and expelled from the Nazi party.

Himmler was not willing to surrender his privileges and appealed to Grand Admiral Karl Dönitz, who had been appointed by Hitler as his successor, for a position in the new government. Still full of self-importance Himmler argued that by regaining control of his security apparatus he would be able to maintain law and order after the war. Dönitz scornfully rejected these pleas and formally dismissed Himmler from all of his positions.

The ex-police supremo fled south from the advancing Soviets seeking to get to Austria or neutral Switzerland. He and his few remaining loyal companions managed to obtain some false papers and Himmler became Sergeant Heinrich Hitzinger. He wore an eye patch and shaved off his moustache. Having shed quite a few kilos in the last months of the war he was difficult to recognise. On May 21st the small party were detained and on the 23rd the three 'non-coms' were taken to the British 31st Civilian Interrogation Camp near Lüneburg.

The British intelligence officers were swamped with work and it seemed almost possible that Himmler and his adjutant might have been released into the civilian population. However, their pristine papers raised a small iota of suspicion in Captain Thomas Selvester's mind. The prisoners were stripped and searched before Himmler's adjutant stepped forward declaring the real identity of his boss.

Himmler then stepped forward and demanded to see Field Marshall Montgomery. The astounded interrogators asked the most hated man in Europe why. Seeking to cash in the last of his political capital Himmler declared that the Soviets were poised to cross the Elbe and attack the British. He then declared that he would be able to bring his remaining SS formations to the side of the British and help repel the Bolshevik hordes.

As realisation dawned on his captors that this sorry-looking individual who they had in their possession was the one remaining Nazi big fish still on the run, a more exhaustive search of Himmler's clothing was made. Seams were picked apart and his shoe linings explored for documents or contraband. Two cyanide capsules were discovered.

It was decided to make a more thorough search which included the prisoner's mouth. Some high profile Nazis had evaded capture by committing suicide with vials of potassium cyanide hidden in cavities drilled into back molars or wisdom teeth. Thin fillings were placed over the implants

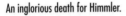

An inglorious death for Himmler.

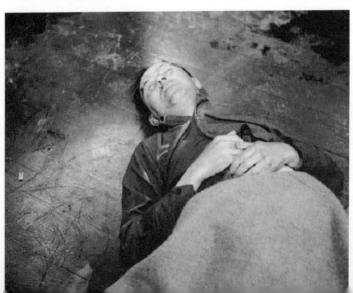

allowing those who wanted to kill themselves to bite down, break the filling and release the poison.

The Doctor who was ordered to examine Himmler was not prepared for the possible consequences of his actions. He allowed Himmler to commit suicide.

Doctor Wells began an examination of Himmler's body and his hair. He decided not to examine the Reichsführer's rectum as he did not believe Himmler would be able to extract a capsule from there and take it without being stopped. Wells was polite and gentle, seeking to reassure Himmler and get his cooperation. The last place he looked was the mouth. Himmler readily opened his mouth for inspection and Wells noted that he had relatively good teeth. There was one anomaly. There was a small blue 'tit-like object' visible between the lower jawbone and cheek.

Unsure of how to proceed he made a fatal calculation that would allow Himmler to escape justice. The German was by no means sure that his insurance policy had been detected and was not likely to commit suicide immediately. If Wells had left the room and got assistance, a soldier could have taken Himmler unawares and knocked him unconscious allowing the implant to be removed. Afterwards Wells himself considered that he should have quickly punched Himmler, winding him and rendering the device harmless for a few precious seconds. Instead he decided to trick Himmler and calmly began another inspection. Himmler was awake to his intentions. Wells thrust his finger into Himmler's mouth to stop him biting down and possibly sweep the capsule out but Himmler struggled and twisted away wrenching the offending digit out of his mouth. He then turned to face the Allied doctor and with a look of haughty disdain deliberately crushed the glass capsule between his teeth.

Himmler's face immediately flushed red and contorted with pain. His neck veins bulged out and his eyes became glassy. In another second he crashed backwards onto the floor, writhing in agony as cyanide entered his system.

Wells called for help and snatched a bowl of water, which he plunged his handkerchief into and used to start mopping out the prisoner's mouth. He also, not considering the danger, gave Himmler a dose of artificial respiration. Other soldiers then leapt on their prisoner, hauled him up and held him upside down. They tried to make him vomit to flush out his throat, all to no avail. Wells reported that there was a slowing series of torturous breaths for half a minute and a pulse for another sixty seconds after that.

In 12 minutes Himmler ceased his struggles and died. The efforts of the British medicos had perhaps slowed the course of the poison but one of the most evil characters in world history had escaped a public trial and execution at the hands of his enemies. He was buried in an unmarked grave near Lüneberg, a grave that has never been located.

10

EXECUTIONS

The post-war executions

Nazis who did not commit suicide were dispatched at the whim of their captors. Trials of Nazi criminals occurred throughout the territories occupied by the Nazis and their quislings. Most of those found guilty of a multitude of crimes were hanged. From Belgrade to Oslo former Nazi officials were strung up with varying techniques and proficiency. Some were hanged by being tipped off a stool while others were dispatched by professionals on a modern gallows.

Apparently it was a fate worse than death to be tried, sentenced and executed by the Serbs. At least one German, on hearing that he was going to be extradited to Belgrade for trial and hanging, threw himself from a fourth floor window to avoid the process.

No doubt those hanged by the British thanked their lucky stars they came under English jurisdiction. Professional English hangmen aided by experienced German executioners pretty much guaranteed a quick and efficient death. Those being hanged by the Russians knew that although hanging was agreed upon as a merciful means of inflicting the death penalty, their deaths would be anything but merciful. The Russian jailers often beat their charges before dragging them to the gallows. No attempt was made to make it a quick process and often the condemned Nazi would be made to wait while the previous victim was cut down, and tossed into a coffin by drunken and jeering Soviet soldiers. The rope would be too short and their death struggles could last for up to 15 minutes. If they were lucky the vodka-swilling killers would take pity on them and stand on their shoulders or tug on their legs to speed up their deaths.

While the Russians were given free rein to torment those that were handed over to them for justice, those who were killed by the Americans were victims of incompetence.

Hermann Göring, like Himmler, managed to cheat the hangman. And it's lucky for him that he did. Master Sergeant John C Woods must go down in history as one of the most incompetent hangmen admitted to the trade. He faked a job history to get the position of American military hangman in Europe in 1944 to escape front line duties as a combat engineer. He had been kicked out of the navy in 1930 due to a poor service record, an inferiority complex and habitual incompetence and clumsiness.

This clumsiness extended to his new career and during 1944 and 1945 he established a reputation for botching his hangings while executing 34 American soldiers. When many of the top Nazis were tried and executed in the Nuremburg War Crimes trials during 1945 and 1946 continued to use a short drop that meant some of his charges struggled for up to 20 minutes before they died. In addition the gallows that he built were faulty and many Nazis hit the side of the trapdoor and suffered broken noses and other facial wounds.

Woods wasn't much fussed with the suffering that he caused and no doubt his superiors didn't mind that the top Nazis suffered a messy execution.

The Nuremberg executions

The Nuremberg trials lasted from late 1945 to 1949 and were a chance for the Allies to put Nazi war criminals on the stand. Conducted by American British, French and Russian authorities they were intended to bring the worst Nazis to account for their actions and deal out appropriate punishments. Nuremberg was chosen for several reasons, it was seen as an ideological heartland of Nazism and its large Palace of Justice and jail was still intact.

The first major trial dealt with 24 surviving top Nazis and lasted most of 1946.

Many were sentenced to death and on the 16th of October 1946 a rogues' gallery of Nazi criminals was dispatched by Woods. Göring managed to avoid the hangman with a smuggled cyanide capsule.

Hans Frank was one of the greatest villains of the Third Reich. Instrumental in concentrating Eastern Jewish communities into ghettos and forcibly conscripting thousands of Poles into slave labour camps, he was an active participant in the final solution. He followed the party line and encouraged his subordinates to treat the Jews in his domain harshly.

> A great Jewish migration will begin in any case. But what should we do with the Jews? Do you think they will be settled in Ostland, in villages? We were told in Berlin, 'liquidate them yourselves.' Gentlemen, I must ask you to rid yourself of all feelings of pity. We must annihilate the Jews wherever we find them and whenever it is possible.
>
> *The "Final Solution": Hans Frank's Cracow Statement*, December 16, 1941. http://www.jewishvirtuallibrary.org/jsource/Holocaust/frank_on_jews.html

Frank found some tiny redemption after the war. Converting to Catholicism during his trial he approached the scaffold with a nervous smile on his face and sought to atone for his crimes bravely. When asked for a last statement he replied in a low voice, 'I am thankful for the kind treatment during my captivity and I ask God to accept me with mercy.'

Whether he received any mercy is unknown but given the millions of innocent deaths he contributed to, Frank would have had to have done a lot of praying.

Following Hans Frank on that gloomy morning was

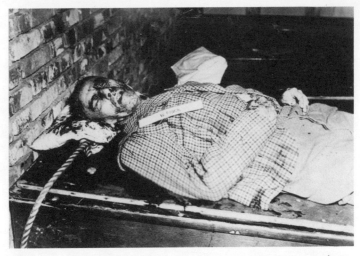

Wilhelm Frick ... bloodied and bruised after being hung by the incompetent Sergeant Woods.

General Albert Jodl. Spoken of disparagingly by his fellow Wehrmacht officers, Jodl was distinguished by his supine attitude to Adolf Hitler as millions of German soldiers were sacrificed by on the Eastern and Western Fronts. He was obviously nervous as he approached the gallows, constantly wetting his lips and looking drawn and haggard. He had good reason to be nervous and after uttering his last words, 'My greetings to you, my Germany' he was dropped by Woods. It took him an estimated 18 minutes to die, kicking and writhing on the end of the rope.

While Wilhelm Frick had not taken an active part in the Holocaust he had been an active proponent of targeting the Jews and was responsible for writing the Nuremberg Race laws. Entering the execution chamber he could not see his anti-Semitic comrade Rosenberg who was still dangling at the end of the rope below the scaffold. He was nevertheless reported as being the least steady of his peers and as he approached the gallows Frick had stumbled several times while ascending towards the noose. His only words were, 'Long live eternal Germany,' before he was hooded and dropped through the trap.

Asked if he wanted to make a final statement before meeting his maker Alfred Rosenberg was alone among his co-defendants in simply saying, 'No.' Sadly he was not so reticent in the early years of the Nazi regime – Rosenberg had been one of the chief architects of the myth of Aryan supremacy. He propagated the myth of the Nordic Aryan master race, destined to rule inferior races. He placed the Jews firmly on the bottom of his racial ladder. He was rabidly anti-homosexual and saw lesbianism as a particular danger to the expansion of the Nordic population. His ideals informed Hitler's plan to obtain *Lebensraum* in the East and set up German colonies that would exploit Slavic labour until they were no longer needed. His writings hinted at a second Holocaust. One that would dispense with the Slavs when they no longer served the needs of their German overlords.

Not just a theorist, Rosenberg put these racist policies into practice when Hitler appointed him as Reich Minister in charge of the occupied Eastern Territories in 1941. Rosenberg ruled the Baltic States and parts of the Ukraine with an iron fist ensuring that *Einsatzgruppen* effectively cleared out Soviet elites and remaining Jewish communities. By the end of 1941 more than half a million Jews had been annihilated and he was able to report proudly that Estonia was the first German occupied territory to be declared free of Jews. His administration ensured that any Jews who were unlucky enough to end up in his jurisdiction were either killed immediately or sent to labour camps where they soon expired.

Although Julius Streicher had fallen out of favour with many in the Nazi elite and had not actually physically contributed to the Holocaust, his earlier anti-Semitic ravings and the coining of the notorious phrase 'the Jews are our misfortune' ensured that he was convicted for crimes against humanity. During the war his propensity for carousing with prostitutes, corruption and slanderous attacks on top Nazis such as Göring led to his sidelining from the Nazi administration. Despite this his American captor, Major Henry Plitt, knew he had caught a significant Nazi big-fish when he arrested Streicher in the town of Waidring in Austria on 23rd May 1945.

Streicher was later to claim that he had been mistreated in numerous ways by Allied soldiers after his capture. He alleged that he had been stripped in his cell and burnt with lit cigarettes that he then had to extinguish with his bare feet. His captors made him drink the water out of the toilet bowl and kiss the feet of Negro soldiers before beating him with a bullwhip. Additionally some soldiers forced his mouth open while others spat into it. Perhaps these tales of suffering were a result of Streicher's overheated imagination. What is not in doubt is that he suffered one of the worst of Wood's botched hangings.

Deciding not to go out with a whisper like Rosenberg, Streicher put on a bit of a song and dance routine. As he was hauled to the scaffold with his hands tied behind his back the Nazi bullyboy yelled out '*Heil* Hitler!' The American authorities were originally going to let the condemned prisoners walk unfettered to the gallows but after Göring's suicide they decided not to take any chances and shackled the condemned men's arms behind their backs. On ascending to the gallows platform Streicher made disparaging references to Jewish history before yelling, 'The Bolsheviks will hang you one day.' as the hood went over his bullet head. His last words before he was dropped were 'Adele, my dear wife.'

He went down kicking and this may have dislodged the hangman's knot, which usually snaps the spine, from its location at the back of the neck. This led to a long agonising death for the Jew-hater. Eyewitnesses to the execution heard him groaning under the scaffold and saw the rope twitching for several long minutes. Woods intervened and went under the gallows to finish the job. What he did is unknown. Maybe a sharp blow to the head or else a heavy pull on

Streicher's contorted limbs. Whichever option he chose, the Jew-baiter's struggles soon ceased.

The other top Nazis hanged that day sought to alleviate their guilt at the destruction their murderous regime had wrought upon the German people.

It was 1.11am when Joachim von Ribbentrop, the first to be hanged in Göring's place, walked through the gymnasium door, his face white but set, his grey hair ruffled. Ribbentrop said firmly, 'God protect Germany,' and then, 'My last wish is that German unity should remain and that an understanding between the east and west will come about and peace for the world.'

It was 2.45 when Artur Seyss-Inquart – shouting, 'I believe in Germany!' – fell to his death.

Ernst Kaltenbrunner, Heydrich's successor, asked if he had any last words, said in a mild voice, 'I have loved my German people and my Fatherland from the bottom of my heart. I have done my duty by the laws of my country. I regret that my people were not led by soldiers only and that crimes were committed in which I had no share. I fought honourably. Germany – good luck.'

Talk about closing the stable door after the horse has bolted.

Death of Göring

Hermann Göring was no stranger to violent death. As a crack fighter pilot in wwi he had stared death in the face many times. The other big three of the Nazi regime, Hitler, Goebbels and Himmler, had all dispatched themselves at a time of their own choosing and Göring was determined not to be the odd man out. As a decorated soldier he was determined not to be dragged to an ignominious death on the end of an American rope.

During the Nuremburg trials Göring has slimmed down from his wartime bulk and was able to assert his dominance over his co-defendants. This was in contrast to the war when the chief of the Luftwaffe had largely disappeared from the public gaze as he retired to his many mansions and concentrated on collecting artworks while using a staggering range of amphetamines and narcotics. Even though he was removed from the public gaze he was viewed fondly by many members of the German public and this was partly due to the heroic reputation he gained in WWI as an elite fighter pilot.

Göring was born in Rosenheim, Bavaria in the year 1893. His father shared many of his son's characteristics and had an immense girth in later life as well as a love for dressing up in impressive German uniforms. His father was the first governor of German West Africa and treated the local population fairly sympathetically.

Hermann grew up in military schools and, although something of a daring and reckless youth, he adapted well to the demands of a military upbringing. In 1912 he was commissioned as a lieutenant and was posted to Alsace where he formed a cutting-edge cyclist corps. In 1915 he was convinced to join the air corps and became the observer for his friend Bruno Loerzer and the two earned the Iron Cross First Class for their daring exploits while conducting reconnaissance missions over enemy lines. They flew the *Rumpler*, an excellent biplane whose ceiling far exceeded that of most allied fighters allowing recce missions to fly with only a limited chance of being shot down.

Göring wanted more action and was sent to fighter training school at Courtrai. After this he and his comrade Loerzer were assigned to *Staffel 5* which was equipped with Fokker E3s. He rapidly made a name for himself and displayed enormous skill and courage. Loerzer, with a malfunctioning machine gun, was surrounded by French fighters but his young comrade came to his aid and chased off the French, downing several in the process.

Göring was unafraid of taking on multiple enemies and

soon became an ace. A flight of Spads jumped the young fighter and he only just managed to land in a field near a military hospital. By May 1917 he had accounted for seven enemy planes and was promoted to commander of *Jagdstaffel 27*, a unit made up of raw pilots fresh out of training school. His flying abilities and charisma allowed him to weld the unit into a tightly disciplined outfit who fought British and French fighters over the Western Front around Arras and Cambrai. By the end of 1917 he had accumulated 16 kills and by June he had 21. Göring had many near escapes and saw his propeller shot away and his fuel tank riddled. He did have that other component needed to survive – good luck.

Göring was rewarded with the Pour Le Mérite, the highest decoration handed out during the war, as well as command of the Richthofen Group in July. Although some of the pilots in this crack unit had more kills than the new commander he proved to be a popular leader who was dedicated to the wellbeing of his men. After the war his heroism was recognised and he took up the glamorous career of a show flier and married his first wife, Baroness Karin von Fock-Kantzow.

Göring's aristocratic background and his prestige as a war hero made him a prize recruit to the infant Nazi Party. Becoming a valued member of Hitler's inner circle he was appointed to command the SA Brownshirts in December 1922. Nazism offered the swashbuckling Göring the promise of action, adventure, comradeship and an outlet for his unreflective, elemental hunger for power. In 1923 he took part in the abortive Beer Hall Putsch. He was seriously wounded and forced to flee from Germany for four years until a general amnesty was declared. He escaped to Austria, Italy and then Sweden, was admitted to a mental hospital and, in September 1925, to an asylum for dangerous inmates. During this hospitalisation he got his first taste of morphine, something that later became an addiction.

Returning to Germany in 1927, he re-joined the Nazis

and was elected as one of its first deputies to the Reichstag a year later. During the next five years Göring played a major part in smoothing Hitler's road to power, using his contacts in conservative circles, big business and amongst army officers to reconcile them to the Nazi Party and orchestrating the electoral triumph of 31 July 1932 which brought him the Presidency of the Reichstag.

The ex-fighter pilot showed his ruthlessness when he was made Commander in Chief of the Prussian police and head of the newly-formed Gestapo. With Himmler and Heydrich he was able to establish the police state that ruthlessly smashed any opposition to the new regime and set up the network of concentration camps. It is believed Göring organised the Reichstag fire which allowed Hitler to claim emergency powers. He then helped plan the Night of The Long Knives and settled many scores with old enemies.

Göring used his position to indulge in ostentatious luxury, living in a palace in Berlin and building a hunting mansion named after his first wife Karin (she had died of tuberculosis in 1931) where he organised feasts, state hunts, showed off his stolen art treasures and uninhibitedly pursued his extravagant tastes. Changing uniforms and suits five times a day, affecting an archaic Germanic style of hunting dress (replete with green leather jackets, medieval peasant hats and boar spears), flaunting his medals and jewellery, Göring's transparent enjoyment of the trappings of power, his debauches and bribe-taking, gradually corrupted his judgment. The 'Iron Knight,' a curious mixture of condottiere and sybarite, the 'last Renaissance man' as he liked to style himself with characteristic egomania, increasingly confused theatrical effect with real power. Nevertheless, he remained genuinely popular with the German masses who regarded him as manly, honest and more accessible than the Führer, mistaking his extrovert bluster and vitality for human warmth. This lack of human feelings was on display when

Herman Göring (left) at the Nuremberg trials. He took his life soon after.

he ordered Heydrich to find a 'final solution' to the Jewish question on 31st July 1941.

After his air force lost the battle of Britain and long-range allied bombing raids began to penetrate deep into the German hinterland Göring rapidly sank into lethargy and a world of illusions fuelled by drugs, alcohol and looting. By this time Göring had become a bloated shadow of his former self, discredited, isolated and increasingly despised by Hitler who blamed him for Germany's defeats. Göring's personality began to disintegrate as he sought to escape from reality and when Hitler declared that he would remain in the Berlin bunker to the end, Göring, who had already left for Bavaria, misinterpreted this as an abdication and requested that he be allowed to take over at once. He was ignominiously dismissed from all his posts, expelled from the Party and arrested. Shortly afterwards, on 9 May 1945 Göring was captured by forces of the American Seventh Army and, to his great surprise, put on trial at Nuremberg in 1946.

During his trial Göring, who had slimmed in captivity and had been taken off drugs, defended himself with aggressive vigor and skill, frequently outwitting the prosecuting counsel. The American lawyer charged with bringing the top Nazis to book asked open-ended questions which allowed Göring to defend himself and the Nazi regime. With Hitler dead, he stood out among the defendants. His was the dominating personality, dictating attitudes to other prisoners in the dock and adopting a pose of self-conscious heroism motivated by the belief that he would be immortalised as a German martyr.

Göring failed to convince the judges, who found him guilty on all four counts – of conspiracy to wage war, crimes against peace, war crimes and crimes against humanity. No mitigating circumstances were found and Göring was sentenced to death by hanging.

The Luftwaffe chief was determined to cheat the hangman. On 15 October 1946, two hours before his execution was due to take place, Göring committed suicide in his Nuremberg cell, taking a capsule of poison that he had somehow obtained. There are many theories that seek to explain how Göring managed to get his deadly package. It is unlikely that he kept it from the guards during his eighteen months of captivity. The Allies were determined that he would not be able to kill himself after Himmler managed to choke on cyanide while in captivity. It is more likely that an American soldier smuggled in the capsule for financial rewards although one theory explains that a honey trap was used.

This theory postulates that a guard GI began a sexual relationship with a beautiful German civilian who asked her new beau to smuggle drugs into Hermann's cell in a black pen. Explaining that they were vitamins and medicine that the ex-Reischmarshall desperately needed she disappeared after her unsuspecting lover delivered the deadly package.

Throughout the Nuremberg trial the defendants had displayed an amazing ability to obtain and hide contraband. Razors, broken glass, nails and other potentially lethal objects were regularly found. Robert Ley managed to kill himself as the trials began. The Americans were determined that no other prisoner would be given the opportunity to kill himself and guards were posted on each cell door 24/7. They were instructed to observe their prisoner at least once every minute. During the night it was mandated that the guards had to keep a light fixed on the face of the Nazi in their charge. Each young soldier was equipped with a long pole and if the sleeping prisoner happened to turn away while sleeping the soldier was to poke the prisoner with the pole until he woke up and turned back to face the cell door. Three guards were responsible for each cell and they would rotate after a three-hour shift.

This unimaginably boring task was only broken by the kind of high jinks that young men are likely to get up to in such a situation. The Americans teased their captives, spoke loudly in funny voices and in one instance made model gallows out of match sticks which they held in front of the accused Nazis. Not surprisingly the defendants got little or no sleep. At one time the most powerful men in Europe, any pictures of the accused in the docks at Nuremberg show them to be shabby and careworn, sleep-deprived and old.

There was one chink in the gaolers' armour, one small corner in each cell where the prisoners had a morsel of privacy. In the far corner of the cells was the latrine and a prisoner could spend a moment here without the light from the corridor illuminating their every move. Robert Ley was Hitler's labour organiser and he performed quite an amazing feat. Above the latrines were old style water cisterns. Ley tore out the zipper from his jacket and fashioned it into a noose. He suspended it from the water tank and hanged himself while sitting down on the toilet. Ley stuffed his underpants into his mouth so that no gagging sounds would alert the guard.

Göring used a similar ruse. Without the guard noticing any unusual movement, Göring – who had asked for a soldier's death before a firing squad and had been refused – slipped a phial of cyanide of potassium into his mouth and crushed it with his teeth while sitting on the toilet. It is likely that he concealed the deadly phial in his rectum and removed it while pretending to wipe his bottom. Like Himmler, Göring died quickly and evaded the noose.

The execution of Göring was intended by the allied authorities to be the main attraction of the trial. He was to lead the parade of condemned Nazis to their death. Although he sabotaged their plans they were determined that he take his place among his dead peers and his dead body was bought into the Nuremberg gym and shown to the gathered media and Allied representatives.

The guards carrying the stretcher set it down between the first and second gallows. Göring's big, bare feet stuck out from under the bottom end of a khaki-colored United States Army blanket. One blue-silk-clad arm was hanging over the side. The colonel in charge of the proceedings ordered the blanket removed so that witnesses and Allied correspondents could see for themselves that Göring was definitely dead. The Army did not want any legend to develop that Göring had managed to escape. As the blanket came off it revealed Göring clad in black silk pajamas with a blue jacket shirt over them, and this was soaking wet, apparently the result of efforts by prison doctors to revive him. The face of this twentieth-century freebooting political racketeer was still contorted with the pain of his last agonising moments and his final gesture of defiance.

English hangings

Albert Pierrepoint was responsible for killing Nazis that were to be executed by Great Britain. No doubt they thanked their lucky stars that he was going to give them the ultimate reckoning rather than the Russians or Americans. He was probably the most efficient hangman in history and could dispatch his victims, from cell to noose, in as little as eight seconds.

Pierrepoint was kept busy during the war and as well as hanging British servicemen had been given the task of hanging a German spy called Karel Richard Richter who was arrested as soon as he dropped into England by parachute. He was one of the few men to give the great English hangman a difficult time. Rather than going quietly to his death he put up a fierce fight and sought to escape out of his cell door. Such was his fury that once he had been pinned to the floor by four warders so that Pierrepoint could place a new leather pinion around his wrists, he broke the thick leather with a twist of his arms. Even on the scaffold he continued to struggle and it took 18 minutes to execute the German spy.

Pierrepoint utilized the 'Drop Tables' issued by the English Justice system. These combined the height of the person to be hanged with their weight in a precise formula that allowed the hangman to determine the length of the rope required to guarantee an instantaneous death as soon as the trapdoor dropped the condemned. A lighter person required a longer 'drop' to ensure that the neck snapped while a heavier individual required less rope. However, several times he was given the task of hanging American servicemen. He was required to use American methodologies which included an American noose (Cowboy coil) with the predetermined length of five feet. This, combined with the American practice of keeping the condemned on the gallows for at least five minutes, guaranteed a slow and painful death.

At least the Americans put on a good feed, something to be appreciated in the frugal conditions of wartime Britain. When called upon to execute five German POWs in Scotland, Pierrepoint was able to organise the schedule to his liking and the five executions went off without a hitch.

During the Nuremburg trials each of the major powers were given the task of executing some of the condemned Nazis. Pierrepoint was the official English executioner and was given the task of eliminating some of the most notorious concentration camp personnel including Irma Greese, Elisabeth Volkenrath and Josef Kramer. Kramer was known as the 'Beast of Bergen Belsen' and rose within the concentration camp hierarchy due to his unremitting brutality.

Greese and Volkenrath were particularly savage female guards who delighted in beating and killing prisoners, often with the aid of fierce guard dogs. These individuals along with nine others were housed in a long corridor at Hameln prison and were the first batch of Nazis to be executed by Pierrepoints in one day. At the end of the corridor were the two gallows which the English hangman and his assistants utilized to efficiently kill his victims. The day before their execution Albert discreetly observed the Germans through windows in the cell door. Utilising the home office drop-tables he calculated the required length of rope that would ensure he would snap the condemned necks as soon as they dropped through the scaffold door. If the rope was too long their head could be torn from their neck and if it was too short they would slowly asphyxiate. The drop-tables allowed the executioner to correlate the subject's weight with the required rope length. As an experienced executioner Albert knew that the build of the subject had an effect of the required rope length. A bull-necked subject would require a slightly longer drop while a scrawny elderly person would be given a slightly shorter drop than the tables recommended. Pierrepoint usually observed his charges discreetly so they were not aware of his rather dark purpose.

By the time he retired to run a pub Pierrepoints executed 435 individuals. Many of these were due to his hanging of Nazis. On the 27th February he carried out the 15 executions between 9.00 and 12.00. The first batch of two were Hauser Friedrich and Friedrich Opitz who 'kicked off' proceedings at 9.00 o'clock. The rest were killed in pairs every half hour or so except for Josef Greimer who was executed on his own, as an odd number, at 12.08.

One can only feel sorry for poor Greimer who would have heard the crashing trapdoors resounding through the prison walls as he awaited his fate. Pierrepoint's efficiency must be commended though, given that he had short breaks for a cuppa between his appointments. He was uncomfortable with one aspect of these hangings. Unlike in England, it was his role to weigh the prisoners before execution and he was unhappy that he had to meet his victims before hanging them. He did try and spare the feelings of his victims. Once shackled they were hooded and dispatched with a minimum of fuss.

Convicted Nazi criminals who were hanged by the Allied nations didn't fare as well as those executed by Pierrepoint. Rudolf Höss was a commandant at Auschwitz and he suffered a prolonged death on a short drop after sentencing by a Polish court. This might seem a minor punishment given the enormity of his crimes. When accused of killing three and a half million people, he retorted that such a number was erroneous and he only had two and a half million victims.

His callous attitude is evident in this description of his camp.

So when I set up the extermination building at Auschwitz, I used Zyclon B, which was a crystalised prussic acid which we dropped into the death chamber from a small opening. It took from three to fifteen minutes to kill the people in the death chamber, depending upon climactic conditions. We knew when the people were dead because their screaming stopped. We usually waited about half an hour before we opened the doors and removed the bodies.

After the bodies were removed our special squads took the rings and extracted the gold from the teeth of the corpses. Another improvement on Treblinka that we made was building our gas chamber to accommodate 2000 people at a time, whereas at Treblinka their ten gas chambers only accommodated 200 people each. The way we selected our victims was as follows: we had two SS doctors on duty at Auschwitz to examine the incoming transports of prisoners.

The prisoners would be marched past one of the doctors who would make spot decisions as they walked by. Those who were fit were sent into the camp. Others were sent immediately into the extermination plants. Children of tender years were invariably exterminated since by reason of their youth they were unable to work.

Still another improvement made on Treblinka was that at Treblinka the victims always knew that they were about to be exterminated whereas at Auschwitz we endeavored to fool the victims into thinking that they were to go through a delousing process. Of course, they often realised our true intentions and owing to that we sometimes had riots and difficulties. Very often women would hide their children under their clothes but of course when we found them we would send the children to be exterminated.

We were required to carry out these exterminations in secrecy but of course the foul and nauseating stench from the continuous burning of bodies permeated the entire area and all the people living in the surrounding communities knew that exterminations were going on at Auschwitz ... From time to time we conducted medical experiments on women inmates, including sterilisation and experiments relating to cancer. Most of the people who died under these experiments had already been condemned to death by the Gestapo.

Rudolf Franz Ferdinand Hoess, "Affidavit, 5 April 1946" in *Trial of the Major War Criminals Before the International Tribunal, Nuremberg, 14 November 1945, 1 October 1946* (Nuremberg: Secretariat of the International Military Tribunal, 1949), Doc. 3868PS, vol. 33, 27579.

Transferred to a Polish prison the commandant was executed on a makeshift gallows constructed by German POWs and there is a possibility that his masked hangman was also a German prisoner. Höss was typical of many SS guards. He had a natural predilection for violence and fled home at the tender age of 15 so that he could join up for the front in WWI. He proved to be exceptionally brave sustaining several wounds and earning many decorations. Never losing his taste for violence Höss fought communist insurrections with the *Freikorps* in the Ruhr and Polish separatists in Silesia. He was arrested for murdering a communist leader in 1924. Joining the Nazis in 1924 he became a member of the SS in 1933. Himmler and Hoess had met each other in the twenties and when they met again in 1934 Himmler recommended he join the camp SS. Transferring into Dachau, his cold-eyed ruthlessness was noticed by Eicke who transferred him into the Commandant Staff. By 1940 he was placed in charge of a small camp in a little known town of Auschwitz. The rest is history.

SELECT BIBLIOGRAPHY

Addison, Paul and Jeremy A Crang (eds), *Firestorm: the Bombing of Dresden, 1945*, Pimlico, 2006

Bower, Tom, *Klaus Barbie: Butcher of Lyon*, Michael Joseph, 1984

Butler, Robert, *The Gestapo*, Casemate, 2004

Carruthers, Bob, *The Gestapo on Trial: Evidence from Nuremberg*, Pen and Sword, 2014

Chamberlain, Peter and Hilary L Doyle, *Encyclopedia of German Tanks of World War Two*, Orion, 1999

Deighton, Len, *Blitzkrieg*, Pimlico, 2007

Delarue, Jacques, *The Gestapo: A History of Horror*, Frontline Books, 2008

Drury, Ian, *German Stormtrooper 1914–1918*, Osprey, 1995

Goldhagen, Daniel Jonah, *Hitler's Willing Executioners: Ordinary Germans and the Holocaust*, Abacus, 1997

Höss, Rudolf, *Commandant of Auschwitz*, Orion Publishing Group, 2000

Klee, E, W Dressen, V Riess (eds), *The Good Old Days: The Holocaust as Seen by Its Perpetrators and Bystanders*, The Free Press,1988

Linton, Robert Jay, *The Nazi Doctors: Medical Killing and the Psychology of Genocide*, Basic Books ,1986

Mojzes, Paul, *Balkan Genocides*, Rowman and Littlefield, 2011

Noakes, Jeremy and G Pridham (eds), *Nazism 1919–1945, Volume 3: Foreign Policy, War and Racial Extermination: A Documentary Reader,* University of Exeter Press, 1988

Norman, Andrew, *Hitler: Dictator or Puppet,* Pen and Sword, 2011

O'Donnell, James P, *The Berlin Bunker*, Arrow Books, 1979

Owen, James, *Nuremberg: Evil on Trial,* Headline, 2006

Posner, Gerald L and John Ware, *Mengele: The Complete Story*, Queen Anne Press, 1986

Seaton, Albert, *The German Army*, Weidenfeld and Nicholsan Ltd, 1982

Stolfi, R H, *Hitler's Panzers East: World War 2 Reinterpreted*, University of Oklahoma Press, 1991

Thomas, Hugh, *The Strange Death of Heinrich Himmler*, St Martin's Press, 2002

Wachsmann, Nikolaus, *KL: A History of the Nazi Concentration Camps*, Little Brown, 2015

Zaloga, Steven J, *Operation Pointblank 1944: Defeating the Luftwaffe*, Osprey, 2011

www.holocaustresearchproject.org

www.operationbarbarossa.net